NEIL YOUNG

HEART OF GOLD

HARVEY KUBERNIK

OMNIBUS PRESS

London / New York / Paris / Sydney / Copenhagen / Berlin / Madrid / Tokyo

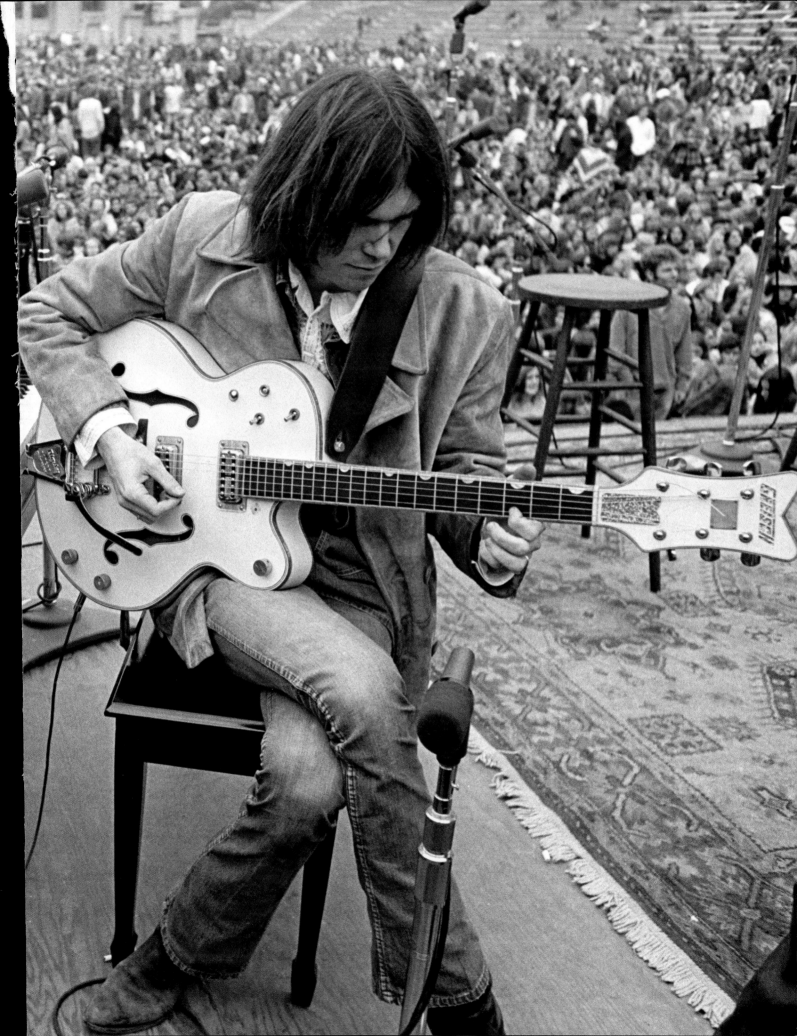

For Marshall Herman Kubernik
(July 14, 1922–December 7, 2014)
"Every day after World War II is a good day."

This edition published 2015 by Omnibus Press
(A Division of Music Sales Limited)

ISBN: 978.1.78305.790.0
Order No: OP56221

Exclusive Distributors
Music Sales Limited,
14/15 Berners Street,
London, W1T 3LJ.

A catalogue record for this book is available from
the British Library.

Visit Omnibus Press on the web at
www.omnibuspress.com

Design and layout © 2015 Palazzo Editions Ltd
Text © 2015 Harvey Kubernik
Please see picture credits on page 223
for image copyright information

Created and produced by
Palazzo Editions Ltd
2 Wood Street, Bath, BA1 2JQ, United Kingdom
www.palazzoeditions.com

Publisher: Colin Webb
Art Direction: Extra Strong
Managing Editor: Joanne Rippin
Editor: James Hodgson
Photo Editor: Sally Claxton

Printed and bound in China by Imago

Endpapers: Neil Young's Gibson Les Paul and
Martin acoustic guitars in front of vintage tweed
Fender amplifiers on stage at the Olympiahalle,
Munich, June 17, 2009.

Page 1: Wiener Stadthalle, Vienna, July 23, 2014.

Pages 2-3: Tuning up before CSNY's concert at
Balboa Stadium, San Diego, December 21, 1969.

CONTENTS

Introduction 6

Aurora 12
Expecting to Fly 30
Everyone I Love You 56
From the Middle of the Road to the Ditch 72
More to the Picture than Meets the Eye 92
Lost in Space 106
Keep on Rockin' 124
A Long Road Behind Me A Long Road Ahead 142
War and Heavy Peace 158
Long May You Run 178

Contributors 194
Discography 197
Further Reading 221
Sources, Credits, and Acknowledgments 222

BACK by Popular Demand TONIGHT

"ROCK 'N ROLLING" NEIL YOUNG
and THE SQUIRES

Enjoy the swinging music of Neil Young and The Squires, just recently returned from an Eastern Tour. Recording stars under the "Vee" label.

FLAMINGO
CLUB — TAVERN

344 N. MAY. ST.   DIAL 623-8458

INTRODUCTION

"There really wasn't anything
more important in my life
than playing music.
And you had to really want
to do it and you had to make
music first in your life."

— NY, 1992

"I never did interviews because they always got me into trouble. Always. I said more by not saying anything."

— NY, 1975

I deliberately missed Neil Young's October 2012 Alchemy show at the Hollywood Bowl, having decided that the $500 for a pair of tickets, dinner and drinks, stacked or preferred valet parking, or a shuttle bus, was too high a price even for the privilege of seeing Neil and Crazy Horse under our formerly smoggy skies (binoculars required).

I had already seen Neil play the Hollywood Bowl with his other two main bands, Buffalo Springfield in 1967 and CSNY in 2006, so it was a tough choice to miss out on the trifecta.

The afternoon of Neil's scheduled 2012 Hollywood Bowl booking, I comically lamented to photographer Harold Sherrick, "Well, I guess I'm not seeing Neil Young tonight." It was before an interview and photo job we were doing that day when Harold and I drove over to an organic market in the San Fernando Valley.

Outside in the parking lot, I ran into my friend Burton Cummings, of Guess Who fame. He sang the band's 1967 version of "Flying on the Ground Is Wrong," the first recorded cover of a Neil Young song. Burton was leaving the store but touted the delicious Mary's Gone Black Pepper Crackers available inside.

"Go in and get some," was his directive. Always listen to a Canadian. I've been listening to Burton since 1969; why stop now?

I then saw a big tour bus in the same parking area. I thought, "What kinda band can afford this place?" As we were about to walk through the front door, standing outside, against the brick wall, was Neil Young. He was wearing a hat, carefully avoiding the UV rays and the phosphorescent bright lights that loomed inside. I looked at Harold and said, "There's Neil. I guess I saw him today after all."

In spring 2014, I did make it to the Dolby Theatre on Hollywood Boulevard and Highland Avenue to see Neil Young in a solo acoustic setting. Second-row balcony seats. Free parking.

Before the show, there was a mandatory stop at the Musso and Frank Grill on Hollywood Boulevard. F. Scott Fitzgerald used to proofread his novels in a booth there. William Faulkner liked the Mississippi Mint Juleps. Gore Vidal once said, "Coming into Musso's is like stepping into a warm bath." I've encountered all kinds of people there, from GNP Crescendo Records owner Gene Norman and jazz great Barney Kessel, to film director Curtis Hanson and even John Wayne. Jack Nitzsche

Opposite: A rare moment of relaxation at the height of Buffalo Springfield's fame, c. 1967.

Page 6: Journeying through the past at the Dolby Theatre, Los Angeles, April 1, 2014.

Overleaf: Buffalo Springfield rock the second annual KHJ appreciation concert, Hollywood Bowl, Los Angeles, April 29, 1967.

loved Musso's, had a regular booth, and Keith Richards hosted a party there in 1997. I closed my first two book deals using an old pay phone in the back of the joint …

Directly across the street from the Dolby is the former HQ of Mercury Records. One afternoon in 1970, their West Coast radio station promo man, Rodney Bingenheimer, an early Neil Young supporter, picked up David Bowie at LAX in a convertible, took him to Hollywood for the first time, and then over to Lewin Record Paradise, a British-owned specialty record shop.

In my mind are these indelible images on the Lewin's wall, next to the front counter, of Bowie's UK import LP jacket of *The Man Who Sold the World* right next to a cover LP slick jacket of the "lost" second Buffalo Springfield album, *Stampede*.

I would have never imagined way back then that Bowie would ask Rodney, now a DJ on KROQ-FM, to introduce him on stage at his 2004 Wiltern Theatre show in Los Angeles, and that during that tour Bowie would perform Neil's prophetic "I've Been Waiting for You."

On the Dolby stage that evening in 2014, it wasn't just a case of Neil reworking and restaging his catalogue or digging up new ground on that sacred corner of my youth. He joked about being a rich hippie, boasting about purchasing a guitar in Tennessee that Hank Williams formerly owned.

And then, a revealing psychic moment, an instance of geopiety at the very spot where Neil's Hollywood dreams and schemes began in 1966. He introduced "Flying on the Ground Is Wrong" as he sat at the piano. "Yeah, where the wall begins and this building begins there was a street called Orchid Avenue. And the building was called the Commodore Gardens and I used to live there. And I wrote a song there."

And he looked at the audience and he turned around and stated, "I wrote the song right here." Everyone laughed. Neil stared at the floor like it was an epiphany, not showbiz shtick.

He was acknowledging his first archeological dig in Hollywood while exposing deep-seeded songwriting roots. When he proudly told us this anecdote, and performed the tune, it honestly felt like he was finally reclaiming his own song.

Like a miner who just might have a Heart of Gold.

Harvey Kubernik, Los Angeles, California

AURORA

1945-1966

"I knew when I was thirteen or fourteen what I wanted to do. There was nothing else that interested me."

— NY, 1992

Timeline

Near right: Exterior of the Flamingo Club, Fort William, Ontario, 1964.

Center right: Neil at the center of the Earl Grey Junior High yearbook committee, Winnipeg, 1961.

Page 12: Ad for a show at the Flamingo Club, c. 1964 (Neil left).

1945

November 12:
Neil Percival Young born, Toronto General Hospital, Toronto, Ontario.

1945–48

Lives with his mother and father, Edna (Rassy) and Scott, and his elder brother, Robert (Bob, born April 1942), in a three-bedroom bungalow in Toronto.

1948

The Young family relocates to Jackson's Point, Ontario.

1949

The family moves again—to the small town of Omemee, Ontario.

The family moves back to Toronto.

1958

Back to Toronto and then to Pickering, a town just east of the city.

1954

Another move, this time to Winnipeg, Manitoba.

1953

September:
Neil is hospitalized with polio during the epidemic sweeping Canada.

1951

December 25:
Neil receives first musical instrument, a ukulele, as a Christmas present from his parents.

1960

August:
After a series of marital rifts, parents finally break up. Mother Rassy moves with Neil to Winnipeg.

Fall:
Enrolls at Earl Grey Junior High in Winnipeg.

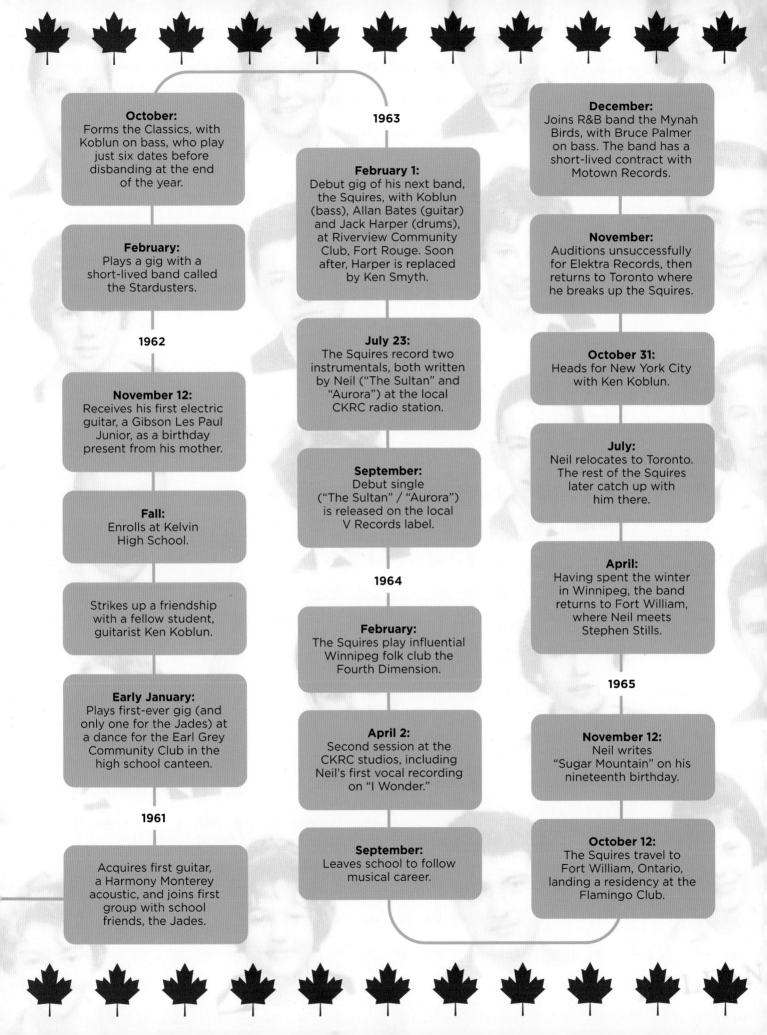

October:
Forms the Classics, with Koblun on bass, who play just six dates before disbanding at the end of the year.

February:
Plays a gig with a short-lived band called the Stardusters.

1962

November 12:
Receives his first electric guitar, a Gibson Les Paul Junior, as a birthday present from his mother.

Fall:
Enrolls at Kelvin High School.

Strikes up a friendship with a fellow student, guitarist Ken Koblun.

Early January:
Plays first-ever gig (and only one for the Jades) at a dance for the Earl Grey Community Club in the high school canteen.

1961

Acquires first guitar, a Harmony Monterey acoustic, and joins first group with school friends, the Jades.

1963

February 1:
Debut gig of his next band, the Squires, with Koblun (bass), Allan Bates (guitar) and Jack Harper (drums), at Riverview Community Club, Fort Rouge. Soon after, Harper is replaced by Ken Smyth.

July 23:
The Squires record two instrumentals, both written by Neil ("The Sultan" and "Aurora") at the local CKRC radio station.

September:
Debut single ("The Sultan" / "Aurora") is released on the local V Records label.

1964

February:
The Squires play influential Winnipeg folk club the Fourth Dimension.

April 2:
Second session at the CKRC studios, including Neil's first vocal recording on "I Wonder."

September:
Leaves school to follow musical career.

December:
Joins R&B band the Mynah Birds, with Bruce Palmer on bass. The band has a short-lived contract with Motown Records.

November:
Auditions unsuccessfully for Elektra Records, then returns to Toronto where he breaks up the Squires.

October 31:
Heads for New York City with Ken Koblun.

July:
Neil relocates to Toronto. The rest of the Squires later catch up with him there.

April:
Having spent the winter in Winnipeg, the band returns to Fort William, where Neil meets Stephen Stills.

1965

November 12:
Neil writes "Sugar Mountain" on his nineteenth birthday.

October 12:
The Squires travel to Fort William, Ontario, landing a residency at the Flamingo Club.

"To me, Canada is my family, where I grew up, memories of being young and being open to ideas. And then tryin' to get outta Canada because it was limiting … So I'm proud to be Canadian but I don't let it hold me back—part of the planet, not part of the nation."

— NY, 1992

Timing, as they say, is everything. And Neil Percival Young, son of Scott and Edna "Rassy" Ragland Young, arrived at the portal to a post-war era bursting with possibilities unimaginable to almost any previous generation.

Born in Toronto, Canada, on November 12, 1945, Neil was a fully paid-up "baby boomer." His life trajectory has propelled him through the protean changes that transformed society throughout the momentous 1960s and beyond. It would take a mountain man's strength and guile to survive and he was uniquely equipped to keep his footing.

Life in the Young household was never settled. Neil and his elder brother, Bob, were buffeted by the unhappy marriage of their parents. As a novice journalist, Scott Young was often on the road, his family trailing dutifully behind, and pitching camp like army postings. In 1949, they moved east, to Omemee, Ontario, which Neil later immortalized in his song "Helpless."

Sharry Wilson: Omemee was a small town in Ontario. I think the total population when the Young family was living there was about 700. Everybody knew each other. There was one public school. They would go fishing. There was a train track that ran behind their home. That's when Neil got fascinated with trains. All the things that he's really passionate about like cars, chickens, and trains—that was all established in his childhood.

Neil raised chickens as a child, had a small but thriving egg business, and a few years later was considering the possibility of eventually enrolling in the Ontario Agricultural College at the University of Guelph to become a chicken farmer.

Neil's first instrument was a plastic Arthur Godfrey ukulele given to him by his father after Neil saw it in a shop window and expressed interest in it. He bought his first acoustic guitar in Winnipeg shortly after he arrived in August 1960.

Scott Young was a writer who scrambled for jobs at the beginning and wasn't making that much money. Rassy assisted Scott in typing, proofreading, and mailing out his work to magazines like *Argosy* and the *Saturday Evening Post*. Even though the family's finances came under strain at times, the children were never deprived of anything. They lived in modest homes in small towns and rural environments, but also grander homes in solid upper-middle-class neighborhoods in Toronto later on when Scott's economic situation improved.

Scott wrote a daily column for the *Globe and Mail* from 1957 to 1969. Many of his columns included amusing anecdotes about his family life. Scott was then sports editor at the *Toronto Telegram* from 1969 to 1971, and then he returned to his daily columnist position at the *Globe and Mail* in 1971. Scott worked for *Maclean's*, an iconic Canadian magazine. During his childhood, Neil was around writers all the time who were guests in the Young home: Robertson Davies, June Callwood, Trent Frayne, and Pierre Berton with his wife, Janet. Scott was also well known as an announcer/interviewer on *Hockey Night in Canada*, a position he held from the late 1950s to the early 1970s. *(2014)*

Larry LeBlanc: Scott was a celebrity and this was in an age when there weren't a lot of celebrities in Canada. Scott had a real presence. He was very soft spoken and very commanding. There's no question that both of Neil's parents were very strong characters. *(2014)*

At the age of five, Young contracted polio, a disease that afflicted tens of thousands of children throughout North America at that time. Prior to the introduction of the Salk vaccine in the mid-1950s, polio was often fatal and those who survived it would contend with aftereffects ranging from pain, muscle weakness, and fatigue to severe cases that could lead to paralysis and deformity.

"Polio is the worst cold ever."

— NY, 1984

Sharry Wilson: Neil's was considered a "lucky polio." He suffered no permanent paralysis, but the muscles on his left side had weakened considerably. His parents thought wintering in New Smyrna Beach, Florida would aid in Neil's recovery. *(2014)*

The physical travails of his childhood would find a troubling symmetry with the collapse of his parents' relationship. It had always been rocky, but by the time Neil entered his teenage years it was more or less over.

At fourteen, he was put in the wrenching position of relocating to Winnipeg with Rassy, while brother Bob remained in Toronto with Scott. As bitter as his mother was over the breakup, Neil retained a deep respect for Scott. There would continue to be a palpable unease between them; affection was muted, circumspect. Or maybe that was simply the Canadian way—a cautious upper lip.

Neil aged seventeen in his high school year book (left). Neil's mother, Rassy, shown in 1986 (below left) and his father, Scott, in 1977 (below right). Toronto General Hospital, where Neil was born on November 12, 1945 (background).

"I wanted to say to Elvis Presley and the country that this is a real decent, fine boy, and wherever you go, Elvis, we want to say we've never had a pleasanter experience on our show with a big name than we've had with you."
— Ed Sullivan, following the last Elvis performance on The Ed Sullivan Show, 1956

Winnipeg, "Gateway to the Golden West," had long been a magnet for those in search of a new beginning. The vast, featureless prairie allowed for an interior reconstruction, all that emptiness waiting to be filled by emotional baggage.

Neil quickly became part of this rich, loamy connective tissue. Rassy had a history with Winnipeg; it was where she had been born and raised in a prominent local family, the Raglands, and also where she had met Scott, then writing for the *Winnipeg Free Press*. Her father, Bill, and one of her sisters, Toots, still lived there; Bill's last years were spent in the home she shared with Neil.

The geographical remoteness of Winnipeg only amplified that quaking sense of being an outsider, a "loner." Rassy didn't give two hoots; she was a shoot-from-the-hip, straight-talking gal who gave as good as she got. She doted on Neil, who was sometimes embarrassed by her salty tongue and unapologetic manner, but revered her with a deeply personal pride.

Neil soon carved his own place within the Balkanized social hierarchies of junior high school. He played guitar (following on from the ukulele), which caught the girls' attention, and cut a free-spirited path around the jocks who judged him warily at a distance.

The early 1960s was a time for Brylcreem and malt shops, Bazooka Joe and lonely teardrops. The Earl Grey Community Centre became a favorite hangout for Neil and his friends. Not everyone favored ice hockey during the endless winter months.

Classmate Sid Rogers recalls this time with crystal clarity: "I saw Neil heading to the [Earl Grey] club with his guitar. I tried to talk him into coming to play but he insisted that he had to go and practice. So I said to him, 'Neil, give it up, you're never going to make it. You might as well play hockey.' Those words still haunt me."

Neil had witnessed Elvis Presley's performances on *The Ed Sullivan Show* in 1956, and was as electrified as his fellow Mouseketeers. Six years later it was heart throbs with great hair who ruled the pop charts. The Jades, Neil's first band, contented themselves with covers of the Ventures and Pat Boone.

By 1963, though, Winnipeg and the world had begun to spin on a different axis. Bands were bursting forth like fields of wild flowers in spring, Top Forty AM radio (CKY, CKRC, CJOB) was tuning into some hipper sounds, and local scenes were gravitating around particular clubs and groups. *American Bandstand* aired on CJAY-TV, an afterschool hitching post for the latest in sights and sounds, and before too long, on CFTO-TV, there emerged *Hi Time*, a Canadian equivalent.

Neil, meanwhile, was drifting through Earl Grey Junior High and then Kelvin High, honing his craft in a succession of bands like the Stardusters and the Classics. College really wasn't an option. "I wasn't into school," he later said, to no one's surprise. "I had a pretty good time there but I really didn't fit in because I wasn't very good in school and I wasn't interested in being very good in school. I used to spend my time at Kelvin drawing amplifiers and stage setups. I was always flunking out."

Despite evidence of a keen, thoughtful intelligence that would have served him well at university, Neil made his position clear: His declared major would be … troubadour, much to the chagrin of his concerned father, whose own success reflected a deep regard for academia. Rassy, equally anxious, was nonetheless unconditionally supportive.

Sharry Wilson: Rassy always supported Neil and his aspirations. She was his number one fan and helped him in many ways. She bought him his first electric guitar for his sixteenth birthday—a Gibson Les Paul Junior—and loaned him her car to get to gigs.

She also bought him his first decent amplifier—an Ampeg piggyback unit. A crisis developed when this amplifier blew up at a high school dance. Neil needed a new amplifier and asked his father for a loan of $600. Scott was not willing to discuss the loan until he saw evidence of better grades from Neil. Rassy wrote to Scott to inform him that she would make sure Neil got his amplifier and that she didn't think very highly of his tactics.

Rassy was seen as being quite exotic by Neil's friends. She was a regular panelist on a quiz show in Winnipeg called *Twenty Questions*. When not involved with tapings for the show, she spent most of her time at the country club playing golf and tennis. She was often away from home and left Neil to his own devices. Neil's friends envied his freedom. Rassy was a force to be reckoned with because she held strong opinions and was not afraid to let them be known. Neil's friends didn't know quite what to make of her. She was definitely not a traditional mom. *(2014)*

February 1, 1963 saw the debut of the Squires, Neil's latest and most ambitious undertaking. With their homemade gear (heavy on distortion even then) and irrepressible earnestness, they worked the school auditorium and community club circuit like old-school road dogs. Bookings came in, gigs with top talent upped their game. Most memorably they shared the stage with Chad Allan and the Reflections, the biggest band in Winnipeg. The Reflections would become the Expressions before morphing into the

Guess Who, Canada's biggest band, featuring prairie rock icons Randy Bachman and Burton Cummings.

Lorne Saifer: If you look at Winnipeg in the early sixties, there was Chad Allan and the Expressions, the Deverons, the Shondels, the Squires, the Mongrels, the Fifth. Neil went to Kelvin High School, which was in a good upper-middle-class area. He lived upstairs on Grosvenor Street.

"**The drinking age in Winnipeg was twenty-one. Therefore you had a tremendous community club business in the city. There must have been two dozen of them. Every one of them ran dances on the weekends.**"

— Lorne Saifer, 2014

Opposite: Elvis Presley's electrifying performances on *The Ed Sullivan Show* in 1956 had a profound impact on the ten-year-old Neil Young.

Above: The Squires (Neil center) play a dance night at their school, Kelvin High, in Winnipeg, fall 1964.

Kenny Smyth lived across the back lane from me in Winnipeg. One Sunday afternoon I go into the back room and there's Kenny on the drums and Neil Young on guitar. Kenny Koblun playing bass and Al Bates on rhythm. The Squires. At that point they were an instrumental band. They were playing a tune by the Shadows [hugely popular 1960s British instrumental band]. They did "Apache."

I knew Kenny Smyth. I went to school with him. I had been in some bands. I gravitated to them and ended up kind of managing them.

Canada, at that point, was very British. A lot more influence from Britain than the United States. You got a lot of British records in Canada before they were available in the United States. My friend's cousin came back from England and brought back an album called *With the Beatles*. He gave me this Beatles LP which hadn't come out in Canada or America yet. I put it on and went nuts. Phenomenal. I ran over to Neil's house and played it for him and gave it to him to listen to. Neil flipped out over the Beatles album. And he goes crazy over "It Won't Be Long," the opening track on the LP. Neil decided he wanted to do a Beatles song at their next gig—Friday night at the Kelvin High School cafeteria. Only problem was, we had one amp and no microphones.

To show you the British influence, Neil picks me up in his mother's soft blue Vauxhall. All these British cars came into Canada that you never saw in the States. My first car was a Hillman. So Neil picks me up before the gig and says, "Where are we gonna get a microphone?" I replied, "I know. Drive me over to the Shaarey Zedek synagogue." I had my Bar Mitzvah there.

I go into the temple where they had a table set up in the banquet room and there was a big old mic. I take the mic and the stand and go out the side door. Neil's looking at me. "Let's get out of here!" Off we go.

He plugs the microphone into his big Ampeg amp. The first time Neil Young sang in public was through that microphone. He sang lead on "It Won't Be Long."

I was with the Squires for maybe a year. We went out to eat a couple of times after the shows. I don't know that Neil was so much a loner as just passionate about music. The first song Neil Young ever wrote and recorded was "I Wonder" and it was his first vocal. *(2014)*

Gary Pig Gold: Nearly two-and-a-half minutes flat of chaste, chugging, all-Canadian Merseybeat, "I Wonder" could have *so* easily found its place right there upon the latest Swinging Blue Jeans B-side. But the X-factor, then as now, was young Neil's pleading, while slightly menacing lyrics ... *and* vocal

delivery. Sure, his guitar is still tipping frets toward mentor Randy Bachman, but even today one can picture young Winnipeg lasses swooning under the song's sway within the local community center. While their out-of-depth boyfriends cast daggers Neil's way from the sidelines, that is. *(2014)*

Lorne Saifer: The first time Neil Young ever saw Randy Bachman, I took him. Randy had a big orange Gretsch guitar. We went to River Heights Community Club and that is where I introduced Neil to Randy. I know that Neil loved Randy's playing and his guitar. *(2014)*

NY: Randy was definitely the biggest influence on me in the city. He was the best. Back in those days he was years ahead of anybody else in the city. He had a homemade Echoplex from a tape loop on an old tape recorder. He did that Shadows style better than anybody else. He was playing a big orange Gretsch guitar and I got one like his. I still play an orange Gretsch like that one today. My heroes were guys like Bachman and [bassist] Jim Kale. I always thought Randy's guitar playing was great. I'm like an ax compared to him. *(1992)*

Randy Bachman: I remember playing with Al Bates and the Silvertones, Chad Allan and the Reflections, which were all the same band but with name changes, and also I remember being introduced to Neil Young, who came to our shows at high school dances in Winnipeg. I had gone to see Neil and his band play the Twilight Zone many times.

Right: Neil acquired a Gretsch 6120 Chet Atkins guitar in Winnipeg and still plays one like it today.

Above: The Beatles arriving at JFK on their first visit to America, February 7, 1964 (top). Another British band, the Shadows (center), was also a major influence on Neil and fellow Canadian musicians like Randy Bachman (bottom, in Union Jack cape).

Sometimes Neil would borrow bass player Jim Kale's Fender Concert amp, which had two channels and two inputs to each channel. All of the Squires could plug into this amp. Neil would call and ask Jim if we had a gig on such and such a date, and if we said, no, we weren't booked, then Jim would loan Neil the Concert amp for his gig. Then we'd all go and see Neil and the Squires play their gig.

Because of my guitar buddy Lenny Breau, as well as Chet Atkins, Duane Eddy, Eddie Cochran, my dream guitar was an orange Gretsch 6120 Chet Atkins model. I finally got one and it was beautiful and had amazing tone. I played it on "Shakin' All Over" as well as "Taking Care of Business." Neil got his orange Gretsch from Jon Glowa, who I replaced on guitar in Chad Allan's band.

When I joined the Reflections, Bob Ashley was the piano player, and Bob's mother had a German Korting reel-to-reel tape recorder with a switch to play both the record head and the playback head, thus creating an echo. For trying to copy the Shadows guitar sound, this was the magical machine to use.

Both Neil and I loved the Shadows. Hank Marvin's echo-laden Stratocaster leads and Bruce Welch's amazing rhythm guitar work. My first recorded instrumental was "Made in England" and Neil's were "Aurora" and "The Sultan," both Shadows-inspired songs. *(2014)*

Gary Pig Gold: Cut direct to two-track somewhere inside CKRC Radio during the summer of 1963 for a local label specializing in polka music, "Aurora" sounds like some pre-Mothers Zappa spaghetti western dinner fused with an incongruous, yet somehow perfect walking bass line; the same kind of bass style none other than Bruce Palmer would soon be bringing to Jack London and the Sparrows about 900 miles to the south-by-southeast in Toronto.

Meanwhile "The Sultan"—quite possibly *still* the only record, Canadian or otherwise, to feature a gong as its lead instrument—adds precisely the correct amount of prairie fuzz to its unashamedly Shadows-by-way-of-Bachman rattle. Neil still plays this song, very occasionally, in concert. Apparently, at least 300 seven-inch copies of 'V' Records # 109 were pressed … for "Winterpeg," that wasn't bad. *(2014)*

As if to put an exclamation point on the changin' times, the "British Invasion" hit North America in early 1964. The Beatles and their co-congregants brought a sense of wonder to the inchoate admixture of pop frivolity and teen angst that defined the current state of rock 'n' roll.

Their music shouted out "Now!" with an exhilarating urgency, galvanizing their youthful enthusiasts. On that hallowed first American tour in August 1964, the Beatles even touched down in Winnipeg (only for refueling, alas). In the ensuing hubbub, doors were thrown wide open to groups that previously couldn't get arrested.

The Squires, with their Beatle boots, longish hair and chiming electric guitars, landed a plum gig at the legendary Fourth Dimension coffeehouse in February 1964. The "4-D" had long been the key showcase for blues and folk artists and their beatnik following. And now … shazam, it became a bastion of railing amps and howling, discordant singers. This volte-face led to a predictable tension between sensitive folkies and the hirsute interlopers.

> "I always believed I could find someone else that might have the determination. The only thing that kept me going was thinking that the next guy was going to share the same attitude that I had. I probably asked almost everybody in Winnipeg ... I was looking for people who wanted to take a chance. Maybe that's why I couldn't find any."

> — NY, 1992

In September 1964, Neil left school and the Squires became his all-consuming passion. And what self-respecting band could function without the proper horsepower to shuttle them from gig to far-flung gig. So begins his storied relationship with the internal combustion engine. It was love at first sight—a 1948 Buick Roadmaster hearse, which he nicknamed Mortimer "Mort" Hearseburg. A more appropriate name for the wheels of a shambolic pop group could scarcely be imagined. The Squires put thousands of hard-fought miles on Mort; from Fort William on the coast of Lake Superior to the Hudson River port of Churchill, they blazed a fur trapper's trail, bringing their wares to a hungry audience.

Not everyone shared Neil's commitment. Players came and went, driven off by the unforgiving elements, and general fatigue in the face of his inexhaustible appetite for rehearsing and gigging.

In October, Neil's frustration with his hometown convinced him to relocate with the Squires to Fort William, halfway between Winnipeg and Toronto. "I always knew that I could never get to be the biggest band in Winnipeg." The key was to establish a presence somewhere else, where "you have all the advantages of being someone unique that no one has seen before."

The new arrivals soon landed a five-night residency at the town's Flamingo Club, where they caught the attention of Ray Dee, a popular DJ at the local radio station CJLX. Dee recorded several songs from the band at the station's two-track recording studio on the evening of November 23, and worked hard to help the Squires build their name in the area.

On April 18, 1965, the Squires played at the Fort William branch of the 4-D, sharing the bill with a folk outfit out of New York called the Company. They featured another hell-bent-for-leather true believer with a sweet voice and slinky guitar style named Stephen Stills. Stills recognized a kindred spirit in the tall, lanky, orphan-voiced singer who stood center stage, wielding an orange Gretsch like a lumberjack. It was a sound that would soon become a chart-topping signpost of pop music's next big thing. That very week, Columbia released the Byrds' "Mr. Tambourine Man." Folk rock's time had surely come.

Above: Neil met Stephen Stills in Fort William and eventually followed him to Los Angeles, where he is pictured here in October 1966.

Opposite: With their leader toting his orange Gretsch, the Squires storm the 4-D in Fort William, 1965 (left). By the time they left Winnipeg, the band had already cut their first single, "The Sultan"/"Aurora" (right).

Neil was equally impressed by Stills. "His voice was phenomenal. His guitar playing was marginal. He was the rhythm guitarist and he played a big red Guild acoustic guitar. He didn't really get into playing lead until the Springfield. He was more of a singer. He'd been with several singers in the Au Go Go Singers and the whole hootenanny thing in New York, so he had voice training and knew harmony."

NY: We got into a thing in Fort William where we did classic folk songs with a rock 'n' roll beat and changed the melody. We did a really weird version of "Tom Dooley" which was like rock 'n' roll but in a minor key. And then we did "Oh Susannah" based on an arrangement by a group called the Thorns. Tim Rose was in the Thorns. We saw them at the 4-D. We also did "Clementine" and "She'll Be Coming Round the Mountain" with all new melodies I wrote. We totally changed them with rock 'n' roll arrangements. It was pretty interesting. *(1992)*

Stills and Young dialed into a regime of jamming, drinking, carousing around town in Mort, and built a relationship that would ultimately pay dividends

beyond their wildest reckoning. The Company returned to New York while the Squires bashed away in the north. Money was nonexistent, the exigencies of the road were taking their predictable toll.

In the summer of 1965, Neil abruptly left for Toronto, leaving loyal band mate Ken Koblun behind. Sadly, the long drive southeast was too much for Mort, which wheezed to its inglorious demise near Iron Bridge, on the north coast of Lake Huron. Neil completed the journey by motorbike, then crashed at his father's place. It was time to regroup and take the pulse of the city's clamorous music community.

Neil immediately headed for the vibrant district of Yorkville. Joni Mitchell practiced her magic here, as did Zal Yanovsky, who would soon form the hit-making Lovin' Spoonful. Denny Doherty, from Halifax, paid his dues here before heading south for "California Dreamin'" with the Mamas and the Papas. Ian & Sylvia, Gordon Lightfoot and countless others crafted a singular Canadian sound in Yorkville before spreading their gospel to the States and beyond.

Peter Goddard: When Neil arrived in Toronto in 1965, Canada and Toronto were becoming different things.

"We didn't succeed in taking Toronto by storm. It was a tough time. We were small fish in a big pond, had no reputation, and really there was nothing special about us in the big city."

— NY, 2012

If you grew up outside Toronto, you grew up around beer, hockey, *Hockey Night in Canada*.

Neil arrived when the city was becoming spectacular. Jane Jacobs, author and activist, had arrived and suddenly Toronto became the model for all cities in the world. The Toronto Symphony Orchestra had [musical director] Seiji Ozawa starting in 1965. It was a hotbed of art and classical music.

The UOT was the hippest university in the world. Let me go further: Ryerson University, which was our tech college, invited Marcel Duchamp with John Cage. They would show Andy Warhol movies on Yonge Street.

Toronto never became famous, because it seemed to be a copy of New York or Los Angeles. But it really was quite unique. And Neil in 1965 and very early 1966 would have seen a city that did not exist five years earlier. *(2014)*

Yorkville was happening—perhaps not quite Hollywood's Sunset Strip, London's Soho, or New York's Greenwich Village, but it rocked to an authentically native beat. Surrounded by a financial and cultural metropolis, it staked its claim as Canada's

little bit of bohemia. Bands like the Sparrow with John Kay (later of Steppenwolf) and Levon and the Hawks—soon to become the Band—raged late into the night at Le Coq d'Or, the Colonial, and any other gin-soaked barroom scene serving up that winning trifecta of booze, babes, and a bruising bottom end. Bernie Fiedler operated the Riverboat coffeehouse. Neil played there and later wrote about the venue in "Ambulance Blues."

At one point Neil cut off his hair and took a brief job as a stock boy at Coles bookstore to repay a loan from his father. (He recounts this experience in an anecdote titled "Bookstore Rap" on *Sugar Mountain: Live at Canterbury House 1968*.) He was struggling but he wasn't aimless. The guitar was a stalwart companion, his eyes and ears ever alert to a flicker of inspiration for songs that continued to come.

Opposite: Heading for Fort William with band mates Ken Koblun (left) and Bob Clark (right) in his beloved Pontiac hearse, Mortimer "Mort" Hearseburg, 1965.

Above: Upon arriving in Toronto in 1965, Neil soon gravitated toward the vibrant Yorkville district.

"Neil has a drive to be creative and to be expressive. It doesn't matter if there are ten people or ten thousand people in the audience. He just gets in that zone when he is on stage. People always say, 'How come he doesn't talk a lot on stage and interact?' But, if you see him after his shows, he's poured everything into that show. Alone with an acoustic guitar, with Crazy Horse or whoever backed him up. It's the intensity about him."

— John Einarson, 2014

In fall 1965, Neil, together with his long-suffering musical confederate Ken Koblun, decamped for New York. He had an audition with Elektra Records and was eager to reconnect with that hot shot from the Company, Stephen Stills, whose address he'd kept close. Stills, apparently, had left for Los Angeles according to his roommate, Richie Furay, another itinerant busker and former Au Go Go Singer. Well then, said Neil, mind if I show *you* a new song I've worked up? The song was "Nowadays Clancy Can't Even Sing."

Richie Furay: I thought it was a real fantastic song. It had a haunting melody. Maybe it was the way Neil sang it. It was like nothing I was used to listening to. It had metaphors and allegories about this classmate named Clancy who was just one of those guys everybody picked on. I couldn't begin to tell you what it's all about but I love to sing it even to this day.

Neil seemed very sure of himself, of where he was going and was very intense. He impressed me so much as an artist and songwriter. *(1992)*

Wherever he was going, it was not to be with the Squires. Upon returning to Toronto in late 1965 having flunked the Elektra audition, Neil told the rest of the band that it was time to call it a day.

Sharry Wilson: Ken Koblun and Neil were the only two members of the Squires who were with the band the entire time—three years in total. Ken also wanted to succeed with music and he saw Neil as his guiding light. He felt that Neil abandoned him in Fort William

An early solo performance at the Riverboat coffeehouse in Yorkville, Toronto, 1965.

The MYNAH BIRDS

RICK MASON – DRUMS
JOHN TAYLOR – RHYTHM GUITAR
BRUCE PALMER – BASS HARMONICA
RICKIE MATHEWS – VOCAL, MOUTH ORGAN
TOM MORGAN – LEAD GUITAR

A great band, exciting, showy and different. The Mynah Birds released the Mynah Bird Hop on Columbia. They have appeared on HI TIME, MICKIE A GO-GO, and other shows throughout Ontario. Their ability to entertain well is proven each time they step on stage.

when he went to Toronto after Mort broke down near Blind River. He was again abandoned in Toronto once the Squires split up. [Ken would later have a very brief stint with Buffalo Springfield in February 1967, replacing the absent Bruce Palmer.] *(2014)*

NY: We were together a long time, even longer than Buffalo Springfield. We were pretty young and just learning the business and we were pretty naïve. But we had a lot of fun back then. They could have made it. I just wanted it more than they did. *(1992)*

Neil was now alone, hustling gigs as a solo act, digging deep into his folk roots to sustain a semblance of a career. Just when he needed it, he met someone who threw him a lifeline. Bruce Palmer, already an experienced performer at nineteen, was a familiar face on the Yorkville scene. His band, the Mynah Birds, needed a guitarist. They were a mashup of R&B and rock, with a charismatic black singer named Ricky James Matthews (who would famously reinvent himself as the 1980s funk master Rick James). Although this wasn't really Neil's thing, he needed to eat, the pay was good, and he didn't have to take the responsibility of leader.

The Mynah Birds had financial backing from John Craig Eaton, a member of the lordly Eaton family, whose fortune was made in retailing. Neil received a Rickenbacker guitar and a Traynor amp to augment his twelve-string acoustic.

Above: After the breakup of the Squires, Bruce Palmer invited Neil to join his R&B group the Mynah Birds.

Opposite: Neil Young and Joni Mitchell were just two of the ambitious young Canadian musicians who headed south in the mid-to-late 1960s.

They were then signed to Motown Records—one of the label's first "white" acts—and sent to Detroit ("Hitsville, USA") to record their debut album with producers R. Dean Taylor and Mickey Stevenson.

Gary Pig Gold: If the lone (semi-)released Motown Mynah track, "It's My Time," can be any indication, this was a band who had expertly absorbed all the characteristics of the Toronto Sound—Yankee ex-pat R&B, British Invasion harmonies, jangle-folk guitar—and slung atop it a vocalist of rare kick and confidence. "I'll Wait Forever," also cut at these Detroit sessions, sounds like some sort of Young Rascals/Seekers hybrid, while "I've Got You in My Soul" could have fallen off the rear end of the Stones' *12 x 5* given half a chance. *(2014)*

Bill Munson: The Mynah Birds headed down to Detroit to record in early 1966. They'd already auditioned for and been signed by Motown, so were now treated as an investment to be protected. They were put up in a nice hotel, the Pontchartrain, they were assigned to some solid in-house producers (notably fellow Canadian R. Dean Taylor), they were recorded professionally with, at times, vocal backup by big-name Motown veterans including the Four Tops, they were fitted out for suitable Motown clothing, and they were even schooled in Motown stage moves. *(2015)*

The future was certainly looking bright, but what came next for the Mynah Birds was a disaster. Ricky James Matthews turned out to be not just American but an American who was AWOL from the United States Navy. Motown convinced him to turn himself in, and he was taken off for a stretch in the navy brig while his case was considered.

The four remaining band members were left high and dry, without a front man and without a recording contract. Neil soon found himself back at square one in Toronto, with just Bruce Palmer at his side.

Larry LeBlanc: Neil had to go to New York or Los Angeles to make it. Here's the gist of Canadian music. We had two-track studios. Nobody got an album. Bands got singles for $500. If you had a bunch of singles, then you did an album.

The sole ambition of the whole Canadian music industry from 1963 to certainly 1975 was to get into the States somehow. Either sign with an American label or play New York. Nobody dreamt of Los Angeles. The Sparrow went to New York and San Francisco before they became Steppenwolf and came to LA. Bernie Finkelstein had the Paupers. They went to New York.

"Canada just couldn't support the ideas I had. There wasn't an audience for the music I wanted to do. I just couldn't get anyone to listen. By 1966, I knew I had to leave Canada, and the sounds I was hearing and the sounds I liked were coming from California. I knew that if I went down there I could take a shot at making it."

— NY, 1992

The thing was, the downfall in Canada was that nobody was writing music. There weren't a lot of songwriters. Basically they were copying what was out there. Each city had a scene. Winnipeg, Vancouver, Ottawa, Montreal, Toronto, and the scenes were rotated around the radio stations. The DJs in a lot of cases managed the bands and financed their records. There was no national scene. That came later, in the late 1960s and early 1970s.

Neil knew he had to get out of town. And he was writing songs. *(2014)*

Peter Goddard: In Canada, whether you were a musician or filmmaker, you either had a huge sense of inferiority or you simply went and did it.

I was pretty actively covering the scene and Neil Young just sort of went through it and disappeared. Joni Mitchell played Toronto a number of times. She was here. Neil Young was like a ghost. He showed up, materialized, then de-materialized and left. Whereas Joni almost made a point of getting hurt, getting

pissed off, leaving for LA—"Fuck you guys, I'm not coming back"—Neil was just so far from caring about all that stuff. *(2014)*

Bruce Palmer: Neil and I were sitting at the Cellar club in Yorkville one night in March just after the Motown deal fell flat. He turns to me and says, "Let's go to California." I thought that was a good idea. There was nothing else happening. So we decided then and there to head out to LA. *(1992)*

NY: Bruce and I pawned all the equipment. It was the only way we could go. The band had broken up. Bruce and I were the only ones who wanted to be in the band. Ricky was in jail. It was really Eaton's equipment. *(1992)*

Years later Neil would accept full responsibility and reimburse the outstanding Eaton debt from a concert fee in Toronto. But for now it was time to pay his dues in the City of Angels.

EXPECTING TO FLY

1966-1969

"Something was
happening, but we
didn't know what it was.
It was fucking
Buffalo Springfield,
that's what it was."

— NY, 2012

Timeline

1966

March 22:
Neil leaves Toronto on a road trip to the US West Coast with Bruce Palmer and others.

Below: Buffalo Springfield band photo, 1967. Jim Fielder (second from right) filled in for Bruce Palmer when the bassist was temporarily deported back to Canada.

Previous page: The original lineup, 1966. Left to right, Stephen Stills, Bruce Palmer, Neil Young, Richie Furay, and Dewey Martin.

April 1:
Arrives in Los Angeles, soon linking up with Stephen Stills and forming Buffalo Springfield.

April 11:
Buffalo Springfield plays its debut gig, at the Troubadour, Hollywood.

Early May–mid-June:
The band plays a seven-week residency at the prestigious Whisky a Go Go club on Sunset Boulevard.

Summer:
Neil suffers his first epileptic seizure.

June:
The band begins recording sessions at Gold Star Studios, Los Angeles.

July 25:
Buffalo Springfield plays as a support act to the Rolling Stones at the Hollywood Bowl.

January-September:
Recording of second album, *Buffalo Springfield Again*, mainly at Sunset Sound, Los Angeles.

1967

December 5:
Release of debut album, *Buffalo Springfield*.

August:
Buffalo Springfield debut single, the Neil Young composition "Nowadays Clancy Can't Even Sing," is released on Atco, an Atlantic subsidiary.

April:
First chart entry— the rereleased *Buffalo Springfield* hits #80 in album best sellers.

June:
Neil announces his departure from Buffalo Springfield.

August:
Rejoins the band.

October 30:
Buffalo Springfield Again released.

November–May 1968:
Main recording phase of the band's final album, *Last Time Around*.

1968

May 5:
Buffalo Springfield makes its final appearance, at the Long Beach Arena, before officially disbanding the following week.

June:
Neil signs a management deal with Elliot Roberts.

December:
Release of debut solo single, "The Loner."

December 7:
Marries Susan Acevedo.

November 12:
Release of *Neil Young*.

October 23-28:
Solo concerts at the Bitter End club, New York City.

August-October:
Records tracks for his first solo album with producer David Briggs.

August:
Moves into a newly purchased house at 611 Skyline Trail, Topanga Canyon.

July:
Neil signs to Reprise Records with a $20,000 advance.

July 18:
Release of *Last Time Around*.

"I was listening to the radio and heard the Byrds. The sound of their electric guitars and voices made me think that LA was the place to be. Neil wanted to be Bob Dylan, I wanted to be the Beatles."

— Stephen Stills, 1992

lush with cash, Neil and Bruce Palmer hit the road, blazing behind the wheel of a 1953 Pontiac hearse, natch. Finally, in early April 1966 they arrived in Los Angeles, in search of Stephen Stills and musical dreams held desperately dear.

Coincidentally, Stills had been anxious for Neil to join him as well. Richie Furay, another gypsy, was back with Stills, the promise of a band his inducement to come west. Ken Koblun decided to pass, preferring the grounded locale of Toronto to the talk-talk of Hollywood hopefuls.

Where was Neil? Having given up their search for the mercurial Stills, Neil and Bruce decided to head to San Francisco and what sounded like a promising music scene.

In one of the most fortuitous encounters in the history of pop music, an early April afternoon on Sunset Boulevard saw our two protagonists come to a traffic stop at the exact same moment—one going east and the other going west. But, good heavens, who else but Neil would be driving a hearse with Canadian license plates in LA? And thus one of the enduring creation myths was born.

"Bruce and I were just leaving to go to San Francisco. We were on Sunset stopped at a light. The traffic was heavy. Then Stephen and Richie saw us. Stephen saw the hearse with Ontario plates and said, 'I know that guy, it's Neil!'"

— NY, 1992

John Einarson: When the light of recognition went on in Stephen's head, he jumped out and ran to the driver's side of the hearse where he banged on the window, startling Neil at first. Once Neil realized who this frantic person was, the two pulled their vehicles into nearby Ben Frank's [Coffee Shop] parking lot and everyone exchanged hugs all round, laughing at the quirk of fate which had brought them together again. *(1992)*

Los Angeles, the city of noir and city of light. For all its enticing charms—the vaguely toxic vermillion sky, the lustrous undertow of the adjacent Pacific—it could induce a palpable ambivalence.

By 1966, the city was going through a vivid reimaging, like a film set readying itself for its next call to "action." The Watts riots of August 1965 had slapped the dreamy denizens into social/political consciousness, the smog-shrouded basin taking on an acrid, burnt-brown hue.

There was, indeed, something happenin' here, something best documented in the melodies and words of young troubadours who found in pop music the ideal platform to address all those roiling, inchoate concerns. Los Angeles was the epicenter of this sonic youth-quake. The strum of a D minor chord, the hurt in an orphaned voice, a transformative backbeat, a pulsing bass line, the sting of a lead guitar, this was the recipe for rebellion with a bullet, turning protest into publishing.

This page: "What a field day for the heat." Martin Luther King Jr. visits the Watts district of Los Angeles on August 17, 1965 (above left), with tensions running high after six days of rioting (above right). A fur-clad Sonny & Cher support a less violent protest—against strict enforcement of curfew restrictions on Sunset Strip, December 1966 (below).

Opposite: Stills and Young tuning up at the Whisky a Go Go, April 1966

Above: The band got its name from a sign hanging on a steam roller.

Above right: Rehearsing at the Whisky a Go Go, April 1966.

Right: Buffalo Springfield made its debut at Doug Weston's Troubadour on April 11, 1966.

Dickie Davis: I met Stephen Stills when he was in the Au Go Go Singers in Houston. In 1966 I was now working at Doug Weston's Troubadour in Hollywood selling tickets and running the Hoot nights. Neil Young and Bruce Palmer come into town and I hear about it. Stephen and Richie connect with a drummer, Billy Mundi. They were good. I'm watching Steve, Richie, Bruce, with Billy Mundi, and at this point their manager Barry Friedman asked me to help out with the band. Sort of like a road manager thing. Dewey Martin joined as drummer replacing Billy.

Returning from the Troubadour in my faded red 1963 Volvo P1800, Richie and I pulled to the curb on Fountain Avenue outside Barry Friedman's place. I stopped immediately behind a steam roller and noticed a small metal sign hanging loosely from it.

"How about that?" I said. "I've heard of Mercedes-Benz, and Alfa Romeo, but there's a Buffalo Springfield. Never heard of that one before."

Everyone laughed and got out of the car. We proceeded to try to get the sign off the roller. It was hanging from only one bolt but it wouldn't come loose. As they went inside I drove away. Later,

possibly the next day, I was at Barry's. Stephen showed me the sign and said he'd decided that we should use it as the name of the group. I liked the idea. It had a contemporary, sort of Jefferson Airplane ring. *(2014)*

Chris Hillman of the Byrds helped Buffalo Springfield get their first Whisky a Go Go show, which secured a subsequent residency in May and part of June 1966.

Henry Diltz: Buffalo Springfield was great on stage. My first impression of Neil Young was that he was kind of a quiet guy. Neil played so well. And that is the thing about Buffalo Springfield. You had Stills and Young on the guitars. Both of them spurring each other on and feeding off each other. Just like a good jazz group would do. One guy plays a solo and the other guy takes off from there and tries to maybe build on that. Or do something better. The two of them with dueling guitars and then Richie Furay with that amazing voice soaring above all that. And then they had harmonies, and their drummer, Dewey Martin, had been our drummer in the MFQ

at the Troubadour. And Bruce was a nice guy and a phenomenal bassist. *(2014)*

Chris Darrow: I first started recording in Los Angeles in 1966 as a member of Kaleidoscope and Barry Friedman produced our first album, *Side Trips*. I saw Buffalo Springfield at their fifth gig at Covina High School in 1966. They shared a bill with the Byrds and the Dillards. Neil Young had a thin, almost whiny, voice, and a detached manner, that gave him a more mysterious vibe. *(2014)*

Howard Kaylan: I did see Buffalo Springfield at the Whisky a Go Go. The band rehearsed in the house that Mark Volman and I shared in Laurel Canyon on Lookout Mountain. Richie and Stephen slept on our floor. I moved out after a failed drug bust—didn't know if the house was being watched. Paranoid, Richie moved into my room and the group practiced and wrote there. We all knew well before they played show number one that they would be stars. In the Canyon, we were used to our friends becoming stars. *(2014)*

"The real core of the group was the three Canadians—me, Bruce Palmer, and Dewey Martin. We played in such a way that the three of us were basically huddled together behind, while Stills and Furay were always out front. 'Cause we'd get so into the groove of the thing, that's all we really cared about. Time meant nothing. We were ready."

— NY, 1997

Above: The band at their pulsating best, with Furay and Stills front and center, at the Whisky a Go Go, October 1966.

Overleaf: Looking heavy in this 1967 portrait by Jini Dellaccio.

"I always liked fringe jackets.
I went out and bought one
right away with some pants
and a turtleneck shirt.
Oh yeah, I thought
I was heavy."

— NY, 1997

Charlie Greene and Brian Stone, two rascally East Coast PR flaks fled Manhattan in 1960 and set up shop in Hollywood. A turn at running a nightclub in Canoga Park failed miserably. Finally, inevitably, they landed—crashed— on the Sunset Strip, the music business being the last refuge for them. Luck and business savvy led them to sign up Sonny & Cher to a management contract just before the duo struck gold with "I Got You Babe."

Dickie Davis: Charlie Greene and Brian Stone came on the scene. I brought them. They're hot on the charts with Sonny & Cher. I knew they could sell anything. Charlie was one of us, like it or not. Brian, not one of us but knew how to behave. *(2014)*

Brian Stone: Dickie said, "I have this act and they're really great. And you gotta hear them." Dickie, by the way, was originally a full one-sixth member of the group. Not as a manager but as the publisher. He suggested us.

Charlie and I got blown away when we saw Buffalo Springfield at the Whisky. It was electric. They were all minors or barely out of their teens and we had to have all their parents sign and take them all to court. And we got them places to stay. Neil was quiet and shy. He was this extraordinary and co-equal talent and writer and Neil had songs. He was such a genius; Neil was writing this advanced stuff.

Nobody in the group wanted Neil to sing any leads on songs because they didn't like his voice. It was brought up in the studio a lot. Stephen would say, "I want to sing that song." Originally, when we first signed them, it was written down that Richie Furay was the lead singer. But positions were still being defined in this group. Neil would say, "I want to sing this song. I wrote it. It's my song."

We took Buffalo into the studio and made decisions about tunes, and what songs we would try to do. Neil Young and Stephen Stills were two sensational players. How they sang and acted together, worked together. Played off each other. I loved the bass player, Bruce Palmer.

We had already been all over the world with Ahmet Ertegun, the founder of Atlantic Records, and we called Ahmet and got them signed to Atco, an Atlantic subsidiary, for a big advance. Ahmet used to say to me all the time, that "next to the Beatles, Buffalo Springfield was the best rock group ever of all time." It was very rare to have two—if you want to include Richie Furay as well, three—extraordinary singers and players in the same group. *(2014)*

John Einarson: Greene and Stone were pivotal not only to Buffalo Springfield's career but Neil's career. They already had Sonny & Cher, and in fact the first press attention that Neil got back home after leaving Winnipeg was a notice in the local papers that said "Ex-Winnipegger Neil Young is now writing songs for Sonny & Cher." Somebody must have got their wires crossed. *(2014)*

Denny Bruce, from Lancaster, Pennsylvania, Amish country, was holding down the drum chair behind a bunch of pick-up gigs in Philly when one-too-many harsh East Coast winters finally took its toll. The prospect of endless summers and the jingle-jangle soundtrack percolating out of Los Angeles proved irresistible. He found Lowell George wandering around a San Fernando Valley Junior College campus, was in the Western Union and kept time for Frank Zappa's earliest incarnation of the Mothers and was a Sunset Strip regular, where the wayfaring tribes were beginning to gather. It was a helluva time to be smart, acerbic, and twenty-one.

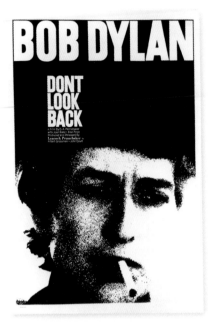

Denny Bruce: In 1965 I was staying at Jack Nitzsche's house in the Hollywood Hills after he split with his wife, Gracia.

I first met Neil in 1966 when he was living in an apartment at the Commodore Gardens in Hollywood. I saw Buffalo Springfield play all the local clubs. The Whisky, Gazzarri's, and smaller places. After performing Neil would go to his apartment still wide awake and write songs. Neil and I had a casual friendship and he was a true fan of music. Neil was always interested in my opinion about all things pop.

Jack liked to hang out at the Greene and Stone offices on Sunset, which were always open all night just in case anybody wanted to show up. There was a pool table. One night I introduced Neil to Jack.

Neil was doing guitar stuff, and always trying to make his guitar a little bit different, and he said, "Do you know where that sound is coming from, Denny?" I responded, "I know it's not the Ventures." And he said, "Close. Hank Marvin, the guy in the Shadows. See, in Winnipeg we had BBC Radio and I heard them."

We constantly had chats about music. Records, performers like Ian & Sylvia, and he loved Dylan. Neil would constantly talk to Jack about his work with the Rolling Stones, Sonny Bono, and Jackie DeShannon. Jack and I became his mind-trust. Neil loved imagery as much as songwriting and performing.

Neil also indicated to us that he wanted to create a musical and lyrical mix of the Stones and Dylan. In 1966 Jack took me to one of the Stones' *Aftermath* sessions at RCA he was working on where Andrew Loog Oldham was producing.

Neil and I watched the D. A. Pennebaker Bob Dylan documentary *Don't Look Back* at the Los Feliz Theater. Neil had his mind blown and asked me if we could see it again. *(2014)*

Keeping one's equilibrium within the squall of a rising rock band would test the resolve of the Good Samaritan. Neil had the added burden of managing an epileptic condition that was becoming increasingly disruptive. A seizure could strike without warning, often resulting in a debilitating convulsion, which, left unattended, might prove fatal.

Dickie Davis: Neil's first seizure happened in spring or summer of 1966 at the Teen Fair held in the parking lot of the Hollywood Palladium on Sunset Boulevard. I heard about it immediately. Somebody called and said, "Neil's in trouble." It was very scary and to the best of my knowledge Neil had no idea of the problem at that point.

I had seen one epileptic seizure before. At the Whisky. So we banned strobe lights at shows. But he had seizures regardless of strobe lights. After the Teenage Fair he had a doctor. And Neil had been diagnosed. I know Neil was epileptic. I know he was scared to death. I know it hurt physically. This was scary because the man could get hurt. He could fall into lights or fall off the stage. *(2014)*

At the Melodyland Theater in Anaheim, Neil had an epileptic fit mid-set and was carried off the stage.

Brian Stone: We put Neil into the UCLA Medical Center in summer 1966. No musicians had health insurance then. Sometimes Neil could not play a set. This happened a few times. Neil would say, "I'm sick, man. I don't know what's happening." We told Neil, "We have to take you in," and that's when he went to UCLA for that week or so. *(2014)*

The pressures of fame. As Buffalo Springfield's reputation grew, Neil suffered a spate of epileptic seizures. Portrait by Jini Dellaccio, 1967.

"One day, I was there at Teen Fair with
a few friends ... when the sky started to spin
a little and I felt a bit sick to my stomach.
I started to fall. The sky was getting dark
and the sounds were all echoing, a hollow
reverberation inside my head."

— NY, 2012

Buffalo Springfield started recording their first album at Gold Star Studios on Santa Monica Boulevard in June 1966. Owners Dave Gold and Stan Ross and engineer Larry Levine had welcomed artists from Johnny Mercer, Dimitri Tiomkin, and Eddie Cochran through to the new generation like the Turtles, Love, and the Seeds.

Stan Ross: Gold Star brought a feeling, an emotional feeling. Dave [Gold] built the equipment and echo chamber. Gold Star was not a dead studio, but a live studio. It was all tubes. When you have tubes, sound expansion doesn't distort so easy. We didn't use pop filters and screens around the microphones when we recorded vocals.

Buffalo Springfield was a self-contained group. I was always impressed by the songwriting abilities of the Buffalos. Neil Young, especially. He had an unusual sound. Very nasal and country. *(2001)*

Dan Kessel: I grew up at Gold Star. My stepmom, B. J. Baker, sang background on Phil Spector's records and my dad played guitar on those as well. I performed handclaps on the Crystals' "He's a Rebel" when I was ten. My dad played on Sonny & Cher recordings. So, I was always welcome there as far as studio owners Dave Gold and Stan Ross were concerned.

One day I walked into the booth with Ahmet Ertegun and engineer Doc Siegel and sat in on a recording session for the first Buffalo Springfield album. The band didn't seem to mind.

Buffalo Springfield had a new voice and a new sound and would have made a good album under most any circumstances. The band was in good hands at Gold Star with Doc Siegel. Stan Ross and Larry Levine were the main engineers there but Doc often subbed for them.

Neil was using his mainstay orange Gretsch 6120 Chet Atkins guitar, Steve had his Guild Starfire, and Richie was playing what looked like an Epiphone Riviera or a Gibson ES-335.

> **"Neil's voice was kind of like Roy Orbison going sideways. Very compelling."**
> — Dan Kessel, 2014

Neil seemed to inhabit his own space, which is not to say he wasn't communicative or friendly. He and Stills were the most vocal about the arrangements and didn't always agree on everything right away or sometimes ever but that's not unusual with artistic collaborators. *(2014)*

Released in December 1966, *Buffalo Springfield* was a decidedly mixed blessing. While it announced the arrival of a vital new musical force—a shotgun marriage of Northern folk and Southern rock, chiming Gretsch guitars and rueful harmonizing—the recording lacked the sound and fury of their live performances. "Produced" by their gimcrack managers, Greene and Stone, it may have been weak tea sonically—the band loathed it—but there was no gainsaying the fact that a worthy successor to the Byrds and Love was eyeing the prize.

Brian Stone: When Charlie and I first heard "Clancy" we loved it! That's the song we wanted to put out as the first single. *(2014)*

Kirk Silsbee: It was very smart to give those "Clancy" vocals to Richie Furay. Neil had an odd voice, with a haunted edge to it and lacking warmth. Richie's voice, on the other hand, was far more engaging and even sweet, in the best sense of the word. But listen to "Clancy"—it's quite a poignant vocal performance. The lyrics are emotionally torturous, which seemed to be Neil's stock-in-trade at that time. *(2014)*

Brian Stone: After everyone signed off the first album, we sent it to Ahmet and he said, "The fuckin' thing is beautiful." *(2014)*

Ertegun was even more taken with the epoch-defining Stephen Stills song "For What It's Worth," inspired by the Sunset Strip curfew protests of late 1966. The song was recorded just after the release of the first album and reached the Top Ten when it came out as a single in January 1967.

"Neil's harmonics on 'For What It's Worth' were done by plugging straight into the board in the studio. The notes are so clear because there's no amplifier or microphone involved. It wasn't really a technical decision. It was kind of like, Neil's gonna sit in the booth and do this. It was that simple."

— **Dickie Davis,** 2014

Neil played the debut album to the members of the Guess Who at Christmas 1966 when he came back to Winnipeg to visit his mom. The band then cut one of his contributions, "Flying on the Ground Is Wrong," in London in March 1967. Neil was absolutely thrilled that his old pals had recorded the first cover of one of his tunes.

John Einarson: Buffalo Springfield's debut LP got some action in Winnipeg because Neil was the hometown boy. The album was nothing at all in Canada. For us in Winnipeg it was cool because on the back of the album in the individual band member blurbs, Neil says Winnipeg is his home. "Wow! That's amazing. There's Winnipeg."

Richie Furay still insists that it's the only Buffalo Springfield album. But what is missing is the sound quality. The songwriting is there. The performances are there. The playing is there. The sound quality is flat. Even despite the fidelity deficiencies, listen to Bruce Palmer's bass playing. It's absolutely brilliant. He had a style that was intense. *(2014)*

Above: Rehearsing at home in Malibu, 1967.

Opposite: At the legendary Gold Star Studios, where Buffalo Springfield recorded its self-titled debut album in 1966.

"Even then, though, you could sense that Buffalo Springfield wasn't built to last—a dozen great songs and ... kablooey! But that's always been Neil and Stephen's MO."

— Kenneth Kubernik, 2014

In January 1967, just as the band was making a name for itself, bassist Bruce Palmer got into some immigration problems and was deported back to Canada. They employed various fill-in bass players (Ken Koblun, Jim Fielder, and Bobby West) until he was able to return in late May, but then Neil, frustrated at Stephen Stills's domineering attitude to the band, quit the following month, only to rejoin in August.

Meanwhile, the label, Atco, just wanted to get another album out quickly to capitalize on the success of "For What It's Worth." In the end, they decided to re-press and rerelease the first LP in March, with "For What It's Worth" in place of "Baby Don't Scold Me."

John Einarson: It was an attempt to get a new album together from a band that wasn't together, because Bruce is gone and as far as everybody is concerned he is the glue that keeps the band together. They are doing sessions. Atco had all intentions of putting an album together. And then Neil left the band just as they are accumulating all these tracks. Things are kind of in limbo.

Neil comes back to the band in August and that's when things go into high gear for the second album. They'd already recorded "Mr. Soul" and "Bluebird," but then Neil comes in with "Expecting to Fly," which he's been working on with Jack Nitzsche. He brings in "Broken Arrow," and Stills comes in with "Rock & Roll Woman."

Neil wrote "Mr. Soul" in the hospital. It's Neil pointing a bit of a jaundiced finger at the whole Hollywood music scene and the fame that the band was starting to experience. He pulled that kind of lick from "Satisfaction." Buffalo Springfield went to New York with Charlie Greene and Brian Stone to record at Atlantic. Otis Redding wanted to do the song. Neil said no. Charlie Greene told me that. Ahmet was there. And he didn't want Neil to sing it. So Stills sang it and Richie sang it, and Otis is there and he wants to take the song. Then Neil put his foot down for the first time and said, "No. It's going to be my song. And I'm going to sing it."

Neil left the band and the reason he came back was that he couldn't get a deal and he couldn't get out of Atco Records. So he had no money. And Jack Nitzsche pitched Neil on the idea he could be a solo artist. He could be a "Roy Orbison." *(2014)*

Kenneth Kubernik: Ninety-three cents is what I paid to see the "totally groovy" second annual KHJ appreciation concert at the Hollywood Bowl on April 29, 1967 with the Fifth Dimension, Johnny Rivers, the Seeds, Brenda Holloway, the Supremes—and Buffalo Springfield.

I loved that Neil and Stephen played those ornate Gretsch guitars, as gold-plated and stylish as a Louis Quatorze furnishing. I remember them as being both rowdy and detailed in their music and their deportment; those fringe jackets nailing that carefully cultivated pose of lawlessness.

There was nothing transgressive about them— they were no threat to the state like the Doors or Love. They strived for a more authentically American sound; though they didn't have a great keyboardist on board, something of the Band lurked around their edges. *(2014)*

Opposite: In June 1967 Neil decided to leave the band. Although he returned two months later, this marked the beginning of the end for Buffalo Springfield.

Below: Songwriter, arranger, and producer Jack Nitzsche was a key influence in Neil's decision to go solo.

Before recording for the second album, originally to be called *Stampede* and then renamed *Buffalo Springfield Again*, began in earnest, Denny Bruce went up to Neil's cabin in Laurel Canyon.

Denny Bruce: He had his jumbo acoustic twelve-string guitar and he's halfway through a song that turned out to be "Expecting to Fly." There was always a different tuning and Neil was also really good at using various time changes.

Then Neil starts talking about "Expecting to Fly" and said, "I hear it as a song for the Everly Brothers." I agreed and mentioned the song to Jack Nitzsche, who was about to work with the Everly Brothers. Jack and I went over to Neil's place and he played "Expecting to Fly." Then Jack said, "Never mind the Everlys. This is for Neil Young. We can make a great record." *(2014)*

"Neil now had confidence building from Jack and Gracia Nitzsche, and myself. Jack really believed in Neil's music. And Jack knew Neil would eventually become a solo star. He knew he wasn't meant to be in a band."
— Denny Bruce, 2014

Don Randi: Jack Nitzsche called me to play keyboard on some dates in 1967 at Sunset Sound. Bruce Botnick was the engineer. When I walked into the studio I didn't realize it was for Buffalo Springfield.

I thought it was for a Neil Young album, because he was supposed to be breaking away and going on his own. Hal Blaine and Jim Horn are on the track. I played piano and organ.

When Jack and Neil asked me to play on the end part of "Broken Arrow" they were both waving me on to keep playing. I kept looking up at them, "Are you ever gonna tell me to stop?"

I'm on "Expecting to Fly" with Russ Titelman, Carol Kaye, and Jim Gordon. I had some little head chart arrangement to work from and another of the tunes might have been sketched. It was pretty wide open with the chord changes. And all you had to do was hear Neil sing it down with an acoustic guitar and you sat there, "Oh my goodness."

You have to realize that, as great a musician and as great a songwriter as he is, Neil would also realize talent himself. Neil liked to experiment. He was smart enough to know what he wanted and knew how to get it. *(2014)*

"On Buffalo Springfield Again, the songs were so strong, and so were the performances. We had two massively prolific writers, Stills and Young, and there was constant tension between the two—creative tension that would manifest itself in either one of them, you know, losing it for a few minutes. And then they would get back together and hug like crazy and do the songs."
— Bruce Botnick, 2014

NY: "Expecting to Fly" took a long time to write. It came from two or three different songs that I molded together and changed around to fit it together. We spent three weeks recording and mixing it. Some people have said that they can't hear the lyrics too well. I like to hear lyrics and I can hear the words to it. They are buried in spots, but the general mood of the song is there. That's what matters in that particular song. It's not like a modern recording; it's based on an old theory. The new style is to try to hear every instrument clearly. The old way of recording is the Phil Spector idea of blending them all so they all sound like a wall of sound. *(1997)*

During 1967, Buffalo Springfield broke with the Greene and Stone management team. Dickie Davis helped negotiate the settlement, one of the key features of which was that individual band members would now hold publishing rights for their own songs.

The end of October saw the release of the second album, *Buffalo Springfield Again*, which guaranteed the band's legacy with iconic readings of Neil's "Mr. Soul," "Expecting to Fly," and "Broken Arrow" and Stephen Stills's "Rock & Roll Woman" and "Bluebird." Taking over production from Greene and Stone, these two ambitious young guns finally corralled that layered, textured sheath of sound—stacks of guitar tracks arrayed like a tasty parfait—which came to define an entire musical genre.

Buffalo Springfield Again was a defining moment in Los Angeles music history; like Brian Wilson before them, the Springfield meshed song craft with new recording techniques, elevating the music to a rarefied eloquence. If not the paradigm shift of *Sgt. Pepper*, the record furthered the claim by a cohort

of young talents that the artists themselves were fit for command. Stills and Young would see their captaincies awarded in very short order.

Richie Furay: We were always comfortable singing someone else's song early on. On the first album and some of the second, you can hear the cohesiveness, the group effort; there was not the possessiveness of, "This is my song, this is my baby, I'm singing it because I wrote it." The individual members brought their own take to the song. We liked the Beatles with John and Paul singing harmony. Stephen and I did a lot of that unison singing. That we picked up from the Beatles but then there was a lot of experimentation. *(2001)*

Kirk Silsbee: "Broken Arrow" was Neil's *SMiLE* [legendary lost Beach Boys album]. The self-referential obsession found in the song wasn't something we were used to hearing from these musicians—not just the Springfield but all of the musicians in the genre. Dylan talked about other people and he crawled up their asses with microscopes. But he didn't talk about himself. Then Neil Young laid himself open, rolled up his sleeves, showed his track marks the way Miles Davis did on "It Never Entered My Mind." Neil wasn't afraid to show himself as vulnerable or scared on Jack Nitzsche's sonic highway. But the orchestration has Nitzsche responding to the words and the spare chords that Neil gave him. *(2014)*

Photographer and friend Nurit Wilde perfectly captured Neil's introspective side in this 1967 portrait.

"Neil and I hung out briefly when he was living in Laurel Canyon. One day we decided we would take some photos and try to make him look like a movie idol. They weren't really posed. He sat on the bed and there was a nice natural light coming in through the window and Neil was wearing a poncho and had a guitar in his hand and was kind of strumming, thinking and looking."

— Nurit Wilde, 2014

In early 1968, Buffalo Springfield did two US tours of the South with the Beach Boys and the Strawberry Alarm Clock. Bruce Palmer had again been deported, in January, and was replaced by Jim Messina. The band spent less and less time together and relations became increasingly difficult. Eventually, in May, Buffalo Springfield announced its breakup.

Dewey Martin: We were fighting internally, and then Neil left the band finally. Stephen said, "I can't go on breaking in new guitar players." I think it was impossible because of where everybody's head was at. It wasn't just one guy's fault. *(1997)*

Dickie Davis: One of the reasons, I think, that Neil left the band was because he didn't want to go back on tour and get tight with them again. Because if that happened in town we drifted apart. On tour we became friends again.

  By that time we hardly spoke to each other while we were in town. When we were on the road everybody started playing together and going to each other's rooms and working on songs and being friends again. *(2014)*

NY: I just couldn't handle it toward the end. So I'd quit, then I'd come back, 'cause it sounded so good. It was a constant problem. It just wasn't me scheming on a solo career, it wasn't anything but my nerves. Everything started to go too fast. I began to feel like I didn't have to answer to or obey anyone. I needed more space. That was a big problem in my head. I just wasn't mature enough to deal with it. I was very young. We were getting the shaft from every angle, and it seemed like we were trying to make it so bad and we weren't getting anywhere. *(1997)*

Mark Guerrero: I saw the Buffalo Springfield's farewell performance at the Long Beach Arena, May 5, 1968. It was a great show, one of its highlights being a hot version of "Uno Mundo," but it was sad to know it was the end of the road for the band. *(2014)*

Rodney Bingenheimer: I went to Buffalo Springfield's last concert in Long Beach. Neil was back in the band. I really liked drummer Dewey Martin and at the gig he dedicated "Good Time Boy" to me. I was on the side of the stage. I was really sad when the band broke up. I was really bummed out when I heard Buffalo Springfield was ending. *(2014)*

Denny Bruce: Neil, Jack, and I went to the final Buffalo Springfield concert in a limo. Jimmy Messina came home with us. Head down and crying. "I can't believe it's over." It was a sense of relief for Neil. He was glad it was over.

I was going to have some sort of band or music project with Neil and Jack once Neil was through with Buffalo Springfield. Jack placed a transatlantic phone call to Mick Jagger and dropped in a casual question to Mick about the three of us moving to London. That's when Mick said to Jack how much all of his music friends, like Graham Nash, said "Expecting to Fly" was their favorite record at the moment. Mick "green-lit" the move, saying, "If you have Neil as a solo artist you won't have any problems doing business here!" I sold my car. I had to get money for this move. I got rid of my drum set. We got passports. Then one day Neil impulsively changed his mind and our trip didn't happen. *(2014)*

Buffalo Springfield's third and final album, *Last Time Around*, was released in July 1968, two months after the band had broken up. Few of the songs featured more than two or three band members playing together at a time, and even the cover photo had to be montaged. One of Neil's two contributions, "I Am a Child," was recorded completely separately from the rest of the band.

Richie Furay: The band was that first album and it was never captured again. That album represented the five of us together in the studio. After that it started to fall apart. It got worse with the next two albums. There were a lot of people being used other than the five of us. *(2001)*

"The only good album we made was the second one. But the first one was better than the second one," Neil told Pete Johnson of the *Los Angeles Times* in October 1968. "If the production on the first album had been anything near the production on the second one, we'd have had a much better thing."

Jim Messina: Neil cut "I Am a Child" by himself. He had booked another studio at Sunset Sound, a little four-track room which had some sort of German console in it. He probably was uncertain about what he wanted to do at that point. Gary Marker contributed bass to the track. I don't remember Neil being around much then. He delivered a completed tape of "I Am a Child" to us. That was it.

The minute Steve left the band, there was no Buffalo Springfield. He was committed and wanted to keep the band together. Neil wasn't. I just knew Neil always wanted a solo career and that Buffalo Springfield was his security. *(2004)*

NY: There have been better albums. I didn't have much to do with this one. I only sing on it and only wrote two. I was going to quit the group anyway even if they stayed together so I wanted to save my own songs for my own albums. *(1968)*

Opposite: Another Pleasant Valley Sunday by the pool at Peter Tork's house. Photograph by Henry Diltz, 1969.

Below: Even the cover of Buffalo Springfield's final album showed that Neil was headed in a different direction from his band mates.

"Neil could not see himself as second fiddle. He couldn't and wouldn't see himself as just a member of the band, one of the five guys."

— Richie Furay, 2004

One of cinema's most indelible images is of Alec Guinness collapsing on the plunger in *The Bridge on the River Kwai*. A more fitting symbol of Neil Young's career could hardly be imagined; blowing up—and later mending—bridges seems to be his *raison d'être*.

A case in point: Neil's relationship with his longstanding manager Elliot Roberts. Roberts arrived at the tail end of Buffalo Springfield, a smooth operator schooled at New York's William Morris Agency. Having already secured a long-term recording contract at the Warner Bros. subsidiary Reprise for Joni Mitchell, he was eager to expand his stable of artists within the thriving Los Angeles scene. It was Mitchell who in 1968 introduced Roberts to Neil while recording her debut album. Neil was in an adjacent studio with Buffalo Springfield.

Roberts thought he'd hit pay dirt with Buffalo Springfield, who were floundering without professional management or direction. He appeared to be the man with the plan. Until Neil, in one of his many acts of bull-headed caprice, terminated the arrangement over Roberts's transgressive act of hitting the driving range instead of tending to the nursery, um, band. The die was cast; throughout his brilliant career, Neil's changeable nature would drive his friends, lovers, and musical associates to blithering distraction. And then … wham, he turns around and *hires* Roberts to manage his solo career.

NY: First of all, I fired Elliot from Buffalo Springfield because he was out playing golf. I was in a bad mood or somethin'. It was just before the Springfield was gonna break up, so everything pissed me off. So you could even say I was like a spoiled little brat or whatever and it would probably be true. No problem

with that. Because I know how long it took me to learn some things—to grow up.

But still—my feelings were, "This guy's a fucking jerk." I liked him, but he was a jerk. No way I wanted him to manage Buffalo Springfield … But when I said, "I don't want him to manage the band," I wasn't thinking to myself, "I'm gonna get this guy. He's gonna manage me." *(2002)*

Jack Nitzsche had initially introduced Neil to Mo Ostin at Reprise; that meeting eventually resulted in a solo recording artist album deal, with a near $20,000 advance, negotiated by Elliot Roberts.

Daniel Weizmann: What Reprise knew, and, indeed, represented in the late 1960s, was the stone fact that the lid had popped off the square world, that the square world was no more. Other labels played the middle. "House style" at Reprise was Go All the Way: Captain Beefheart, the Fugs, Tiny Tim. No experiment too esoteric, no flip-out too outrageous. And here comes Neil, who had already broken the barriers with his band, played too loud, jammed too *out* … but now clearly wanted to push the envelope even further.

In an era of excess, Neil Young was reaching for *satori* through the greatest possible extremes, highest volumes, and brittlest sensitivity. Reprise knew they had found their man. *(2014)*

Above: Neil's first solo deal was negotiated by Reprise label boss, Mo Ostin (left), and Neil's manager, Elliot Roberts (right).

Opposite: Portrait by Nurit Wilde, 1966.

Overleaf: Neil moved out of Los Angeles in late 1966, first to Laurel Canyon and then in 1968 to Topanga Canyon.

Having initially left the city in late 1966 to rent a cabin in Laurel Canyon, Neil now spent his solo advance on a house in Topanga Canyon. He moved there in August 1968 and began work on his first solo album.

Tosh Berman: Topanga Canyon is a very remote area between Santa Monica, Malibu, and Woodland Hills. It is a fortress of sorts—a very closed community. It was good if you were an artist. It could give somebody like Neil Young the space and privacy to do his work away from the big city. On the other hand, there is always a darkness and a lightness. You're pretty much cut off from people and a lot of things.

I remember one time in 1967 a huge envelope came from England and it was a letter from Brian Epstein wanting my dad [multimedia artist Wallace Berman] to sign a permission to use his image on the front cover of the Beatles' *Sgt. Pepper* LP cover. Brian Jones and Keith Richards came by our house once. John Locke of Spirit was a friend of my dad's.

I must have first met Neil in 1968 at a social setting. A party as a kid. Actors and artists like Russell Tamblyn, Dean Stockwell, and George Herms were always around. Neil would hang out at Russ's house. It wasn't Wallace, Dean, or Russell teaching Neil directly about how to be an artist but maybe more of Neil observing them. I think Neil was watching what was happening and observing the scene and watching Russell work in his studio. *(2014)*

Another Topanga resident was to become Neil's pulsating pole star over the next three decades.

A bad ass from the high plains of Wyoming, David Briggs hustled his way to Los Angeles at seventeen, a rebel with a cause. He could play a little guitar, could talk a mean streak, and was hell bent on making records, making it happen. There was no Plan B. Briggs had a stint at Tetragrammaton Records, producing an album for comedian Murray Roman, and during the very late 1960s he worked with Jerry Williams, Spirit, and Grin.

In another of those "could only happen to Neil" acts of far-out serendipity, Briggs stopped to pick up a tattered scarecrow bumming a ride on the highway. It was, of course, Neil.

With support and guidance from the more experienced Jack Nitzsche, Neil and Briggs commuted to a trio of Hollywood studios to cut tracks for the album with accomplished session musicians including Hal Blaine, Jim Messina, George Grantham, and Ry Cooder, and vocalists Gloria Jones and Merry Clayton.

NY: We just went through it together—learning how to make records. David didn't know much more than I knew. But he knew how to keep on top of me and keep things organized. *(2002)*

Merry Clayton: I worked with Jack and Neil in 1967 on "Expecting to Fly" and then in 1968 on "The Old Laughing Lady" and "I've Loved Her So Long." You know, when you feel stuff. You can feel that music and you can get a tingle from the back of your neck and up your back. It had magic. When you surround yourself with soulful, beautiful people can't nothing come out of you but soulfulness. And beauty. *(2008)*

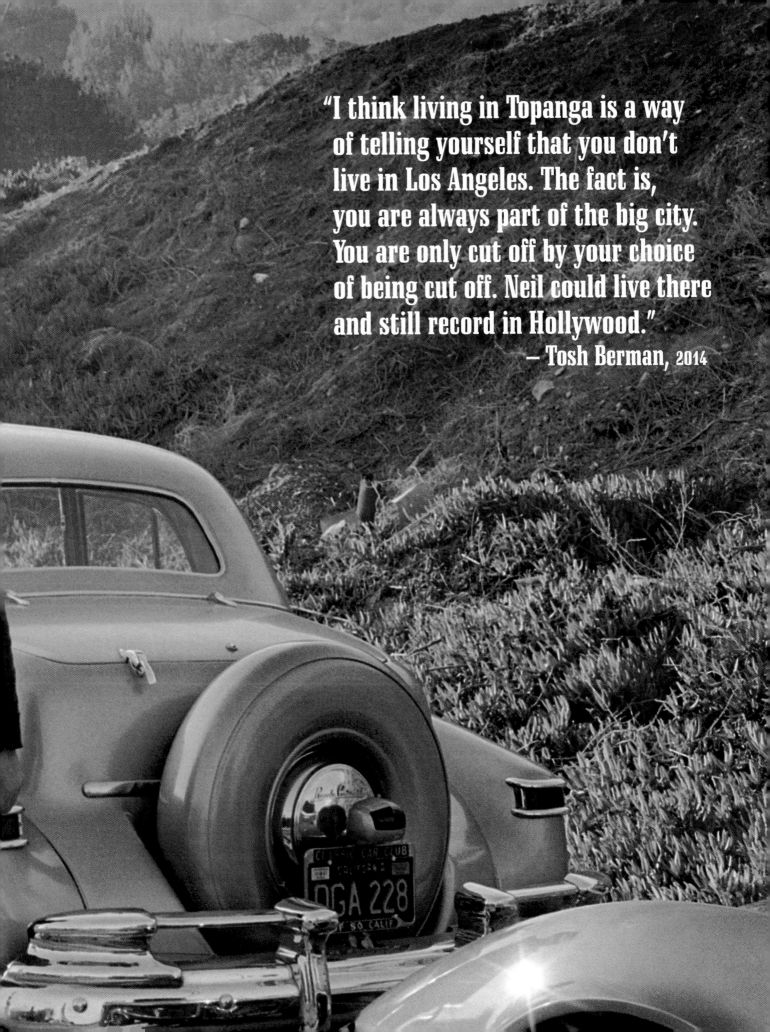

"I think living in Topanga is a way of telling yourself that you don't live in Los Angeles. The fact is, you are always part of the big city. You are only cut off by your choice of being cut off. Neil could live there and still record in Hollywood."
— Tosh Berman, 2014

Nils Lofgren: From David Briggs, Jack Nitzsche, and Neil Young I learned early on that you must be authentic and passionate about what you are doing first. At all costs. You must never let go of that.

In my band Grin and then with Neil, David Briggs was in our corner musically. He would chase the David Geffens and Elliot Robertses out of the room. He'd say, "Get out of here. We're not talkin' business!" And they were like, "Look, man. This is our artist."

David was the guy who burned every bridge with the executives. And he didn't care. He was like, "I know you have to talk to Neil Young about business. You're not doing it when we're making music. Get out!" And that was his mantra. "We're making music and take that shit out of here." *(2014)*

Once recording was complete, Neil played his first dates as a solo artist, a six-night residency in October at the Bitter End club in New York.

NY: I plan to perform as a solo artist but not in the same areas that I was performing before. I don't want to perform for big crowds. I want to feel closer to the audience and able to communicate with people. I don't care about making it commercially any more. *(1968)*

Then, on November 12—his twenty-third birthday— he released his self-titled debut LP. Although a commercial flub, *Neil Young* gave tantalizing hints of what was to come. Songs like "The Loner," and "The Last Trip to Tulsa" with its Pynchon-esque goofball paranoia, captured the spirit of the time with buckskin acuity.

"The Loner" and "The Last Trip to Tulsa" regularly featured on FM radio request lines. Also receiving airplay were "The Old Laughing Lady," with its seductive chorus of female singers, and the wishful "I've Been Waiting For You," its phased and flanged-sounding guitars anticipating the arrival of T. Rex and David Bowie. Indeed, thirty-four years later Bowie covered the song for his album *Heathen*.

NY: On my first album I liked "The Loner." I felt like I was getting into something different there. Starting to, anyway. "The Old Laughing Lady" I think was probably the best song on that. That's really a good one. We did some other things that I really got into. That was a personal album.

They did the compatible stereo [Haeco-CSG encoding system] on my first album and blew it, man.

You couldn't hear the vocals. I went crazy with those idiots. The guy who did that doesn't work at Warner Bros. anymore! My first record they put it through this thing, man ... The vocal disappeared. *(1973)*

Neil would subsequently remix the album in the summer of 1969, telling *Cash Box* magazine in their September 6 issue, "The first mix was awful. I was trying to bury my voice, because I didn't like the way it sounded."

Kim Fowley: The Jack Nitzsche and Neil Young relationship. An alpha male is what Neil Young is and Jack Nitzsche was an interpreter and a passive male who later became an alpha male. Nitzsche also had a Wagnerian aspect to his work. Neil indulged his grandiose musical vision by getting his empty acoustic to resonate in a Wagnerian way modified. Which is how they made those records.

He's great at being Neil Young. He has a radio voice and there's lots of pathos and emotion in it. Neil connects with lonely people. *(2014)*

James Cushing: One of the virtues that Neil Young's music represents was the willingness to expose one's emotional vulnerability. As a survivor of polio and an epileptic, Neil Young had already been through the pain the traditional and new underground media were covering.

He and Joni Mitchell experienced physical disease, immobility, and confinement, all things that tend to make you stand out from other groups of kids and make you more sensitive and aware. Mitchell contracted polio in 1953 and suffered more severely, including some paralysis.

It's important not to be reductive and say, "Oh, they suffered from polio, Neil had a slew of epileptic seizures. Therefore they understand the plight." Their art is a lot more interesting than that. The times required artists able to give convincing musical form to the new inwardness that resulted from the collapse of the 1960s ideals.

Mitchell's and Young's music dramatized how people *as individuals* could pull through dark times. Their Hollywood-birthed albums of 1968 illustrate this. *(2014)*

With his first wife, Susan Acevedo, in 1967. The couple got married in Neil's house in Topanga on December 7, 1968.

To round off another eventful year, on December 7 Neil got married for the first time. The proprietor of a Topanga diner, Susan Acevedo was a few years older and significantly wiser than Neil. She had a young daughter named Tia to raise, and now found herself with another soul to care for. A nurturing presence with a watchdog's attentive eye, she recognized Neil's willfulness as a weakness to be exploited by less honorable companions and she countered by keeping both barrels cocked. Susan was an important companion for Neil. She introduced him to many artists in the region and helped create his clothing designs for touring.

However, the continual absences for touring, rehearsals, and recording, coupled with Neil's immaturity, were too much for the marriage to bear and Susan and Neil legally parted in 1970.

Toward the end of January 1969, Neil went back to Canada to play some solo club dates at Le Hibou in Ottawa, before moving on to Toronto for a week-long engagement at the Riverboat, one of his old Yorkville haunts.

Writing for the *Toronto Telegram*, Peter Goddard was present at the first Riverboat show.

Peter Goddard: Neil had his first album out. Some of the greatest stuff. Purely as an act or the art of constructing a song. I still think it's some of the best things he ever did. It was so complete in and of itself.

The first night I heard Neil, there were four people. And that includes the chief waitress and the owner.

Bruce Palmer was sitting in front of me. Maybe there was one other person in the room.

I saw something that night. And I am very parsimonious when I say this. I could list a number of shows where you watched and you could hear something define itself as you watched it. And the point was, what got me, was how absolutely complete a musician he was.

I think about this concert a lot. Or that night a lot. Because you could see he was working through something. It was all a package in his mind and he did it. *(2014)*

Ritchie Yorke, then a columnist for the *Toronto Globe and Mail*, attended one of the other Riverboat shows.

Ritchie Yorke: Sitting there last night on the stage cross-legged, guitar in lap, dressed in cream Irish fisherman sweater, blue jeans, and well-worn brown boots, Young looked remarkably free of worries. His voice was soft, effeminate on occasion; his guitar-playing a fascinating mixture of tenderness and stridency. The songs had a lifting melodic strength. Some, such as "I Am a Child" (the Springfield favorite), were outstanding. Others were tentative.

In short, Young proved a singer of conviction with a rare sense of purpose. *(1969)*

Afterward, Neil revealed his future plans to Yorke. "I've formed a backup group called Crazy Horse. Three guys—guitar, bass, and drums—and I'm playing lead. I'm the boss."

EVERYONE I LOVE YOU

1969-1970

"It will be a while before people forget
the Buffalo Springfield, I know that.
But someday they'll be asking me
about what's going on now ...
I'm nervous about the whole thing.
It's like I've never been near the upper
reaches of the music business before."

— NY, 1969

Timeline

This page main photo: CSNY at Balboa Stadium, San Diego, December 21, 1969.

Background: Fans climbed the sound tower at the 1969 Woodstock Music and Arts Festival to get a better view.

Page 56: Portrait by Tom O'Neal, c. 1969.

1969

January–March:
Neil records his follow-up album, *Everybody Knows This Is Nowhere*, with Crazy Horse (Danny Whitten, guitar; Billy Talbot, bass; Ralph Molina, drums).

February 12–June 22:
First live dates with Crazy Horse, a series of residencies at clubs including the Bitter End in New York City and the Troubadour in Los Angeles.

October–December:
Recording of CSNY album *Déjà Vu* at Wally Heider's studios in San Francisco and Los Angeles.

August–June 1970:
Recording of solo album *After the Gold Rush*.

WOODSTOCK MUSIC and ART FAIR
SUNDAY   SUN.
AUGUST 17, 1969   AUG. 17
10:00 A. M.   1969
$8.00 Good For One Admission Only

WOODSTOCK MUSIC and ART FAIR
SATURDAY   SAT.
AUGUST 16, 1969   AUG. 16
10:00 A. M.   1969
$8.00 Good For One Admission Only
00950 NO REFUNDS   00950

August 18, 4 a.m.:
CSNY appears at Woodstock.

August 16:
Debut appearance of Crosby, Stills, Nash & Young, at the Auditorium Theatre, Chicago.

July:
Begins rehearsals with Crosby, Stills & Nash (David Crosby, Stephen Stills, and Graham Nash).

May 14:
Release of *Everybody Knows This Is Nowhere*.

December 21:
Final date of the CSNY 1969 US tour, at Balboa Stadium, San Diego.

1970

January 6–11:
European dates with CSNY.

February 25–March 28:
US tour with Crazy Horse.

Crosby, Stills, Nash & Young
WOODSTOCK · HELPLESS
ATLANTIC

March:
First singles chart entry—CSNY's version of Joni Mitchell's "Woodstock" rises to #11.

March 11:
Release of *Déjà Vu*, topping pop album chart and selling over two million copies pre-release.

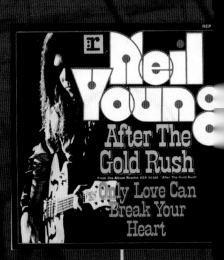

REP
Neil Young
After The Gold Rush
From This Album Reprise REP 44 080 "After The Gold Rush"
Only Love Can Break Your Heart

September 19:
Release of *After the Gold Rush*, reaching #8 on the US album chart.

May:
Writes "Ohio" in response to the National Guard shooting dead four Kent State University students protesting US involvement in Cambodia.

May 12–July 9:
US Déjà Vu tour with CSNY.

April:
First solo singles chart entry (with Crazy Horse)—"Cinnamon Girl" peaks at #55.

"I don't know how it happens, but when I'm singing and playing with Crazy Horse, I'm a different guy. I write a different thing, I see things differently, I see deeper pictures, I'm able to write and express myself much deeper in a certain way than I can do with anybody else."

— NY, 2012

In January 1969, Neil Young checked in to Wally Heider's recording studio in Hollywood to begin recording his second solo album with his new backup group: Danny Whitten on guitar, Billy Talbot on bass, and Ralph Molina on drums.

Kim Fowley: I met Danny Whitten in the early sixties when he was dancer and in a singing group called Danny and the Memories. Danny looked like a young Kirk Douglas and he sang like a Dion DiMucci version of a better Neil Young. I know Danny Hutton was seriously considering him to be the third voice in Three Dog Night. Everything good about Danny Whitten's technique and formula, Neil applied to his own shit. Wouldn't you be bummed out if you were soul-drained? Well, that's what happened to him. *(2014)*

Danny and the Memories had shape-shifted into the Rockets, who recorded an LP on the White Whale label—pure grunge, a loud, sloppy, guitar-driven sound like an open wound, with a backbeat that listed like sailors on leave at Subic Bay. This was a band only Neil Young could find common cause with, and he went to hell and back with them.

Neil saw the Rockets one night at the Whisky a Go Go, appropriated three of the members and rechristened them as Crazy Horse. They became the blank canvas upon which he painted his visceral, unmediated masterworks.

"Danny Whitten, from the day I met Crazy Horse and Neil Young at the Cellar Door in 1969, it was common knowledge, and Neil would be the first to tell you, that Danny was one of his early mentors and influences. Danny had that great deep 'Bee Gees' vibrato, with that California soul and lament."

— Nils Lofgren, 2014

Everybody Knows This Is Nowhere was the fruit of this idiosyncratic partnership. It's a quaking dirge for two guitars, bass, drums, and a voice full of woe. Only in 1969 could such a seeming downer become the signature sound of FM radio. Suddenly, Neil Young is the *next* voice of his generation, whiny and careless, all frayed edges and broken glass.

Peter Lewis: My band, Moby Grape, knew Neil and Buffalo Springfield from shows we did together and recording studios. I was at Neil's house and he spun an acetate copy of *Everybody Knows This Is Nowhere*. I flipped out and told him, "This is just gonna make you a huge rock star, man. Because you finally got that sound that you were lookin' for. It's not "Brian Hyland" and it's not "Jack Nitzsche's take on you." *You* did this. *(2014)*

NY: *Everybody Knows This Is Nowhere*. I don't think there's anything on it that I didn't like. That's when a change came over me. Right then I started trying to just do what I was doing. Just trying to be real. *(1973)*

In 1969, Richard Bosworth was a high-school senior, playing in a band called Jennifer's Friends.

On Friday May 2, the group was on the way home from a gig in Bridgeport, Connecticut when they stopped by the Stone Balloon, a new club in downtown New Haven. The owner gave them a four-night booking as the opening act for Neil Young.

Richard Bosworth: We didn't know Neil Young was in Buffalo Springfield. None of us had heard of him. His name was actually misspelled on a poster for the engagement as "Neal Young."

The following Thursday, Neil walked in the room. He had this glowing aura. Talent and greatness just seemed to be pouring off of him. He said hello to everyone, was very warm and friendly. Neil was talkative, taking out his guitars and letting us check them out. He handed me his orange Gretsch 6120,

which I strummed on for a moment, not knowing that it was his primary guitar in Buffalo Springfield.

He went on with his Martin D-28 guitar and opened up with "On the Way Home" from *Last Time Around*.

Neil had an old black Les Paul with a Bigsby vibrato bar. The other guitarist was playing Neil's Gretsch 6120. The guitar amps were all old Fender tweeds and blond Fender Bassmans, unlike the Marshall amps of the day.

The first song was "Cinnamon Girl." He introduced the band as Crazy Horse. Before the next song Neil cited guitarist Danny Whitten, stating that he'd heard Danny writing a song and it was so good that he felt he better get in on a good thing and co-write it.

They then tore into "Come On Baby Let's Go Downtown," "Down by the River," "The Losing End," "Cowgirl in the Sand."

Backstage on Saturday night, Neil was strumming a guitar by himself while a friend and I were having a discussion about our imminent senior graduation dinner the following month. Neil said, "What are you guys talking about?" I explained it was my job to book a band for the event. He asked, "What does it pay?" I replied, "$250." He went, "Um. That's what I'm getting a night for this gig. Maybe I'll play your senior grad dinner."

Sunday evening, Stephen Stills shows up. He was with a dark-haired guy who turned out to be Dallas Taylor. Backstage between shows Stills was cocky and confident. He and Neil seemed happy to see each other. I asked Stephen what he was doing now after Buffalo Springfield.

"I've just recorded a new album with David Crosby of the Byrds and Graham Nash of the Hollies but we don't know what we're going to call it." Stills told Neil he had just been at dinner with Ahmet Ertegun and Ahmet told him about Neil's New Haven shows, suggesting Stephen drop by to talk.

At the end of Neil Young and Crazy Horse's final set of the four-day run, Neil brought up Stills and Dallas Taylor took over the drums. To end the evening Stills and Young proceeded to trade fiery guitar licks like they had in Buffalo Springfield and soon would again in some new unnamed group in the future. *(2014)*

"Cinnamon Girl" was issued as a single. A different mix from the album version, with Neil's vocal more prominent, it would fall just short of the US Top Fifty.

Neil's LP was constantly in rotation on regional radio stations KPPC-FM, KMET-FM, and KLOS-FM. And he would gain further exposure when Buddy Miles covered "Down by the River" in 1970.

Neil Young and Crazy Horse live at the Fillmore East, New York, March 1970. Left to right, Jack Nitzsche, Neil Young, Danny Whitten, Billy Talbot, and Ralph Molina.

Crazy Horse was the perfect vehicle for Neil's road rage approach—they'd been touring together throughout the recording of *Everybody Knows This Is Nowhere*—but now he decided to hitch his wagon to that hydra-headed enticement Crosby, Stills & Nash.

NY: I think it started with Stephen and Ahmet. Crosby, Stills & Nash were thinking about going out on the road to promote their album. When they started thinking about it, they realized that to have me there would be another addition, just another step. And they wanted to do that to carry that Springfield thing that Stephen and I had going all the way into their thing, you know, with those vocal sounds. I guess that's why they asked me to join.

At that time I was really excited, you know. Because I hadn't been doing really well. I had a couple of records out, neither one was really too successful. And then I joined Crosby, Stills & Nash and did that tour with them and my records started taking off. And so I guess it helped me on all levels, joining them. Besides making what I thought was really great music that was really getting me off, I mean more people were getting to know me as an artist and to get

interested in what I was doing. So it was a really good thing for me. It was a good thing for everybody, I think, 'cause I think I added a lot to them, too, in helping them. *(1973)*

Kenneth Kubernik: An ocean of ink has washed ashore over the years detailing CSNY's sumptuous sound (early on), the prima donna antics (Persian carpets and private chefs), the sordid behaviors (aka the "Frozen Noses"), and the endless fits masquerading as artistic license.

It's an exhausting litany and yet there were moments of such incandescent beauty that the whole tawdry enterprise was not beyond redemption. Bootlegs from the earliest gigs in summer 1969—the Greek Theater in Los Angeles and the Fillmore East in New York—document that ineffable, pitch-perfect rapport between voices and guitars in shimmering balance that tolled like church bells. *(2015)*

Above: The initial July 1969 CSNY lineup: Dallas Taylor, Stephen Stills, David Crosby, Bruce Palmer, Neil Young, and Graham Nash. Palmer was soon replaced on bass by Greg Reeves.

Opposite: A cold one in the pool during rehearsals at Peter Tork's house.

"It was a different band when Neil joined. Crosby, Stills, Nash & Young is a completely different band from Crosby, Stills & Nash. And not a lot of people understand that. They think it's just an added voice. But it's not. It's an added attitude. Neil brings a sharper edge."

— Graham Nash, 2014

In summer 1969, the esteemed Canadian music journalist, author, and broadcaster Ritchie Yorke conducted an exclusive interview with CSNY for his *Rap with Crosby, Stills, Nash & Young* college radio special program that was distributed as a promo by Atlantic Records. Yorke taped the outfit at Peter Tork's house, which they were renting for rehearsals.

NY: Right from the beginning, he [Graham Nash] and I hit it off. Now I'm finding a bunch of new friends and it's groovy. Willie [Graham Nash] knows how to make you feel at home. He's groovy and very honest. *(1969)*

David Crosby: I've known Neil for only the past four years, I guess. I've watched him through the Springfield. We went down to hear them and we were knocked out. That was when I was still in the Byrds. I remember the first time I heard them, I went up to him and Stephen and I said: "That thing that you guys are doing with the two guitars is like singing a duet. You guys gotta keep doing some more of that or else I'm going to be really dragged for a long time." That's really great stuff. *(1969)*

Stephen Stills: Neil is just about my best friend in the entire world, really. We're both people that grew up where our whole clan was kind of different from everybody else around us. There always was a certain sense of alienation from people around us. They're all old things and no amount of analyzing and psychotherapy can ever wash away some of those scars. You have to do it yourself. And we both kind of uniquely know that about one another and it's nice. We can look each other in the eye. We blew it before when we didn't. And we're trying harder now. *(1969)*

On August 18, 1969, CSNY played the Woodstock Music and Arts Festival, only their second live show together. Neil performed "Mr. Soul" and "On the Way Home" for the massive gathering, but he was not to be glimpsed in the Woodstock film documentary which was released the following year. Having felt distracted by the omnipresent cameras, he didn't sign the artist release form for movie exhibition.

NY: Woodstock was a bullshit gig. A piece of shit. We played fuckin' awful. No one was into the music. *(2002)*

Although Neil declined to be in the authorized *Woodstock* frame game, his song "Sea of Madness" was included on the hugely influential soundtrack album. Strangely, though, the version that was chosen for the album was actually taped at a CSNY Fillmore East show a month after the festival.

Jerry Wexler: After the 1967 Monterey International Pop Festival, in the summer of 1969, I got the rights to the *Woodstock* soundtrack album. There was a lawyer named Paul Marshall, he used to be our in-house counsel. He called me up, "Listen. Are you interested in Woodstock?" It was going to take place in two weeks.

Who the hell knew what Woodstock was going to be? He said I could have the rights for seven thousand dollars. I figured, "Seven grand? Let me take a shot." And that was it. I should have also grabbed the film rights but Warner Bros. got them. Thank God that I bought Woodstock. *(2007)*

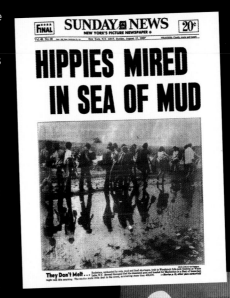

An estimated 400,000 people responded to the Woodstock organizers' offer of "three days of peace and music."

"This is the second time we've ever played in front of people, man, we're scared shitless."
— Stephen Stills, to the Woodstock crowd, 1969

Left: Keeping things tight rehearsing with CSNY. However, Neil was increasingly preoccupied with his next solo album, *After the Gold Rush*.

Overleaf: CSNY at Fillmore East, New York, June 1970.

During the fall of 1969, CSNY shuttled between the stage and the studio, combining a US tour with the recording of their first album as a quartet. *Déjà Vu* was eventually released on March 11, 1970 and became a monster success which subsidized their even more monstrously profligate behaviors.

Bill Halverson: As an engineer for Wally Heider's Hollywood studio in 1968, I did Cream's "Badge" session at Heider 3 with George Harrison, Eric Clapton and everybody. So I had some real good history with Atlantic Records. I then did the Crosby, Stills & Nash album.

I later worked with Crosby, Stills, Nash & Young at Heider's studio C in San Francisco for the first time. The CSNY *Déjà Vu* album was a lot harder than the first one. The *Déjà Vu* band sessions were "Helpless" and "Almost Cut My Hair."

I did some of the overdubs on "Helpless." We mixed *Déjà Vu* at Heider's. Neil didn't like our mixes 'cause it was CSN vocals with Neil, and so he'd go mix them on his own. And, if you listen to "Helpless" and "Country Girl," it sounds like Neil Young with background singers. Neil put the pipe organ on "Country Girl" at the MCA Whitney studio in Glendale. *(2014)*

James Cushing: *Déjà Vu* was supposed to be a unified group. It wasn't. "Helpless" was a Neil Young song on that album the way "Julia" was a John Lennon song on the Beatles' White Album. Neil was never a team player and this is another example. You got the sense Neil was saving the best stuff for a solo album, but this one leaked out.

Neil really wasn't collaborating or recording with the band. He was down the hallway from them at Wally Heider's in Hollywood, or back in San Francisco, or at his home in Topanga. There was a dark cloud around that album, as Graham Nash has mentioned.

When Neil joins the CSN faculty, a whole other wild card element enters the building. 'Cause he has such a distinctive sound and such a strong personality that he makes his mark on all the other people who are there. But yet his own work somehow fits in while being instantly recognizable. *(2014)*

Even while recording *Déjà Vu*, Neil was still returning to the party comforts of Crazy Horse to work on his third solo album, *After the Gold Rush*. In a state of continual overdrive, he marshaled enough discipline through studio sessions and grinding roadwork to burnish the band's splintered surface and approximate a professional sound.

He added the sprightly Nils Lofgren on second guitar and piano, an instrument he was unused to playing, the mischievous Jack Nitzsche on keyboards and attitude, and Greg Reeves on bass. Based on an unfilmed screenplay by the actor Dean Stockwell, a fellow Topanga resident, *After the Gold Rush* delivered on the long-awaited promise of an artist in command of his gifts.

Nils Lofgren: It was just one of those magical moments that reminded me of those days in '69 when David Briggs warned me, "Neil is gonna call you about a project. I think you're gonna like it. I think you ought to do it. I'm gonna produce it. I'm doing this *After the Gold Rush* thing. Want you to be in the core band playing guitar, singing, and playing piano."

"I gave Neil and David the bad news I wasn't a professional pianist. Those two guys looked at me and said, 'You've been playing classical accordion and winning contests for ten years.' I said, 'Right.' 'We just need some simple parts. You'll figure it out.' And it was that kind of passionate foresight that they had a lot more faith in me than I did and at that point I wasn't gonna argue with them. 'OK. I'll do my best.' And it worked out."

— Nils Lofgren, 2014

Briggs knew how nervous I was being a pianist. John Locke of Spirit lived right up the road from David in Topanga. John had a porch with a funky old upright piano. He said, "Nils, the door is unlocked. My bedroom is on the other side. I can't hear this piano. You can come anytime." And I did.

I put a sleeping bag on John's porch at his house and just practiced and practiced. And still, Neil and David, maybe they knew, they were going to get simple, rhythmic, solid things from me and Ralph Molina with a very colorful Greg Reeves underneath providing a lot of movement on bass, kind of like the James Jamerson school of playing, and Neil on top. And they realized they'd get that from me as opposed to a great session player who you would have had to coach to play that simple and who might not enjoy it. *(2014)*

Tosh Berman: The playback party for *After the Gold Rush* was held at Neil and Susan's house. Not a huge place. A typical multi-level Topanga house. It was very casual. Not a record label listening party. An invited group of people, Dean Stockwell and Russell Tamblyn, maybe George Herms, Neil's manager, my dad and mom. Mo Ostin was there. I met Roland Diehl, who painted the cover of Neil's first album. When I first heard *After the Gold Rush* I loved it.

Dean Stockwell had written a script or screenplay with Herb Berman called *After the Gold Rush*. An apocalyptic tale about Topanga where I think it's destroyed. As a kid I read the script. And so I knew *After the Gold Rush* before Neil got involved. I think Dean asked Neil to do a soundtrack or songs for the movie to get money from a studio. So at the time I thought of it as being really tied in with the movie.

When I heard the album playback, I was under the impression that Dean's movie was going on. I know Dean got inspiration credit on the album.

It stayed in my mind, but there were songs I heard that did not make the official released album. It was a different record. The sequencing was changed, songs were moved around and added, I believe. The finished album was not the same one I heard at the listening party.

I remember one specific conversation Neil had with my dad, Wallace. He and Neil really admired the first Paul McCartney album, which came out in April 1970. They had a long chat about that LP. Both were impressed by it. I heard the album and really liked it. Really strong melodies, upbeat rhythms, and really pretty songs. *(2014)*

Iris Cushing: I discovered *After the Gold Rush* this century, after my sophomore year at college. I was drawn to unadorned and authentic feel of some of the songs. Right away I trusted Neil Young. His voice had this truthfulness that was, I think, related to the androgyny I heard in it. I did not find his voice particularly "manly." It was high pitched, soft, and strange sounding. He presented an aesthetic.

In "Till the Morning Comes" and the title track of the album, I feel there's a kind of fragmentary mythology there, that Young's telling stories but you're only getting a small piece of them. And they feel really emotionally significant. You can tell when he's singing them that he's bringing in something very personal, but he's not telling the whole story. And that quality of it, that subtlety of inference, really allowed me to feel like he was talking about my own life. And he made the songs into a very inviting, open text. Not one closed message that he was trying to communicate, but rather something that's always open to interpretation and therefore continually alive.

There are moments where sincerity and heartbreak are meticulously balanced with a subtle sense of humor. The placement of "When You Dance I Can Really Love" toward the end gives a feel like a breath of fresh air. *(2014)*

NY: "When You Dance" is a funky record. Me and Billy and Ralph and Danny and Jack. They were all crazy. Jack plays great—I was pushing him. A lotta leakage, boy. That's a unique take, 'cause that's the only take ever done in the studio by the Horse with Jack playing. *(2002)*

Jack Nitzsche: I think I'd rather work in a gas station than do any more Crazy Horse sessions. *(1970)*

On May 4, 1970, four Kent State University students demonstrating against US military operations in Cambodia were shot dead by National Guardsmen in Ohio. Universities around the country closed in protest and Neil shared the sense of shock and outrage. He was moved to write one of his most memorable political songs, which he recorded with CSNY.

"I wrote 'Ohio' in Atascadero, California. Crosby was there, he picked up the phone and booked studio time and we went in and recorded it the next day. The song was written, recorded, and released in about two weeks, something that would be completely impossible today."

— NY, 1990

Bill Halverson: I was working with Stephen Stills at the Record Plant in LA and got a call from a roadie. "We're gonna bring all the gear over tonight." It was for Neil's "Ohio."

I hated the Record Plant tape machine in Studio A and made them rent a 3M twenty-four-track from Heider. I got some Shure SM 57 microphones from Heider 'cause the whole band was coming. Johnny Barbata showed up and I got a drum sound. Plugged Greg Reeves's bass and set up the amps. I know that they are gonna create the sounds they want and I just need to get it on tape.

They arrive. We rehearsed the song for sixteen bars and they stopped. A couple of takes and we had it. There were no overdubs and all live vocals, even the ad libs of Crosby on the end. I had blinders on working and had no idea that the whole Kent State thing had happened.

I get credit for being the engineer but it was all five of us hovering. We were listening to the mix, it was gonna be a single, and they needed a B-side. We'd been rehearsing "Find the Cost of Freedom" as an encore for CSNY concerts. We recorded it. Done. *(2014)*

Graham Nash: My song "Teach Your Children" is going up in the Top Twenty and Ahmet Ertegun is telling me I was going to have a number one hit. Then there's the killing of four students at Kent State. And we do Neil's song "Ohio." And we think America killing its children is more important than us having another hit record. And so I told Ahmet to pull "Teach Your Children," and put "Ohio" out. *(2014)*

Clem Burke: Neil's protest number "Ohio," with CSNY, was just phenomenal. A great lead guitar riff by Stephen Stills, which, besides the political statement it was making, just sucks you right in. *(2015)*

The impact of "Ohio" spread to England where the lads in Mott the Hoople recorded a live version of it one night in 1970 when they were supporting Free at the Fairfield Hall in Croydon, south London.

Ian Hunter: In his twenties Mick Ralphs had a voice uncannily similar to Neil Young's. We were doing an album called *Wildlife* and Mick had a lot to do with that album—a tad of country common sense in among our usual sea of chaos.

Mick came in with it—sang it—and that's the one you're hearing. I was over on the Jerry Lee side of things. *(2015)*

NY: At the first part in my career, or whatever, I wasn't into politics, you know. And then all of a sudden I sort of got into it. Because of what was going on around me I couldn't ignore it, you know. It was too obvious … I didn't feel I would be typecasting myself as a political person. Writing that song was just a pure reaction to the cover of *Time* magazine. I never really thought about it any other way. *(1973)*

In contrast to the whirlwind genesis of "Ohio," *After the Gold Rush* was not released until September 1970, more than a year after Neil had started recording the album. Surprisingly, given its subsequent elevation to "classic" status, reviews at the time tended be lukewarm. *Rolling Stone*'s Langdon Winner felt that the songs needed more time to mature: "Set before the buying public before it was done, this pie is only half-baked," he wrote. The "buying public" seemed not to agree, as the record broke into the US Top Ten, peaking at number eight. But it would be with his next release that Neil would graduate from star to superstar.

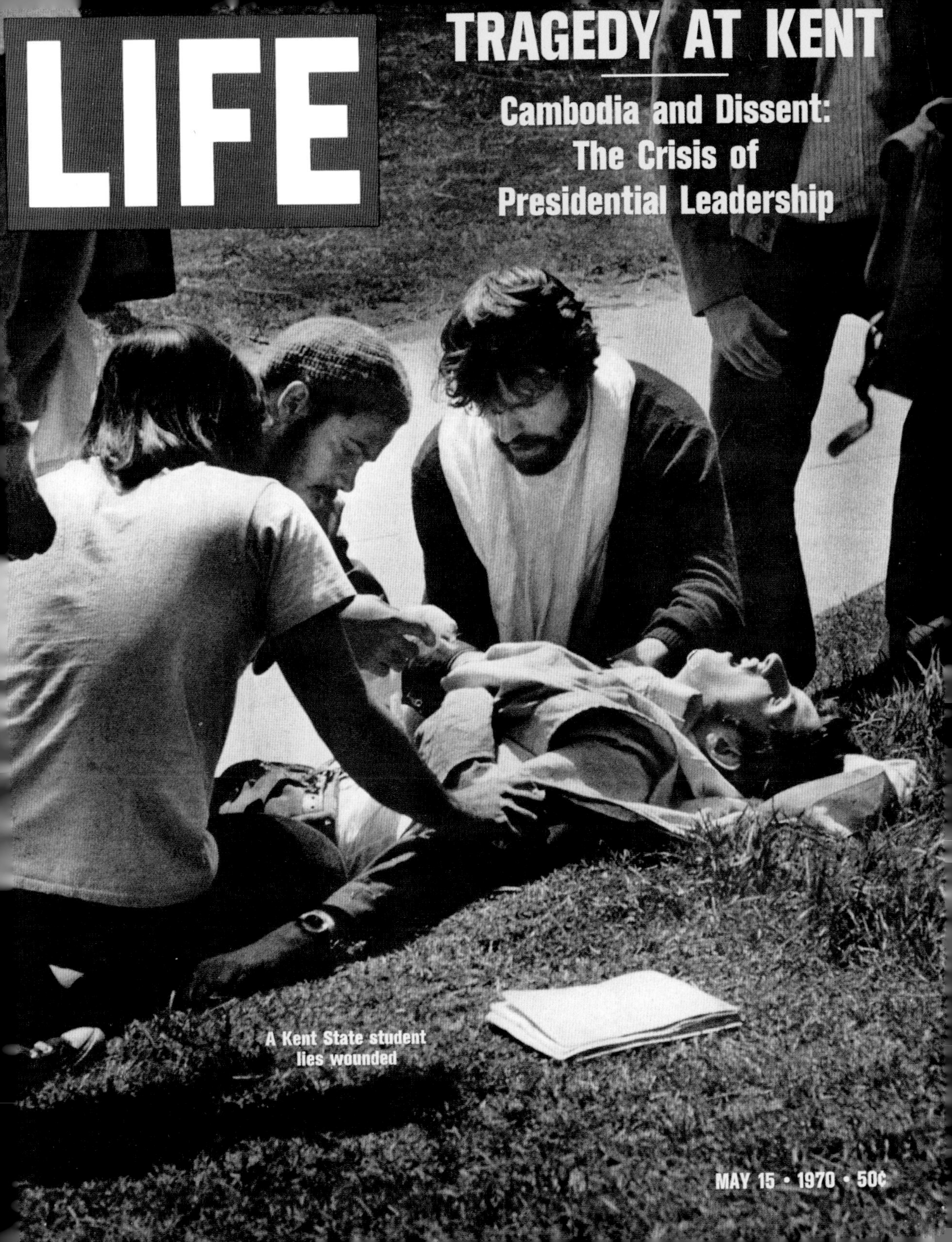

LIFE

TRAGEDY AT KENT

Cambodia and Dissent:
The Crisis of
Presidential Leadership

A Kent State student
lies wounded

MAY 15 • 1970 • 50¢

FROM THE MIDDLE OF THE ROAD TO THE DITCH

1970-1975

"I've been right through that trip of massive audiences and my ego has been satisfied ... But once you've done it, then what? You realize that's not what communicating is all about."

— NY, 1973

Timeline

Right: Neil with the Stray Gators—Ben Keith, Tim Drummond, Jack Nitzsche, Neil Young, and Kenny Buttrey.

Previous page: "Twenty-four and there's so much more" ("Old Man" from *Harvest*). Portrait by Henry Diltz, 1970.

1970

September:
Buys Broken Arrow, a 140-acre ranch at La Honda, California.

October 9:
Wife Susan files for divorce.

November 30–December 5:
A short solo acoustic tour climaxes with two dates at New York's Carnegie Hall.

December:
Meets actress Carrie Snodgress, who moves in to Broken Arrow early in 1971.

1971

April 7:
Release of *4 Way Street*, a live CSNY album from the Déjà Vu tour.

February:
Begins recording *Harvest* in Nashville with the Stray Gators and producer Elliot Mazer, including "Heart of Gold" on February 8.

January 6–February 1:
Journey through the Past solo tour of US and Canada, including two sold-out shows at Toronto's Massey Hall on January 19.

1972

January 17:
Release of "Heart of Gold," Neil's only single to top the US charts.

February 1:
Release of *Harvest*, making #1 album spot in the US, UK, Canadian, and Australian charts.

Early Summer:
Begins work on album and movie *Journey through the Past*.

September 8:
Carrie Snodgress gives birth to Neil's first son, Zeke.

Early June:
Neil's friend roadie Bruce Berry dies of a heroin overdose.

April 8:
The *Journey through the Past* movie opens at the US Film Festival in Dallas, Texas.

January 5–April 3:
Time Fades Away tour of the US and Canada with the Stray Gators.

1973

November 18:
Death of Crazy Horse guitarist Danny Whitten from a fatal combination of Valium and alcohol.

November 7:
Release of the *Journey through the Past* soundtrack album.

August–September:
Recording of *Tonight's the Night* with the Santa Monica Flyers, interspersed with club dates at the Corral in Topanga Canyon and the Roxy in Los Angeles.

October 15:
Release of *Time Fades Away*, a collection of new songs recorded live during the tour of the same name.

October 28–November 23:
Tonight's the Night tour of the US, Canada, and UK with the Santa Monica Flyers, on which Neil plays almost exclusively material from the as-yet-unreleased *Tonight's the Night*.

November–April 1974:
Recording of *On the Beach*.

1974

June:
Work begins on *Zuma*, with Frank "Poncho" Sampedro joining the Crazy Horse lineup on guitar. Recording would continue, on and off, until August 1975.

June 20:
Release of *Tonight's the Night*.

1975

November–January 1975:
Sessions for unreleased album *Homegrown*.

Fall:
Two-year-old Zeke diagnosed with a mild form of cerebral palsy.

Fall:
Separates from Carrie Snodgress.

July 19:
Release of *On the Beach*.

July 9:
CSNY embark on a two-month stadium tour.

"Massey Hall was one of the quietest concerts I've ever been to. It was very stark. I can say it was like watching Neil naked."

— Larry LeBlanc, 2014

Neil Young triumphantly returned to Toronto to headline Massey Hall on January 19, 1971 with two sold-out solo concerts played back to back on the same night.

Larry LeBlanc: Those shows were very important for Toronto. It was Neil Young, local boy, makes good. I was kind of ready. Neil the saint hadn't taken place yet. Our only saints at that time were Robbie Robertson and the Band. This was more like somebody, a football hero, coming home. *(2014)*

Sharry Wilson: You could hear a pin drop at Massey Hall. I felt the audience was being respectful of Neil's performance. A number of the songs had never been heard before.

I loved Neil's simple piano playing, the lovely melody and the references to Canada in the lyrics. Even though the audience remained quiet on the whole, there were some moments that elicited enthusiastic outbursts, especially when Neil sang the line about "north Ontario" in "Helpless."

Neil mentioned to the audience that it was hard for him to bend over to pick up a guitar pick he had dropped. I was aware of a recent back injury he had suffered and presumed he must have been wearing a back brace. That gave me pause. The stage was set very sparsely. It made the concert seem more intimate somehow. *(2015)*

Other changes were afoot. His marriage to Susan Acevedo having broken down, Neil had left Topanga a few months earlier. With his new-found wealth, he purchased the Broken Arrow ranch, paying $340,000 cash for 140 secluded acres south of San Francisco. In time it would become his base of operations for band business, a comforting retreat from the exigencies of adult responsibility, a glorified flop house for his buds, a playpen for the Tom Sawyers and Huck Finns among his roustabout crowd.

Left: "I fell in love with the actress" ("A Man Needs a Maid" from *Harvest*). Carrie Snodgress's Oscar-nominated performance in *Diary of a Mad Housewife* (1970).

Opposite: The new owner of Broken Arrow ranch strumming his Martin D-45, 1971.

Like Crazy Horse, Broken Arrow was a work in progress; the housing was glorified cabins, plumbing optional. A man could lose himself up there, trudging through the tree-lined property, strumming a Martin D-45 without a care or neighbor to consider. A lot of music was born and bred in those sheds, on the makeshift stage, wherever a generator could provide electricity. So, too, did romance bloom and wither like the seasons.

In December 1970, Neil was in Los Angeles resting with a bad back at the Chateau Marmont on Sunset Boulevard when the next major love of his life introduced herself. Actress Carrie Snodgress had ridden the pop-cultural zeitgeist to "It Girl" status with her performance in the Frank Perry movie *Diary of a Mad Housewife*. Neil had read a magazine feature about her and been immediately captivated. When he found out Carrie was in town, performing in a theatrical production in downtown Los Angeles at the Mark Taper Forum, Neil tracked down her number, called her up, and invited her to visit an ailing rock star in his time of need. Irresistible!

Whatever defense she was prepared to play was overmatched by the overwhelming attraction two performers have when circling the red hot sun of celebrity. Carrie was nominated for a Best Actress Academy Award and Neil's music was reaching an audience. They quickly cleaved to each other as lifelines, sharing the high of stardom.

Their relationship ebbed and flowed like cycles of a stalking desert moon. Their son Zeke was born in September 1972. The seeds for Neil's greatest success were planted in this romantic soil. "A Man Needs a Maid" would sprout from this union.

Neil, with Carrie in the house, delivered a stellar solo performance at the Dorothy Chandler Pavilion in the Los Angeles Music Center on February 1, 1971. I sat near Dean Stockwell and dancer/actress Toni Basil. I had to work a full-day shift at the West Los Angeles College library to earn the money for the ticket ...

Denny Bruce: I went with Jack Nitzsche. Neil's voice was really connecting with people then. James Taylor, Cat Stevens, Neil and just a handful of guys were hailed and girls loved it. And Neil was also able to rock so that the guys could dig him when Crazy Horse played loud. *(2014)*

On February 23, 1971, producer/director Stanley Dorfman filmed Neil at London's BBC Television Centre for the *In Concert* TV show. As well as giving Neil crucial exposure in the UK, it enabled him to preview some unrecorded material that would later surface on his breakout 1972 album *Harvest.*

Stanley Dorfman: When we started *In Concert*, BBC2 had just gone color. And the head of BBC2 was David Attenborough. And he liked folk music a lot. So I said, "Let's do singer-songwriters." "Great."

So he sent me to California to find acts. And I met [David] Geffen and [Elliot] Roberts. It wasn't a hard sell at all. The artists couldn't get on television in England unless they had hit records.

The reason Neil Young, Joni Mitchell, and the others connected very strongly with the English audience was because they were folk-music oriented. The British love folk music. Plus, Neil Young citing Bert Jansch and the Shadows in his interviews didn't hurt.

I loved the singer-songwriters of the time. To me they were the poets. Brilliant songs last forever. With all these acts, I never dictated what they should do anyway. They'd come over and we'd have a lunch and a chat. We had marvelous lighting and they lit these things like portraits.

The other thing that I said to them before doing the show was that the editing would be very minimal. We had four cameras, five if you were lucky, no handheld, so the only editing you would do was to cut tunes out. Or put them in. So I told Neil and all the others, if they wanted to they could come to the editing room the next day and kind of decide how to structure the show. And they all liked doing that. Neil came. He was charming, lovely, and delightful. Neil was not elusive in any of my dealings. *(2015)*

The young laughing man. A relaxed moment while writing songs for *Harvest*, Broken Arrow, 1971.

"I told them I wouldn't do a show unless I could bring in quite a few rock stars. I really liked Neil—he was real country and very intense—so I had him on my show twice."

— Johnny Cash, 1997

In February 1971, Neil traveled to Nashville to perform on *The Johnny Cash Show*. An ABC-TV national broadcast. He had a star turn on the "Johnny Cash on Campus" episode aired on February 17, playing "The Needle and the Damage Done" and "Journey through the Past."

"One reason country music has expanded the way it has is that we haven't let ourselves become locked into any category," Cash explained to me during a 1975 interview for *Melody Maker*. When I asked him about his bold policy of mixing established country artists and relative newcomers from other genres on his TV program lineup, Cash replied, "We do what we want."

Guesting around Neil's spot on *The Johnny Cash Show* were James Taylor and Linda Ronstadt.

Huddled around a microphone, these three blossoming talents gave viewers a taste of the burgeoning singer-songwriter movement in early 1970s rock music.

While in Nashville, Neil took time to record some new material. Serendipity played its designated role in his career as always; an encounter with veteran producer/engineer Elliot Mazer, an acquaintance of Elliot Roberts, introduced Neil to a new set of musicians who would profoundly influence his sound from this point on.

With Mazer handling the console at Quadrafonic Sound Studios (which he had cofounded), Neil laid down most of the tracks for what would become *Harvest*, his biggest seller and, for many, his most enduring work.

"Neil's singing and playing on 'Heart of Gold' were magnificent. His tempo was perfect. It was great. All we had to do was make sure we didn't mess him up."

— Elliot Mazer, 2015

Left: Elliot Mazer, the producer of *Harvest*.

Opposite: Performing on *The Johnny Cash Show*, February 1971.

Elliot Mazer: I had a friend who smoked a lot of weed, which I wasn't then, who played nothing but *After the Gold Rush*—a lot. That was the first time I heard of Neil Young. I was interested in the voice. All of a sudden we read about Neil coming to Nashville to tape *The Johnny Cash Show*. I said, "We need to host a dinner."

Neil, Linda Ronstadt, James Taylor, and Tony Joe White attend, have dinner, and I meet Neil. "You work with these Nashville guys. Can I get the studio tomorrow to mess around?" "Sure." I moved a session to accommodate him. And called some musicians. *(2015)*

The future Stray Gators, a bunch of seasoned Nashville session men, covered all the musical bases: rascally Tim Drummond on bass; Kenny Buttrey, the timekeeper from Dylan's immortal *Blonde on Blonde*, on silky smooth drums; pianist John Harris; guitar player Teddy Irwin; and Ben Keith, Neil's future right-hand man, on yowling steel guitar. They would set the table for their irascible leader at countless gigs and studio sessions. For now, it was time to bring in their first harvest, and they all knew it was something special.

NY: I wrote "Heart of Gold" on tour. Wrote it on piano. It was originally part of "A Man Needs a Maid." It was like a suite, and then I decided to make them into two separate songs, and one of them became "Heart of Gold." *(1990)*

Elliot Mazer: I knew "Heart of Gold" was a hit when Neil played it. His songs generally create an overpowering feeling. Kenny, Drummond, Ben, Teddy, and I are in the control room. Small space. Twelve feet by twenty feet. And Neil plays "Heart of Gold" and I look up and Kenny and I both at the same time put our fingers up as "number one." We knew it.

From then it was only a matter of time to get the thing done properly and out. I used a Neumann U67 or 87 microphone on his voice and rode his sound levels.

Neil played "Old Man" and sang it beautifully. I knew that was the take. I would know very early with him if it would be a take or not. I remember after that take, Neil came into the control room and saw Linda and James there and said, "Let's record the backing vocals." And we did the backing vocals right in the control room. James played six-string banjo on it. *(2015)*

Linda Ronstadt: I sang in Nashville with Neil. We were doing *The Johnny Cash Show* and Neil was there. James Taylor was there. After we got finished with the TV show, Neil said, "I'm going to go record. Will you guys come along?" So we recorded "Old Man" and "Heart of Gold." It took all night long. We didn't get there until midnight. It was just before dawn, we came out of there and it had begun to snow.

I remember I had to be on my knees for most of the session because James and I were singing together. But James was so tall, he had to sit in a chair, then I'd have to bend over to sing, so I knelt on my knees. I could just reach the microphone. James was bent over and I was kneeling. So I was really tired by the time we finished. Because it took hours. But we loved the music. It was so good. James was playing a banjo. Actually, it was a guitar with a banjo head on it with six strings. That's James playing banjo that you hear on "Heart of Gold."

Two of the most beautiful, poignant songs. Neil is just the best. He's my favorite writer from that time. I was a huge Neil Young fan. We didn't think in those terms about those songs having an impact. I just went, "This is the best thing I've ever heard. I wanna be on it." I was glad that I got to sing on it. I had sort of learned how Neil's harmonies go by listening to them on the radio. I was just glad to be part of it. *(2015)*

> "More than anyone in rock 'n' roll, Neil Young has the guts to be romantic …
> If "Heart of Gold" is an admission, "A Man Needs a Maid" is an outcry …
> Harvest also sounds better than any other Neil Young album."
>
> — James Cushing, City on a Hill Press, 1972

Elliot Mazer: Neil and Jack Nitzsche went to London and did "A Man Needs a Maid" and "There's a World" live with the London Symphony. Neil recorded "The Needle and the Damage Done" from a concert at UCLA's Royce Hall. His back was hurting him tremendously during the sessions. He had back pain, and the fact that he sat down a lot was really inhibiting him. He then had an operation, which made things a lot better.

We did other tracks that were taped with the Stray Gators inside a barn on Neil's ranch. We used a mobile truck with a UREI tube mixer. "Words," "Alabama," and "Are You Ready for the Country?" Nitzsche was on these sessions. (2015)

While Neil was busy recording Harvest, his fans had to content themselves with the CSNY live double LP 4 Way Street, released in April 1971.

Bill Halverson: I recorded all of it. Neil is wonderful playing live. He makes Stephen better and Stephen makes Neil better. Crosby is probably one of the best rhythm guitar players I've ever recorded. He's just anchoring it with the bass and drums. (2014)

James Cushing: 4 Way Street is loose, more intimate, more spontaneous, more risk-taking and more of that combination of heavenly folk music on the acoustic side and of sublime Buffalo Springfield meets Crazy Horse rock on the second half. (2014)

In his review of the album for the New Musical Express, Roy Carr commented that "Neil Young utterly dominates the proceedings to the extent that at times he almost reroutes the traffic to make it into a one-way street."

Finally released in March 1972, Harvest raced to number one, a defining moment.

James Cushing: Listening to Harvest forty-three years after I reviewed it for my college newspaper, I'm pleased with the country-western flavor Ben Keith's pedal steel contributed to "Out on the Weekend," the looseness of "Are You Ready for the Country?" and the slow, sludgy rock of "Alabama" and "Words (Between the Lines of Age)."

Then as now, the sodden strings on "A Man Needs a Maid" and "There's a World" struck me as a ploy to seduce a long-and-winding MOR audience.

The lyrics had that characteristic Neil Young blend of artlessness and wisdom. A confession that erased ego rather than asserting it. Partly because of the title, the album seemed important. A major statement by a major artist, and as such deserved thoughtful study. (2015)

Matching the album's achievement, "Heart of Gold" hit number one in the singles charts.

Elliot Mazer: In 1972 "Heart of Gold" became a big hit record. I pulled up at Neil's ranch one day. I had a rental car coming from the airport, and as I was about to turn the car off, I hear the DJ on KFRC, "Next we're gonna hear "Heart of Gold." I run into the house, "Neil, come here." I have him sit in the car and he turns it off. I'm not sure what it was about him. I think he loved getting the big checks but publically didn't want to acknowledge that he was a pop success. (2015)

NY: Actually, "Heart of Gold" was never intended for single release. We went into the studio to cut the album and I guess we were hot that night and it was a good cut, but it's gone now. I've seen a few artists who've got hung up on the singles market when they've really been albums people … It's easy to do, but if you're wise, you stay with being what you really are … I just hope there is not a single off my next album. (1972)

Neil's hopes for a single-free album were fulfilled by his next release, *Journey through the Past*, the confused, disjointed soundtrack to his confused, disjointed "trip" of a movie—in short, probably not the follow-up to the multi-million-selling *Harvest* that his record company was envisaging.

Kenneth Kubernik: Not content to lean back on his laurels, Neil decided to branch out into film production; he established Shakey Pictures as the outlet for whatever cinematic whim caught his fancy. And he doubled down on whimsy with his first film. *Journey through the Past*, insipid and inspired in turns, purported to document exactly … well, what, nobody ever really could tell. Filled with scenes of friends babbling incoherently (that would be Mr. Crosby), dramatizations of Neil's subconscious (sometimes a joint is just a joint), *Journey through the Past* was a steaming pile of self-indulgence, with no apologies offered or expected. It sank without a trace and no animals were harmed during its production. *(2015)*

The companion *Journey through the Past* soundtrack album contained television audio source broadcasts with Buffalo Springfield on *The Hollywood Palace* and *The Ed Sullivan Show*, 1970 CSNY live recordings from the Fillmore East, *Harvest* outtakes, one new song—"Soldier"—and excerpts from Handel's *Messiah*, and Miklós Rózsa's musical theme from the *King of Kings* film.

Johnny Rogan: *Journey through the Past* was arguably the start of Neil Young's demythologizing process. Touted as a follow-up to *Harvest*, the work puzzled critics and annoyed many fans, not least because it was a double album with precious new material and a hefty price tag. It might have been better received had it been stressed that it was not a new studio album but a film soundtrack.

The movie became one of rock's best-kept secrets and was banned in the UK as a result of its explicit depiction of a junkie injecting heroin into his arm. Even if everybody had seen the film at the time, the soundtrack probably wouldn't have made sense of it all. As Young correctly observed, "It's got no plot. No point. No stars. They don't want to see that."

As a listener, I enjoyed some of the *Harvest* rehearsals featured therein, but the extended sixteen-minute "Words" strained patience, although these days it sounds more palatable. Young has done much longer songs since. At the time, the general feeling was that there simply wasn't enough Neil Young on this two-record set. "Soldier" was the only new song and even that was poorly recorded, albeit interesting. Hearing the Beach Boys' instrumental "Let's Go Away for a While," where a new Neil Young song might have been included summed it all up in a way. *(2015)*

On November 18, 1972, the prodigiously gifted Crazy Horse guitarist Danny Whitten died from a lethal combination of alcohol and Valium. Neil had watched his friend struggle with heroin addiction and had done what he could to help, giving him repeated chances to get his act together. In the fall of 1972, Neil invited Whitten to Broken Arrow to rehearse with the Stray Gators, then preparing for what was to be the Time Fades Away tour. It soon became clear that Whitten was not going to be up to the job, and so Neil took the tough decision to let him go.

NY: I knew that what I had done may have been a catalyst in Danny's death, but I also knew that there was really nothing else I could have done. I can never really lose that feeling. I wasn't guilty, but I felt responsible in a way. *(2012)*

Taking a walk around Broken Arrow with his dog Winnipeg, 1971. Along with cars and Lionel model trains, dogs are one of Neil's great relaxations.

"I thought Time Fades Away was a very nervous album. And that's exactly where I was at on the tour. If you ever sat down and listened to all my records, there'd be a place for it in there. Not that you'd go there every time you wanted to enjoy some music, but if you're on the trip it's important. Every one of my records, to me, is like an ongoing autobiography. My trip is to express what's on my mind."

— NY, 1975

Above: On the ill-starred Time Fades Away tour with the Stray Gators, Neil replaced Old Black, his iconic 1953 Les Paul guitar, with a Gibson Flying V.

Overleaf: Bakersfield Civic Auditorium, California, March 11, 1973. Neil called up David Crosby and Graham Nash (sharing a mic) for the last month of the tour.

The year 1973 kicked off in earnest with a concert in Milwaukee on January 5. Linda Ronstadt was the opening act. Three months of dates in cavernous arenas were booked for the Time Fades Away tour, during which Neil would be playing a number of previously unheard songs alongside classics like "Sugar Mountain," "Cinnamon Girl," and "Heart of Gold." His band consisted of the core of the Stray Gators: Tim Drummond and Kenny Buttrey provided the rhythm, Ben Keith stoked the engine, and Mr. Hyde, Jack Nitzsche, tinkled the keys.

The tour, frankly, was a disaster. Bathing in the afterglow of Harvest, audiences were willing to applaud even the most woeful performances. Neil was flailing, his band was imploding and even trusty Old Black, the stalwart 1953 Les Paul that had played Babe to Neil's Paul Bunyan, wanted out, replaced by a Gibson Flying V that proved equally uncooperative. Tequila was the tipple of choice and made its presence felt with a vengeance.

The train finally jumped the tracks on March 31 in Oakland, California. Neil walked off stage during the encore, "Southern Man," leaving the audience in an apoplectic fury. It had all become too, too much.

Kenneth Kubernik: This was one sorry lot, shouldering the hurt of Danny Whitten's overdose. Neil seemed to wallow in regret and self-imposed recrimination, Danny's ghastly death some kind of karmic payback for God knows what. Were they all heartless bastards, failing to assist a comrade in need, or was it simply the times, too easy access to too many bad, bad choices which bedeviled all of them to various degrees. Sometimes you had to look the other way or turn to salt yourself. *(2015)*

NY: Those huge concerts. I did it and it was great for my head. To know that I could do that. But you know, even as much as I tried every night to get everybody in those barns off, I couldn't. Because I couldn't even see them, man. And I knew they couldn't see me. I had to cut off all the subtleties of my music and just project it out to eighteen thousand people, you know. I was having a hard time doing it a lot of the time.

Unless you're playing the kind of music where you don't have to listen to the words and you just listen to a feeling. And I think that's a valid thing too. That's like getting together for a war dance or something. Whatever it is it's a very primitive thing. *(1973)*

The resulting *Time Fades Away* album, featuring the new songs recorded live on the tour, did nothing to pull Neil out of his post-*Harvest* tailspin. It was the first of his three "Ditch" albums, the name coming from his sleeve notes for the 1977 *Decade* compilation: "'Heart of Gold' put me in the middle of the road. Traveling there soon became a bore so I headed for the ditch. A rougher ride, but I saw more interesting people ..."

Johnny Rogan: One of my favorite ever music paper headlines was the review for *Time Fades Away* in the *New Musical Express*: "Neil Young Fades Away." It was like reading his epitaph. In the context of the times, it wasn't that surprising. An ill-fated arena tour during which Young's voice gave out was notable for ragged performances and moments where he was apparently berating audiences for their complacency.

Again, it was as far away from *Harvest* as could be imagined. Shortly after its release Young came to England for the Tonight's the Night tour, which left audiences even more confused as the attendant album would not be issued for another two years. Of course, what we were left with on *Time Fades Away* was intriguing. Here was a live album made up of previously unreleased songs. The material was dark, foreboding and occasionally angry. The bluesy "Yonder Stands the Sinner" was shambolic, the title track a rollicking tale of junkies, but there were almost moving ballads like "Love in Mind" and "The Bridge." Anyone doubting Young's talent could always be directed toward "Don't Be Denied" and "Last Dance," two mini-epics, never to be heard in a studio setting.

As I said somewhere in print: "If you got through this one and appreciated the undoubted jewels in the rough, then you were more than ready to follow Young through the most important phase of his career." *(2015)*

Time Fades Away was supposed to celebrate an artist reaching his creative and commercial prime, assisted by musicians hewing to his exacting standards, a healthy appendage to a body of work worthy of all the critical acclaim. Instead, it was a platform dive into a shallow swimming pool. You could guarantee, though, that the one person pulling himself from the attempt would be Neil. He would demonstrate, yet again, the survival skills of a feral cat, landing feet first, impossibly poised and ready to follow his muse past the quicksand the map may, or may not, reveal.

Plotting Neil's moves over the next few years would require the tracking skills of Jim Bridger. He would mix solo acoustic shows with bleeding-ear treks with a reconstituted Crazy Horse, recording in old, owlish barns at Broken Arrow and Hollywood rehearsal rooms, even an outhouse if he thought he could capture the sounds in his head.

Bruce Berry, a longtime crew member held in loving esteem, had died of a heroin overdose in June 1973—the needle doing its damage once again. Still grieving for Danny Whitten and now facing the loss of another friend, Neil responded with an astonishing collection of raw, haunting songs that would become *Tonight's the Night*. Most of the album was recorded in August 1973 in one marathon, tequila-fueled session at an impromptu studio set up in a Hollywood rehearsal facility called Studio Instrument Rentals, but the release was held back until June 1975. The band, which Neil christened the Santa Monica Flyers, was a hybrid of Crazy Horse and the Stray Gators. David Briggs was back, helming the production, riding shotgun on the ensuing tour with the Horse in the fall, another juvenile delinquent running away to join the circus.

The concerts were as much performance art as they were exercises in rock 'n' roll mayhem. Neil himself adopted a vaguely gonzo persona, part Jack Nicholson's Joker, part wasted hipster. The band was equally disorderly—rude, crude, and happy to throw a punch without any provocation. Nils Lofgren remembers this time as a raucous party designed to drown out the lingering darkness with over-amped intensity.

Bristol, England was the setting for Neil's next meltdown, the demons running wild like an all-in *Walpurgisnacht*. Furious with Whitten, with Berry, with his own ruinous excesses, he exploded like a Roman candle, leaving the band and even the roadies to fear for his sanity and the audience to mutter, "What, no 'Cinnamon Girl'?"

Steve Wynn: I bought *Tonight's the Night* when I was fifteen. I had heard "Heart of Gold" on the radio a year or two before that. Who knows? Maybe I thought I'd be getting more of the same. I still remember hearing *Tonight's the Night* for the first time late at night after I had turned off the lights to go to bed. I had never heard anything like it and was mesmerized.

I mean, I was already a fan of some heavy, underground rock—my favorite bands at the time were the Rolling Stones, the Who, Alice Cooper— things like that. But I had never heard anything that was so willfully broken and raw and so wrong in such

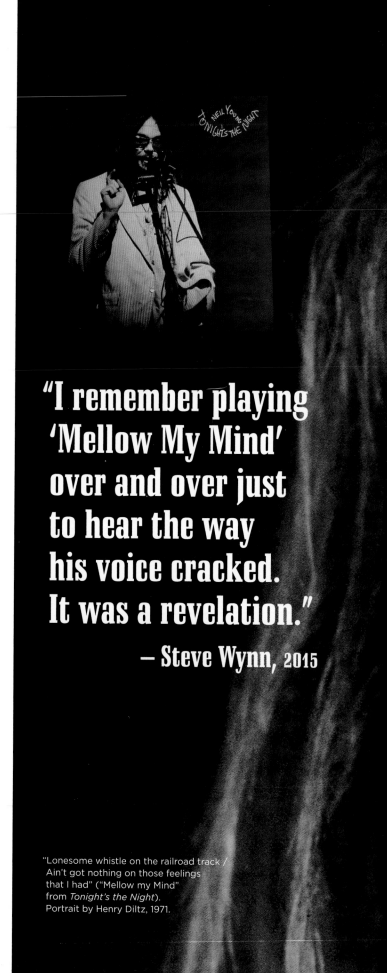

"I remember playing 'Mellow My Mind' over and over just to hear the way his voice cracked. It was a revelation."

— Steve Wynn, 2015

"Lonesome whistle on the railroad track / Ain't got nothing on those feelings that I had" ("Mellow my Mind" from *Tonight's the Night*). Portrait by Henry Diltz, 1971.

Right: Stephen Stills becomes airborne on the final chord of the final date of the CSNY 1974 tour at Wembley Stadium, London, September 14, 1974.

Opposite: In contrast, Neil attempted to stay grounded during the gargantuan stadium tour by spending time with his young son Zeke.

a right way. I had never heard music so human and honest and both beautiful and terrifying. *(2015)*

Neil was recording like a man possessed, stockpiling tracks with a revolving door of Nashville cats and crazy horses, pickin', fiddlin', slip slidin' behind their fearless leader. Released in July 1974, *On the Beach* was culled from these sessions. Another album's worth of songs, *Homegrown*, has never seen the full light of day.

On the Beach was the second of Neil's three "Ditch" albums to be released (although the final one, *Tonight's the Night*, was recorded earlier). The trilogy forms a document of a youth culture in the process of coming apart.

Sharry Wilson: A number of the *On the Beach* songs were influenced by Neil's relationship and breakup with Carrie Snodgress. "Motion Pictures" includes the subtitle "For Carrie." Three of the songs have "Blues" in the title, but none of them is a traditional blues song. There's a laconic and laidback feel to the album, with the tracks running up to nine minutes in length. Neil sings with stark emotion and receives excellent support from the other musicians.

Ben Keith suggested bringing Rusty Kershaw on board and his presence proved to be a big influence on Neil during the recording sessions, many of which were fueled by drugs, most notably honeyslides, a very potent combination of cooked marijuana and honey.

Besides Ben Keith and Rusty Kershaw, other players on the album include David Crosby, Graham

Nash, Tim Drummond, Billy Talbot, Ralph Molina, George Whitsell [one of the Rockets Neil didn't pick when he formed Crazy Horse], and Rick Danko and Levon Helm from the Band. Joe Yankee, a pseudonym used by Neil on the album, is listed as playing electric tambourine and harp on two tracks. All of the tracks were produced by Neil in collaboration with a few other producers, including David Briggs, Mark Harman, and Al Schmitt.

Neil has admitted that the melody for "Ambulance Blues" was borrowed heavily from "Needle of Death" by Bert Jansch, one of his early folk heroes. He heard Bert's eponymously titled first release while staying at a friend's place in Toronto in 1965 and it affected him deeply. Fittingly, Bert Jansch joined Neil in playing "Ambulance Blues" at the Bridge School benefit in 2006. *(2015)*

Jonathan Wilson: *On the Beach* always blows my mind for so many reasons. First and foremost may be the simplicity and starkness of the production. Neil's voice, no tricks, no effects to speak of, just pure tone, true signal, and intention. Of course, you can hear the intention in every corner of this record, every note, every word. Then there's the three-dimensional feeling of every sound. I don't know if it was Briggs, or one of the famous tube mixing consoles they used, but everything has a discrete and perfect place in the spectrum—Ben Keith soaring around, these are brothers in sound at work here.

The drumming is something of note to me on this record, Ralph, and then Levon—what a band. The overall feeling is that of a group of guys who played

a lot together, and they are in total sympathetic accord and control of Neil's vision and the songs. Are they stoned and operating outside time and space? Of course they are. What a heavy guy who could write something like "See the Sky About to Rain."

I love this record, I love the artwork, and I love this time in music so much. This record was released the year I was born, maybe that's why …

I had the opportunity to open for Neil Young and Crazy Horse on their last tour in Europe. I sat every night as close to them as I could get, with my jaw open—I can think of no higher compliment than "There is the sound of a man who understands the human spirit." *(2015)*

"Still, for me, the absolute pinnacle of Neil Young's songwriting career, On the Beach arrived at a time when his importance and relevance were still questioned by the critical establishment. The final three songs ('On the Beach,' 'Motion Pictures,' 'Ambulance Blues') remain among the best single sides of an album ever released. So make sure you play a vinyl copy!"

— Johnny Rogan, 2015

Amid this blizzard of writing and recording, Neil decided to hop aboard the Marrakesh Express once again. CSNY committed to a two-month survey of stadiums in summer 1974.

Bill Graham: Basically, what it amounts to is supply and demand. In the summer of '74, we took Crosby, Stills, Nash & Young, who came to us and said, "We want to play a lot of indoors and outdoors dates." We did a thirty-one-city tour. Seventeen of those dates were in ballparks. That was the beginning. The logistics could work. *(1976)*

On the 1974 CSNY tour, the musicians, the road crew, even promoter Bill Graham, were driven to near-hysterical outbursts by the extravagance, the insensate consumption, the wholesale whoring for pride of place before such rapacious egos.

Zeke Young, a mere toddler, accompanied Neil on the road, a possibly misguided attempt to keep at least one of the shooting stars grounded. Commuting to shows in a maxed-out motor home, desperate to stay as far as possible from the madding crowd, Neil managed to keep his own intake within the bounds of decorum.

Another casualty from this debauched merry-go-round was Neil's relationship with Carrie Snodgress. Zeke's birth had been traumatic and he had suffered lasting after effects, exerting considerable pressures that would have taxed even the most stable of couples; but for two such quixotic individuals, there was no safe harbor in sight. They soon parted around the sea of madness.

MORE TO THE PICTURE THAN MEETS THE EYE

1975-1979

"My career is built around a pattern that just keeps repeating itself over and over again. There's nothing surprising about it at all. My changes are as easy to predict as the sun coming up and down."

— NY, 1995

Timeline

This page main photo: Fans watching the Neil Young concert movie *Rust Never Sleeps* wearing 3D glasses, 1979.

Previous page: US tour with Crazy Horse, Palladium, New York, November 1976.

1975

November 10:
Release of *Zuma*.

December 7-21:
Rolling *Zuma* Revue tour with Crazy Horse at low-key venues across Northern California.

1976

February 16:
Begins recording with Stephen Stills as the Stills-Young Band for *Long May You Run*.

September 20:
Release of *Long May You Run*.

June 23-July 20:
US tour with the Stills-Young Band (brought to a premature end by Neil's sudden withdrawal).

June 7:
Final session for *Long May You Run*.

March 3-April 2:
Tour of Europe and Japan with Crazy Horse.

November 1-24:
US tour with Crazy Horse.

November 25:
Appears at the Band's farewell concert at the Winterland Ballroom, San Francisco.

1977

May 27:
Release of *American Stars 'n Bars*, containing material from various sessions between December 1974 and April 1977.

Spring:
Begins filming movie *Human Highway*.

April 26:
Release of *The Last Waltz*, Martin Scorsese's film of the Band's 1976 farewell concert.

February:
Begins dating Pegi Morton.

Embarks on a brief affair with Nicolette Larson, a vocalist from the Nashville sessions.

November 21:
Final session in Nashville for *Comes a Time*, comprising new songs and overdubbed solo demos from as far back as 1975.

October 28:
Release of three-disc "best of" compilation *Decade*.

July 15–September 2:
Plays a series of club gigs around Santa Cruz, California with local band the Ducks.

May 24–28:
The so-called One Stop world tour, which consists of ten shows (two each night) at the Boarding House, San Francisco. Footage is used for *Human Highway*.

May 27:
After one of his Boarding House gigs, Neil guests with avant-garde rockers Devo at the nearby Mabuhay Gardens club.

August 2:
Marries Pegi Morton.

September 16–October 24:
Rust Never Sleeps US tour with Crazy Horse, including live recordings for a forthcoming album of the same name.

October 22:
Shoots concert at the Cow Palace in Daly City, California for the *Rust Never Sleeps* movie.

October 28:
Release of *Comes a Time*.

December:
Named as Male Vocalist of the Year by *Rolling Stone*.

December:
Rust Never Sleeps voted Album of the Year by readers and critics in *Rolling Stone* magazine.

December:
Named Artist of the Decade by New York's influential *Village Voice* newspaper.

November 14:
Release of double concert album *Live Rust*.

November 14:
Premiere of the concert movie *Rust Never Sleeps*, directed by Neil.

June 22:
Release of *Rust Never Sleeps*.

Spring:
Ben is diagnosed with a severe form of cerebral palsy.

November 28:
Birth of Neil and Pegi's first child, Ben.

YOUNG

"When we get together and play it's just real. I'm a feeling type of drummer and Neil is a feeling type of guitar player and music is a feeling—his emotion draws ours and ours draws his, that's the way it works."

— Ralph Molina, 1997

Out of the maelstrom and into the soothing embrace of Crazy Horse; it had become a ritual, an oasis of sanity in an increasingly insane world (although others might beg to differ). Finding refuge on the beach in Malibu, breathing deep the sea air, cosseted by the vaulted blue sky, Neil hunkered down with that winning combination: Briggs, babes, and the baleful presence of another wild man guitarist. Frank "Poncho" Sampedro was recruited to join the Horse.

Tape was rolling as the waves lapped along the nearby Pacific Ocean shore; it was the closest to a natural high any of them could remember, informing their performances with a rare sense of composure. Zuma Beach is the place where the American Dream runs out of continent. The 1975 album *Zuma* was the result, another collection of derelicts, depressives, and femmes fatales adrenalized by the sound of Old Black, reverberating through a vintage Fender Deluxe amp, a drug in itself.

"*Zuma* was breaking free of the murk," Neil stated in his 1979 Cameron Crowe interview for *Rolling Stone*. "My best records are the ones with Crazy Horse. They're the most fluid. *Zuma* was a great electric album coming from a place where pop leaves rock 'n' roll."

Sharry Wilson: All members of the band gelled as a unit and their efforts paid off on such stellar selections as "Don't Cry No Tears," "Barstool Blues," "Cortez the Killer, "Drive Back," and "Danger Bird." A number of the tracks on *Zuma* reference Neil's breakup with Carrie Snodgress in 1974. And there was the distinctive cover artwork by James Mazzeo. *(2015)*

In his book *Neil Young FAQ*, author Glen Boyd observed that *Zuma* marked Neil's return to a harder rock sound akin to *Everybody Knows This Is Nowhere*.

Glen Boyd: Much like that album's "Down by the River" and "Cowgirl in the Sand," *Zuma*'s two centerpieces are also vehicles that serve as a launch pad for the extended Neil Young guitar solos many fans thought he had abandoned altogether somewhere between *After the Gold Rush* and *Harvest*. For these long-suffering fans, "Danger Bird" and especially "Cortez the Killer" represented a stunning return to ear-shredding, feedback-laden form. *(2012)*

Mark Guerrero: Around my music, I went to school at Cal State Los Angeles where Rick Rosas and I saw Buffalo Springfield on that campus, and earned a BA degree in Chicano Studies. On a cultural level I particularly appreciated "Cortez the Killer" because Cortez is reviled by me and most other Mexican-Americans and Mexican nationals for his "conquest" of the Aztecs and the brutal rule Spain held over Mexico for 300 years. *(2014)*

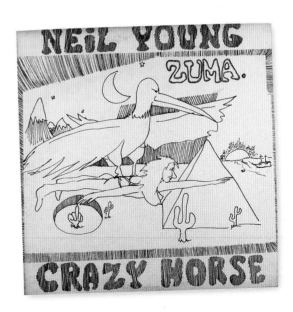

Crazy Horse ramp up the intensity at the Falkoner Teatret, Copenhagen, March 16, 1976.

The following year saw more reckless touring with Crazy Horse, and Neil also recorded an album with Stephen Stills. All four members of CSNY gathered in Miami in February 1976 to make the long-awaited successor to *Déjà Vu*. However, David Crosby and Graham Nash had to leave early to finish another album they were recording together. The remaining pair decided to erase Crosby and Nash's contributions and complete the album without them. Credited to the Stills-Young Band, *Long May You Run* was released in September 1976. This was to be the only time Young and Stills would collaborate as a duo, any prospect of a follow-up made less likely by Neil's abrupt departure from a summer tour after just nine dates. The first Stills knew of Neil's decision was from this notorious telegram: "Dear Stephen, funny how some things that start spontaneously end that way. Eat a peach. Neil."

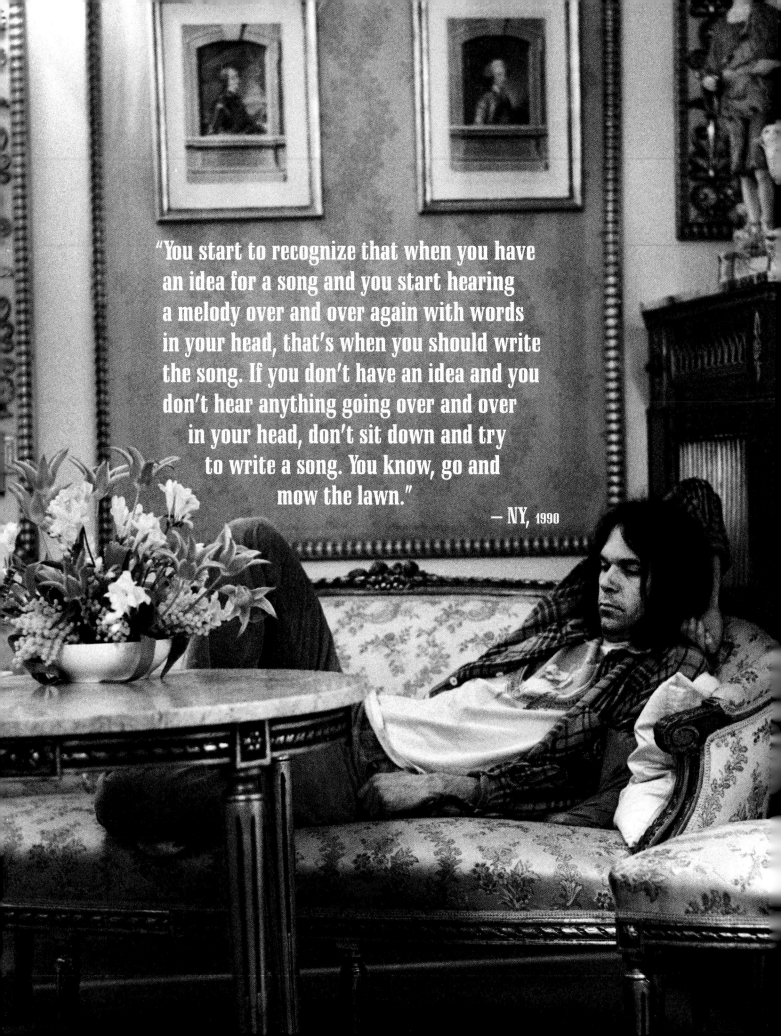

"You start to recognize that when you have an idea for a song and you start hearing a melody over and over again with words in your head, that's when you should write the song. If you don't have an idea and you don't hear anything going over and over in your head, don't sit down and try to write a song. You know, go and mow the lawn."

— NY, 1990

Left: Guesting with Joni Mitchell at the Band's *Last Waltz* farewell show, Winterland Ballroom, San Francisco, November 25, 1976.

Opposite: Downtime in Copenhagen during the 1976 tour of Europe with Crazy Horse.

A Martin Scorsese Film
THE LAST WALTZ

"Before I start I'd just like to say that it's one of the pleasures of my life to be on this stage with these people tonight."

— NY during The Last Waltz, 1976

One show that Neil was determined not to miss, though, took place on the night of Thanksgiving— November 25. Neil was in San Francisco, at the Winterland Ballroom, to join in the filming of the now landmark *Last Waltz*, director Martin Scorsese's homage to the life and times of the Band.

Robbie Robertson: Sometimes you come up with something so right that it takes on a life of its own. When I originally started thinking that we were going to do this and was wondering who we were going to invite, we'd only talked about Bob Dylan and Ronnie Hawkins. And then there were other people who had been so supportive and that we respected so much musically. Eric Clapton, Van Morrison. And then there's our compatriots from Canada, Joni and Neil, and the whole thing just snowballed. *(2004)*

Kenneth Kubernik: Considered by many to be the greatest rock concert film of all time, *The Last Waltz* captured a silvery moment of exultation among a generation's brightest musical lights, a Magnificat of jailhouse blues and Tin Pan pop, of maple-leaf harmonies and punch-drunk soul-stirring, courtesy of the Belfast cowboy, Van Morrison. Neil Young, in a frozen glare, captured on celluloid around the

heart-warming camaraderie, draped his willowy arms around a gaggle of fellow imbibers and truth-seekers. *(2015)*

Performing with the Band, Neil sang "Helpless" and Ian & Sylvia's "Four Strong Winds" (a studio version of which would close his 1978 album *Comes a Time*). I covered and reviewed *The Last Waltz* for *Melody Maker*.

Shortly thereafter, I bumped into Neil one night in Los Angeles at Lucy's El Adobe Café on Melrose Avenue. I was with Bruce Gary, the future Knack drummer, who was a former neighbor and occasional poker opponent of Neil's from his Topanga Canyon days. Bruce and I saw Buffalo Springfield in 1966 and 1967, and CSNY in 1969.

Inside Lucy's everyone was very groovy. We were at adjoining tables with drummer Jim Keltner, who suggested ordering the Barbecue Beef Tostada with extra dressing. Which was not on the menu at the time (my life changed forever ...). It was just before a surprise onstage Band reunion in West Hollywood at the Roxy Theatre that Neil and I both attended. I told him I had just interviewed Robbie Robertson for a *Crawdaddy!* magazine cover story. He grinned, "You must really like Canadians ..."

Having recorded another full album, *Chrome Dreams*, that would join *Homegrown*, that other lost classic, on the shelf, Neil instead decided to release *American Stars 'n Bars* in May 1977, a grab bag of songs gathering dust in the cans; some country-flavored, some lingering statements from years past.

Rob Mitchum: The stark tone of *On the Beach* was only carried over to one track from 1977's *American Stars 'n Bars*, the creepily lo-fi "Will to Love." What fills the remainder of the album is a sort of buffet-style Neil Young, offering up choice leftovers from various failed projects of the era. The peak, of course, is "Like a Hurricane," perhaps one of the finest examples of Neil's willfully untechnical guit-hartic playing style, a chord progression that induces string-popping frenzy in his live shows to this day. *(2003)*

NY: So I'll write a song like "Will to Love." It's a character thing. You get into a character. Subconsciously you could be a whole different person than you are consciously. *(1990)*

Richard Bosworth, who would engineer a portion of Neil's *Landing on Water* album in 1986, sheds some light on Linda Ronstadt's vocal contributions to *American Stars 'n Bars*.

Richard Bosworth: I was recording with Linda Ronstadt at Record One. During lunch one day I mentioned that I'd been working on Neil's new album [*Landing on Water*] and she was really interested in hearing all about it. Linda then proceeded to tell me a story of her work on *American Stars 'n Bars*.

"Neil invited Emmylou Harris and myself to sing on his new album," Linda recalled. "He asked us to come to his ranch in La Honda in Northern California. Neil and his band were in an old barn and it was set up like a live gig with a PA and vocal monitors. We worked all day running down about six songs. At the end of the day Emmylou and I said to Neil that we thought the rehearsals went great and we were looking forward to actually recording the tunes. Neil took us out to the back of the barn and there was a remote recording truck that unbeknownst to us had been recording us all day. And Neil said we were done." *(2015)*

Decade, a three-disc compilation of songs hand-picked by Neil himself, was released in October 1977. There were a few obscurities thrown in to appease the cognoscenti; otherwise, a marking-time gesture from the label that scored commercially, italicizing Neil's position as a revered cult hero with crossover appeal.

The product certainly impressed Vivien Goldman in her *Sounds* review from November 19, 1977. "*Decade* proves that Young's one of the only old-timers whose creativity has remained fresh/strong through his whole career. 'Broken Arrow' still sounds adventurous as do the comparatively new tracks off *Zuma* and *Tonight's the Night* ... an ideal culmination to ten years of unique savage/melodic/tortured/tender vision. No, culmination's the wrong word. Luckily, all the pointers indicate that *Decade*'s not a post-mortem, it's a portent."

Neil struck out into his next decade of creativity with another sharp change of direction: a return to the country-folk stylings of *Harvest*. Upon its release in October 1978, *Comes a Time* broke into the US Top Ten, a position Neil had not occupied since *Harvest*.

Sharry Wilson: *Comes a Time* was originally conceived by Neil as a solo acoustic recording. Mo Ostin at Warner Bros. recommended that he consider adding some rhythm tracks and play with a band. Some consummate studio musicians were assembled for the recording sessions in Nashville in the late fall of 1977, including Ben Keith, Karl Himmel, Tim Drummond, Spooner Oldham, and Rufus Thibodeaux.

Neil also brought singer Nicolette Larson into the fold on vocals. Nicolette, with Neil's blessing, released a cover of "Lotta Love" that met with great chart success upon release. *(2015)*

Mike Grant: With the exception of the bluesy "Motorcycle Mama," *Comes a Time* has Neil in a mellow, almost folk mood and is an album I return to more often than many of his other albums. "Goin' Back," "Comes a Time," "Lotta Love,"

"Human Highway," and his cover of Ian Tyson's "Four Strong Winds" have all made it onto my *California Music Show* radio playlist. *(2014)*

Ian Tyson: When I was trying to put a ranch together, I didn't have much money and I was only playing on weekends. Somebody phoned me and said, "Hey, Neil Young has just cut "Four Strong Winds." I said, "Holy smokes! Hallelujah." To be honest with you, I heard it and I didn't like it. But after the checks started rolling in, I had an immediate affection for it. I got to liking it! *(2015)*

Having become close to Nicolette Larson during the *Comes a Time* sessions in late 1977, Neil was to form a more lasting union with Pegi Morton. He had met her in 1974 when she was working in a bar near Broken Arrow, and after dating intermittently they eventually married in August 1978. Their son, Ben, was born three months later.

Neil's three-disc *Decade* compilation advertised on Sunset Boulevard, scene of the chance 1966 meeting with Stephen Stills that led to the creation of Buffalo Springfield.

"The song 'Comes a Time' is one of my all-time favorite recordings because it just has a great feeling. The song and the performance are a total mesh. Nicolette's singing is beautiful. I can see all the pictures. That is as close to a perfect recording as I ever have gotten."

— NY, 2012

Released in July 1979, Neil's next album, *Rust Never Sleeps*, marked a major shift in artistic direction. Both in its title and its uncompromising style, *Rust Never Sleeps* signaled Neil's recognition that there was a new force in music—namely punk—and that the face of rock 'n' roll would change forever. Name-checking Sex Pistols singer Johnny Rotten and playing club gigs with the post-punk band Devo, he was one of the few members of the Woodstock generation to embrace the young pretenders rather than shy away from them.

NY: When you look back at the old bands, they're just not that funny. People want to be funny now, people want to have a good time. That's why the punk thing is so good and healthy, because the people aren't taking themselves seriously. People who make fun of the established rock scene, like Devo and the Ramones, are much more vital to my ears than what's been happening in the last four or five years. *(1979)*

Sharry Wilson: *Rust Never Sleeps* is an easy album to fall in love with if you're a fan of Neil's work with Crazy Horse. It's bookended by the brilliant "My My, Hey Hey (Out of the Blue)" and "Hey Hey, My My (Into the Black)." Rockers like "Sedan Delivery" and "Welfare Mothers" are played with such feeling and passion. "Pocahontas," "Powderfinger," and "Thrasher" are classics in Neil's canon of work. *(2015)*

"Rust is the finest album Neil Young has ever released … Poignant, perceptive, menacing, dangerous, witty, and cataclysmic. It's a veritable embarrassment of riches. Rust doesn't sleep, it explodes."

— Nick Kent, *New Musical Express*, 1979

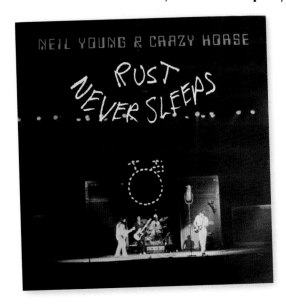

Rust Never Sleeps also made a big impression at the time on a college student named Steve Wynn, who went on to form the Dream Syndicate in 1981.

Steve Wynn: I was going to the University of California Davis, a DJ at the local station KDVS, playing guitar in a new wave band, obsessed with punk rock and often dismissive of the things that came before.

For me and my pals, 1977 had drawn a distinct line in the sand. But *Rust Never Sleeps* felt like it was on the right side of history. It was alternately bare bones, stripped down and then on the other side, as ugly and noisy and raw as anything out there, actually less manicured and mannered than most punk or new wave records. And it even mentioned Johnny Rotten.

I was actually at the Cow Palace 1978 show that was recorded for *Live Rust*. It was the loudest show I ever saw. I felt my clothes move independently of my body. And it was so great—the sound, the staging, the song choices. I was eighteen years old and had already been playing in bands but that show changed the way I felt about playing live music. It probably was as influential as any show I ever saw. *(2015)*

That Cow Palace show was also filmed for a concert movie released in August 1979. *New York Times* critic John Rockwell wrote: "*Rust Never Sleeps* offers some of his strongest songs, both new and old, in performances as fine or finer than those of his recent, partly live record of the same title. The effect here is rougher than the record, less polished with overdubbing; at one point, Mr. Young even mangles the words of one of his best songs. But the intensity of the singing and the playing of Crazy Horse, Mr. Young's longtime partners for electric-rock projects, is as moving as rock can offer."

John Einarson: It's about the intensity of his performance. He's on fire in the movie *Rust Never Sleeps*. And the sense of chronology. Where you've got him waking up on top of the amplifiers and emerging and doing "Sugar Mountain" and "I Am a Child." The idea of the giant amps, too. That came from the notion that he was about to go on tour, just released *Comes a Time* and he looked at all these piles of junk when Crazy Horse was rehearsing. These old amps and he thought it looked awful. Why not build these big giant amps, put the real amps behind them and really show the whole idea that it's about the big sound and making all the musicians look so miniature and so midget around this sound. It was a concept that came to him just before the tour started. Again, this is a guy who just put out *Comes a Time*, which is folky and country, and he goes out with Crazy Horse and then does this thrashing rock 'n' roll tour. And Neil changed his look and got that short haircut and he was wearing pants with braces. Crazy Horse has always been a back-to-basics sound. And Neil embraced the energy level of punk. *(2014)*

Having deftly evaded the rock-dinosaur tag, Neil finished the decade on a high. *Rust Never Sleeps* was named album of the year by *Rolling Stone* and a new generation of fans joined his diehard followers in eagerly anticipating his next move. Seasoned Neil Young observers had grown used to his constant shifts in style, but even they would be taken aback by what he served up over the next phase of his career.

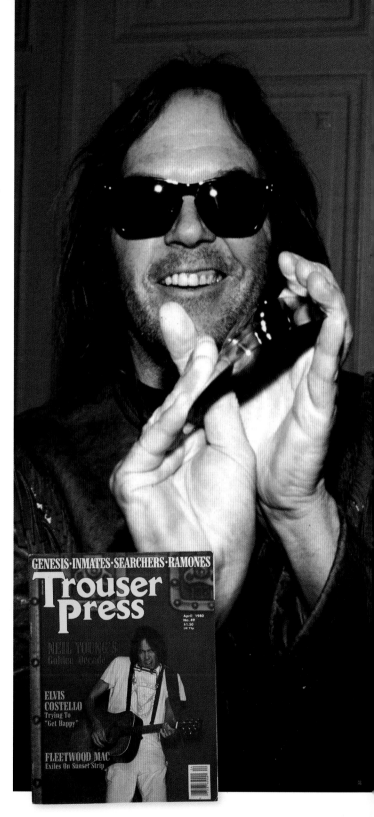

Above: Neil Young's golden decade finished in fine style.

Opposite: New York punk band the Ramones (top), whose irreverent style influenced *Rust Never Sleeps*. The album's opening and closing tracks, "My My, Hey Hey (Out of the Blue)" and "Hey Hey, My My (Into the Black)," cite Sex Pistols singer Johnny Rotten (bottom).

Overleaf: The high-concept Rust Never Sleeps live show was filmed for the 1979 concert movie of the same name. Cow Palace, Daly City, California, October 22, 1978.

LOST IN SPACE
1980-1987

"The fact that I don't go to places where I know my picture's gonna be taken makes people think that I'm hiding. I'm not hiding from anything. I'm just not interested in it."

— NY, 1984

Timeline

Right: Bruce Springsteen guesting on an encore of "Down by the River," Entertainment Centre, Sydney, March 22, 1985.

Below: Wembley Arena, London, September 1982.

Page 106: Sportpaleis Ahoy, Rotterdam, September 1982.

1980

February:
Records side two of *Hawks & Doves* (side one contains previously unreleased material from 1974 to 1977).

March 1:
Release of *Where the Buffalo Roam* soundtrack album, featuring original music by Neil.

October:
Pegi and Neil enroll Ben in a demanding program run by the Institute for the Achievement of Human Potential. This keeps Neil close to home for the next eighteen months.

October–July 1981:
Recording sessions for *Re-ac-tor*.

September:
Release of comedy film *Human Highway*, directed by Neil.

April 14:
Inducted into the Canadian Music Hall of Fame.

1982

October 28:
Release of *Re-ac-tor*.

September–May 1982:
Recording sessions for *Trans*.

1981

November 3:
Release of *Hawks & Doves*.

August 31–October 19:
Trans tour of Europe with the Trans band—his first tour since 1978.

December 29:
Release of *Trans*, the first of five albums for Geffen.

1983

January 5–March 4:
Solo Trans tour of the US and Canada, which finishes early when Neil collapses, exhausted, backstage in Louisville.

1985

1984

1986

1987

August 23–October 26:
Tour of the US and Canada with the International Harvesters.

May 15:
Birth of Neil and Pegi's second child, Amber Jean.

December 1:
Geffen sues Neil for delivering albums that are "unrepresentative" of his music. The suit is later dropped with an apology from label boss, David Geffen.

September 18:
The show at Dayton, Ohio is filmed for the *Solo Trans* movie, released in 1984.

July 27:
Release of *Everybody's Rockin'*.

July 1–October 1:
Another Solo Trans tour of the US, this time with the Shocking Pinks appearing for the encores.

April–May:
Records *Everybody's Rockin'* as Neil Young and the Shocking Pinks.

Late January:
Early sessions for *Old Ways* in Nashville with the International Harvesters, but the country-influenced songs are rejected by Geffen.

February 22–March 22:
Tours Australia and New Zealand for the first time, with the International Harvesters and Crazy Horse.

July 13:
Performs at the Live Aid concert in Philadelphia, playing a solo set and reuniting with Crosby, Stills & Nash.

August 9–September 21:
Tour of the US with the International Harvesters.

August 12:
Release of *Old Ways*.

September 22:
Organizes the first Farm Aid concert with Willie Nelson and John Mellencamp, at Champaign, Illinois.

March:
Main recording sessions for *Landing on Water*.

July 21:
Release of *Landing on Water*.

September 15–November 21:
Live in a Rusted Out Garage tour of the US and Canada with Crazy Horse.

August 13–September 4:
Life tour of the US and Canada with Crazy Horse.

June 30:
Release of *Life*, Neil's final Geffen album, comprising all new songs taken from the November 1986 concert recordings.

April 24–June 6:
Tour of Europe with Crazy Horse.

November 18–19:
Recording of two shows from the Rusted Out Garage tour, at the Universal Amphitheatre, Los Angeles.

October 13:
Pegi and Neil organize the first benefit concert in aid of the Bridge School for children with severe speech and physical impairments, held at the Shoreline Amphitheatre in Mountain View, California.

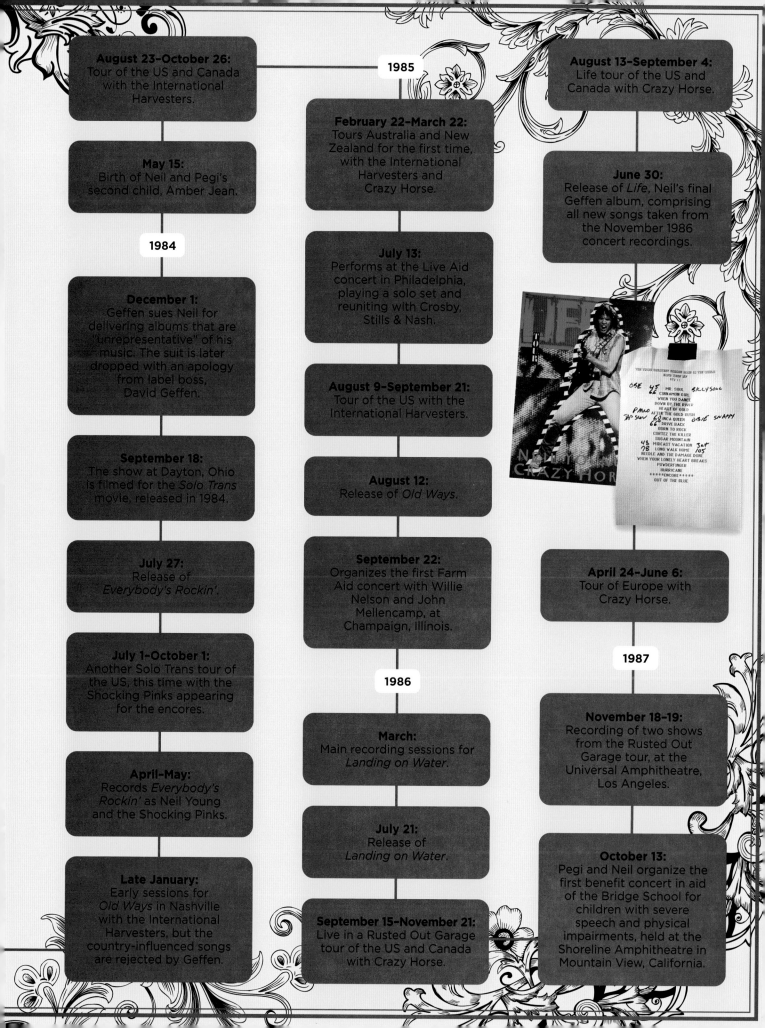

"Neil Young is a great actor. Because what makes an actor great is the ability to truly believe. Believe the situation you're a part of, whether that's being on a spaceship in the future or on a wagon train in the distant past. Neil has always come across as an artist who fully believes whatever he's performing at the time he's doing it. Thrash rock, acoustic folk, pure country, blues … It's not so much that he's a chameleon, it's that he has the ability to put himself into these various characters so authentically that they resonate as real."

— Bill Mumy, 2015

The 1980s began quietly for Neil with *Hawks & Doves*, released in November 1980. This oddball album was a hodgepodge of acoustic and electric songs, some of which were recorded in the mid-1970s, others specifically for the album.

Cynthia Rose: *Hawks & Doves* is no completely unqualified success, despite five cuts of major importance (on the acoustic side one, "The Old Homestead" and the complex, allusive "Captain Kennedy"; on the electric side two, "Comin' Apart at Every Nail," "Union Man," and the title cut). Much of the rest is over-whimsical and veers toward the lightweight, but through the whole album runs a peculiar, pervasive sense of closeness to a mothering force. Some might call it an ideal of community, some hope, others the never-fully-explicable stakes of American rock 'n' roll. *(1980)*

For the music industry, the 1980s began with a massive launch that would upend how bands were broken, careers made and units sold: MTV. In the late summer of 1981, the music cable channel began snaking its way into suburban living rooms all over America with a splashy advert showing a rocket ship launch and an astronaut planting a fluorescent green-and-pink MTV flag on the moon.

The age of music television image-making and album-breaking had begun and a whole new cadre of puppet masters were employed by the record labels to exploit this nascent medium into album and future CD sales: video directors, costume makers, lighting wizards, stylists, hair and make-up teams. By the time Neil, or his 1960s peers for that matter, even knew what MTV was, the charts were being invaded by well-coiffed, designer-suit-wearing bands with New Wave haircuts and trendy videos shot in exotic locales starring cleavage-busting temptresses.

Now MTV programming execs were the ones deciding what would become a hit. What would the new generation now watching hundreds of slickly produced three-minute music videos pumped into their homes twenty-four hours a day think of a mid-thirties singer-songwriter wearing crumpled flannels?

However, during this period Neil had a more pressing situation to deal with: In spring 1979, Neil and Pegi had received the life-changing news that their infant son, Ben, was suffering from a severe form of cerebral palsy.

"I was in shock. I walked around in a fog for weeks. I couldn't fathom how I had fathered two children with a rare condition that was not supposed to be hereditary, with two different mothers."

— NY, 2012

A month before the release of *Hawks & Doves*, Neil and Pegi decided to enroll Ben in a program devised by the Institute for the Achievement of Human Potential. This grueling regime required constant involvement from both parents. With his movements restricted for the next eighteen months, Neil was not in a position to tour the album; instead, he dove right back into his home studio to work on an even more peculiar record. *Re-ac-tor* ultimately sunk Crazy Horse for the next decade, if by nothing else than sheer exhaustion.

Whether Neil was too preoccupied with his family obligations or just not inspired playing with Crazy Horse, or both, the songs fell flat, felt incomplete and seemed to have no vitality to them. Full of meandering electric guitars and sparse, repetitive melodies and lyrics—the Serenity Prayer from the Twelve Step program printed on the back cover—it would be an understatement to say that the album

Neil got to know the post-punk band Devo in 1978 and guested at one of their club gigs in May of that year. He went on to cast them as nuclear garbage men in his movie *Human Highway*.

was wildly out of step with the musical landscape of the time. Reviewing *Re-ac-tor* in the *New Musical Express*, Adam Sweeting described it as "not an album for the squeamish."

If the 1980s had started off bizarrely, things were about to go from odd to downright surreal. Undeterred by the tepid response to his first movie, *Journey through the Past*, Neil Young the cinematic auteur was about to throw another buzz bomb to his followers, daring them to make sense of his latest vision.

Ostensibly a rock 'n' roll narrative featuring Dean Stockwell, Dennis Hopper, and Sally Kirkland, *Human Highway* took four years and millions of dollars of Neil's own money to see through to its ramshackle completion. An impenetrable morass of concert footage and staged scenes, the movie was most charitably viewed as a carryover of the inexhaustible appetite for work, for distraction, that defined Neil during the 1970s.

However commercially disastrous the film was upon its release in September 1982, some of the devotees who saw *Human Highway* enjoyed it.

Sharry Wilson:
I was lucky enough to be

in the audience for the screening of the director's cut of *Human Highway* on September 10, 2014 at the Elgin Theatre during the Toronto International Film Festival. I had viewed a bootleg copy of the 1982 film many years earlier but I relished the opportunity to see it with fresh eyes and with the improvements the Shakey Pictures team had painstakingly worked on.

I immediately noticed that the sound was clear as a bell and the visuals were crisp and clean. I think Neil chose to resurrect the film (with noted improvements) because it still holds relevance today, perhaps even more so. The residents of Linear Valley in the film are complacent about living next door to a nuclear power plant. They go about their daily lives blissfully ignorant of the danger in their midst. Nobody does anything to counteract an obviously earth-shattering situation. The members of Devo are brilliantly cast as nuclear garbage men. *(2015)*

re·ac·tor
south·ern pac·i·fic
b/w mo·tor cit·y

PROMOTIONAL COPY NOT FOR SALE

neil young cra·zy horse

Above: On the set of Neil's bizarre 1982 movie *Human Highway*, in which he starred alongside actor friends Dennis Hopper (bottom), Russ Tamblyn, and Dean Stockwell.

Opposite: Music mogul David Geffen, c. 1980. In the 1980s, Neil recorded five albums for Geffen.

e-ac-tor was to be Neil's last album for Reprise before changing labels for the first time. Founded in 1980 by the savvy music-industry dealmaker David Geffen, Geffen Records quickly began signing up big names: Don Henley, Elton John, John Lennon and Yoko Ono, Joni Mitchell, Peter Gabriel, Aerosmith, Whitesnake—and Neil Young.

Neil's manager Elliot Roberts had been a friend and associate of Geffen's for years and negotiated a seemingly sweet deal: a million dollars an album and complete artistic control. It almost seemed too good to be true. Neil then released his debut album for the company.

Newly released from the restrictions of Ben's Institute for the Achievement of Human Potential program, Neil traveled to Honolulu, Hawaii, with a virtual who's who from his past: Bruce Palmer on bass, Ralph Molina on drums, Ben Keith on the steel, and Nils Lofgren and Frank Sampedro on guitars. The idea was to merge musicians from different periods of his career and "take it further with all those people." They recorded an album with a working title of *Islands in the Sun*. However, when Geffen visited the studio he was not impressed. Neil held his tongue, swallowed his pride, and took a surprising new direction.

Released in December 1982, *Trans* was surely out-there; so avant-garde it went over just about everybody's heads. The album was anchored in Kraftwerk-like computerized synth-pop and anamorphic vocals—rhythms and sounds that Neil hoped would enable him to communicate with Ben.

However, both longtime fans and critics were bemused. Neil originally intended the music to be accompanied by a series of videos, but the budget was not available. So without any videos to promote the album, the new MTV generation never even heard it. Despite this, *Trans* did hit a respectable number nineteen on the *Billboard* charts.

The general sentiment at the time was: Neil Young is lost, Neil Young is over, Neil Young is in the wilderness. Barney Hoskyns of the *New Musical Express* declared him to be a "spectacle of folkie rebel stumbling onto a new toy called the vocoder ... *Trans* is the manifesto of farmyard futurism, a version of tone in which a lanky old cowboy is reassembled as ... well, a lanky old cowboy."

To be sure, however, *Trans has* aged well, its tentacles reaching much farther than the farmyard: Bands such as Radiohead adopted a version of its icy, mechanized sound and eerie alto vocals, and many longtime fans have since rediscovered it. Neil himself has referred to it as "one of my highest moments." At the time, though, he was crushed, taking to heart the critical venom during the six-week tour—his first since 1978—as many of the songs dealt with very personal matters. Songs like "Transformer Man," "Computer Age," and "We R in Control" revolve around Neil's interest in artificial intelligence.

NY: I could see that machines were starting to take over our lives: This image of elevators with digital numbers changing and people going up and down—people changing levels under the control of a machine. I had this whole video thing in mind for the song "Computer Age," starring a guy with a big speaker on his chest, his face was a keypad, and he kept hitting his face. But I couldn't get anyone to believe the fucking idea was any good. *(1988)*

Glen Boyd: *Trans*, to me, when you listen to it now, it does sound a little bit dated. I'm one of the people of that period who liked all the synth pop bands that were coming out at the time. The songs are strong: "Transformer Man," "Sample and Hold." "Like an Inca" doesn't get a lot of love. *(2015)*

Having baffled the world with the futuristic electronica of *Trans*, what would Neil do next? Travel to Nashville and record some acoustic songs in the vein of *Harvest* and *Comes a Time*, of course. However, this artistic lurch was equally unpopular with his new label. Geffen executives rejected the new songs, recorded in early 1983, as "too country" and urged Neil to make some rock 'n' roll.

He took them literally. Released in July 1983, *Everybody's Rockin'* was a twenty-four-minute pastiche of 1950s rockabilly. The subversive intent was clear to everyone at the label, and in early December Geffen Records sued Neil for damages of over three million dollars, claiming that both *Trans* and *Everybody's Rockin'* were "uncommercial" and "unrepresentative of his previous records."

me at all. As far as I'm concerned, that song is just as important as any song that I ever wrote. And it stands up just as well. It's just written in an attitude and a genre that nobody understands. That they don't want to understand! They don't want to see me like that. *(1990)*

> ## "The truth is I fought with him because I wanted him to do better work. I was taking too much of a fatherly role in his life."
> — David Geffen, 2014

NY: I don't really care about what people think about [my songwriting]. I mean, I do care if people like it or not. But that doesn't affect what I'm doing. So I can go ahead and do something like *Everybody's Rockin'* and get completely into it knowing that a lot of people are going to think, "Hey, this is bullshit. Neil shouldn't be doing this. This doesn't mean anything; the songs are meaningless." But that doesn't bother

Whether or not Geffen's cry of too much paternalism echoes true, Neil saw it much differently. Possibly as an antidote to the ugly Geffen lawsuit, which he had now decided to countersue, he unceremoniously announced he was done with rock 'n' roll. Revisiting the 1983 country-tinged sessions that Geffen had rejected, he assembled an all-star cast of country movers-and-shakers, which he christened the

International Harvesters, and made an out-and-out country album called *Old Ways*. (Neil was also taking even more of a "fatherly role" in his own life, as Pegi gave birth to a daughter, Amber Jean, in May 1984.)

Old Ways was not released until August 1985, but before then, in the fall of 1984 and spring of 1985, Neil took the International Harvesters out on the road. The band included Nashville luminaries such as Bennett Keith Schaeufele on pedal steel guitar, Anthony Crawford on banjo, Rufus Thibodeaux on fiddle, and George Jones alum Hargus "Pig" Robbins on piano. The ever-faithful Ben Keith also returned on steel.

NY: I really believe in country music, and I believe in the country music community, the way that people support the music, the more friendly kind of approach of the DJs and the public relations side of it. Everywhere we go, people go crazy. I was very surprised they get off more on hearing the fiddle than they do on hearing a rowdy rock 'n' roll solo ... how many guitar solos can you play? I've had it ... this band is the best I've ever had. *(1984)*

Neil and the International Harvesters crisscrossed the country, with the front man attired in his new uniform: a black shirt, blue jeans, and a tan fringed leather vest topped off with a Harley Davidson cowboy hat. But he wasn't beyond throwing in some old surprises, too.

Kerwin Dean Abramovitch: Neil finally fessed up in 1984 at a Universal Amphitheatre show in Universal City when he was touring with the International Harvesters. While introducing a Buffalo Springfield song he mused, "I'm gonna do a Buffalo Springfield song." The crowd roared, and he slyly added, "I didn't sing this one, but I don't have a chip on *my* shoulder about it." His band kicked into "Flying on the Ground Is Wrong" with Neil singing and playing guitar incredibly. *(2015)*

Some of Neil's inner circle may not have been thrilled with him playing in rodeo arenas complete with horse stalls and cow dung, but the man himself seemed liberated from his personal and professional problems; he even decided to do a few TV appearances to promote the tour, including a memorable slot on *Austin City Limits*.

Opposite: During his solo US tour from July 1 to October 1, 1983, Neil brought the Shocking Pinks on to play songs from *Everybody's Rockin'* as an encore.

Right bottom, and overleaf: Performing with the International Harvesters on the *Austin City Limits* PBS TV show, September 25, 1984.

"I see country music, I see people who take care of their own. You got seventy-five-year-old guys on the road. That's what I was put here to do, y'know, so I make sure I surround myself with people who are gonna take care of me. 'Cause I'm in it for the long run."

— NY, 1985

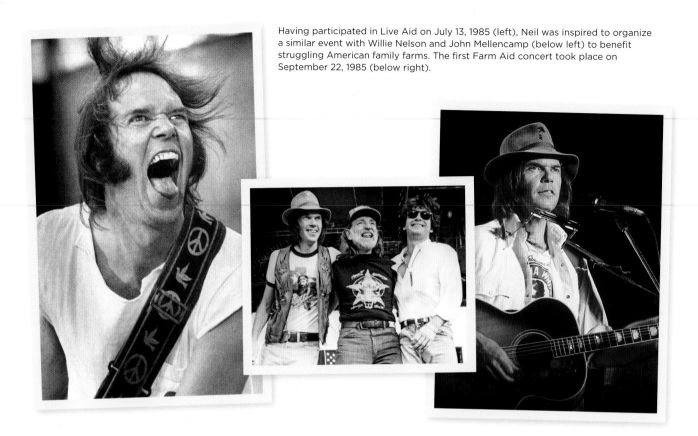

Having participated in Live Aid on July 13, 1985 (left), Neil was inspired to organize a similar event with Willie Nelson and John Mellencamp (below left) to benefit struggling American family farms. The first Farm Aid concert took place on September 22, 1985 (below right).

"His great-grandpa worked this farm. His grandpa worked it and his daddy worked it. He's thirty years old. His wife and children at his side, he stands in the window of the old farmhouse. A car comes up the driveway. A man in a suit is at the wheel, his briefcase at his side. Today is the last day for this family farm. Tomorrow is foreclosure day."

— from "An open letter by Neil Young," 1985

Halfway through the 1980s Neil Young was, to all those who loved him in the 1960s and 1970s, virtually unrecognizable, physically and musically. But then a groundbreaking global fundraising event, and specifically something Bob Dylan would say during his contribution to it, altered his trajectory in more ways than one.

Live Aid was the brainchild of Bob Geldof, lead singer of Irish new wave band the Boomtown Rats, and Midge Ure, Scottish front man of the British group Ultravox. Geldof was so moved by a BBC news report on the scale of the famine afflicting Ethiopia in the mid-1980s he felt compelled to mobilize the music community for a global charity event.

The historic concerts staged simultaneously at Wembley Stadium in London and JFK Stadium in Philadelphia on July 13, 1985 were telecast around the world and raised almost $300 million. Neil played two sets that day in Philadelphia—one with the International Harvesters and one with a specially

reunited CSNY—but both went mostly unnoticed owing to all the other high-octane performers. The Harvesters were sandwiched between acts such as the Cars and Eric Clapton, while CSNY had to follow a Led Zeppelin reunion and then were upstaged by the wildly popular MTV darlings Duran Duran.

During his somewhat shambolic set, Bob Dylan made an offhand comment that it would be cool to see some of the millions being made for starving Africans set aside for American farmers in danger of losing their livelihoods through mortgage debt. Although in the context of the event the comment was perhaps ill-judged, Neil was instantly galvanized. He joined forces with Willie Nelson and John Mellencamp, who had voiced similar concerns, and the trio set about organizing their own fundraiser.

The first Farm Aid concert was held in Champaign, Illinois on September 22, 1985—just two months after Live Aid. As well as the three founding fathers, other performers included Bob Dylan, Tom Petty and the Heartbreakers, Don Henley, Bon Jovi, Billy Joel,

and Johnny Cash. The event raised approximately $9 million for struggling family farmers.

Neil's charitable pursuits were a welcome distraction from his recording troubles. Although the lawsuit with Geffen Records had supposedly been resolved amicably (Neil agreed to cut his $1 million fee per album to $500,000 and David Geffen personally apologized to him), all was not well. Seeking a more commercial sound for his next album, *Landing on Water*, Neil elected to bring in veteran drummer Steve Jordan, who had worked with Don Henley, James Taylor, and Dylan, among others, and guitarist/producer Danny Kortchmar, who had been a hit-making songwriting partner for Henley and Jackson Browne. To be sure, the effect was energizing—at first. However, that exuberance soon faded as Neil struggled to find an original way to deliver the songs while satisfying his record company's hunger for contemporary-sounding hits. He was in no-man's land again.

Eventually, Geffen shut down the recordings complaining Neil was over budget; the artist would have to pay for the rest of the sessions himself. While Neil was trying to emulate the big drum and slicker sound of bands like U2, he had lost sight of his strength as a superior singer-songwriter. He seemed more lost than ever.

Jim Keltner: I first met Neil in 1985 when he was working on *Landing on Water*. My good friend engineer Niko Bolas told Steve Jordan, one of my closest friends and favorite drummers, that Neil wanted the sound of a breaking bottle. It was so far back in the day that nobody knew how to do that. Samplers had just begun and I was one of the first people to have one. I brought it down to the studio and they put me in the bathroom. They set up a microphone in there, threw a bottle, and I sampled it breaking. We put it on tape from my machine. *(2015)*

Richard Bosworth: In December 1985 I was just finishing recording and mixing an album with Roy Orbison in Record One Studio A. Neil had started his *Landing on Water* album in Studio B with Danny Kortchmar co-producing. Anyone who knows Neil Young knows that Roy Orbison is an idol and role model to him. Neil dropped into the Studio A control room many times to check out what we were doing and to say hi to Roy. Every time he dropped by, Roy wasn't there and Neil missed him every time! I remember Neil saying, "That Roy Orbison is one invisible motherfucker!"

Well, I finished mixing Roy's album about a week or so before Christmas and Danny Kortchmar asked me to engineer sessions on Neil's album. Apparently, Neil had wanted to do something digital for a long time but had waited until he had the right people and the right equipment. He purchased two Sony Digital twenty-four-track tape machines that cost $185,000 each and also bought two Synclavier hard disk computer recording systems at $250,000 each, and in 1985 you could buy a decent two-bedroom house for $250,000! We also utilized vocoders on *Landing on Water*, which Neil had gotten into on the *Trans* album. The original vocoders cost about $50,000 and only five had been manufactured. Neil owned three of them! *(2015)*

Niko Bolas: To be honest, Neil is the guy who turned me on to digital. Anything that is just made and might sound good or pushes technology or the envelope, Neil will get two of them and exhaust them.

Neil has taught me to be fearless about trying new stuff. In the end, you close your eyes and you listen. If it has an emotion, you like it. If it doesn't have an emotion or another approach is closer to what you intended, choose that one. *(2015)*

Neil embraced all these new technological developments not only in the studio but also on the road.

Bryan Bell: I was working for Santana on tour and then for Neil to try to help with the high-tech stuff. Neil liked all of the stuff you could do with computers for digital editing and hard-disk recording, but he did not like to play to a click track. He would record something, like a background vocal part or something on the Synclavier, and then he was forced to play in time with the Synclavier. Which he did not like. So I was asked to come up with a solution to trigger the Synclavier for the live drums. It was a box called the Human Clock [a device triggering prerecorded samples for live shows].

The first night in New York at Madison Square Garden Neil asked me to play. "Are you funky?" "Way funkier than you guys." I wanted to play guitar but he said we had too many. He then said, "Bryan. We've done our job for the promoter. We've sold all the tickets. So now we just need to focus on having a good time and entertaining the audience." "What about the critics?" "They get it wrong. We play like shit they say we're great. We play great they say we play like shit. I'm not worried about the critics." *(2015)*

Computer wizard and musician Bryan Bell also observed Neil's recording and production methods at close hand.

HELP!!!!!
THIS @#%^&*+=!:?
THING DOESN'T
WORK!!!!!

1. Is the CLOCK "seeing" what you t
a loose connection to your microphon
other instruments possibly triggerin
whether or not the proper pulses are
clock, simply watch the trigger LED

sing the CLO
tempo are no

nare drum a

n with a lot
st. try feed

place SENSIT
hen retry su

MIDI CLOCKS
+1
+2
+3
+4
+5
+6
+7
+10

MIDI START (

HUM

SPE

OWNER'S MANUAL
AND
OPERATING INSTRUCTIONS

AN AMERICAN INVENTION BY™ *Kahler*

"Neil had an interesting saying. When we were
working on tech, Tim Mulligan and I were still
plugging things in, checking sounds, doing something,
Neil would call it wires and knobs. He would walk
into the studio and say, 'Is it wires and knobs?'
When the tech was done and we're making music,
Neil would say, 'Is it art yet? Are we doing art or
are we doing wires and knobs?'"

— Bryan Bell, 2015

Bryan Bell: I lived in Portland and Neil would call and say, "Let's work today." And I'd fly to San Francisco and stay as long as he wanted me to stay. He actually sang into my cassette answering machine as he was leaving the ranch in his pickup truck to go work out. He sang this beautiful ballad, "I've tried this with the International Harvesters, I've tried this with Crazy Horse, I've tried it alone. Let's try it with the machine. You and the computer. Let's see what we can do."

I loaded the whole track for him. He walked in, "that sucks, this sucks," and throws my stuff out and puts in his own. "I want this snare sound." And we start to build the track. He had a concept and a feeling when he wrote the song and he'd been trying to record it for ten years and never got what he wanted.

As it got recorded, the lead vocal wasn't as good as the answering machine tape. And Neil likes to do vocals under the full moon. We were losing the moon, right. About three days of full moon. When the moon came up again we'd start doing rhythm tracks and then at the full moon we'd do vocals. But his vocal wasn't as good as the cassette tape. So, Tim Mulligan and I took the truck to the front steps of the studio. We put super-good microphones in the ceiling, pointed the truck at the full moon and did the vocal in the truck. And we got it. Gorgeous. We put it away in the computer and I go away. *(2015)*

Despite absorbing a considerable investment of time, energy, and money, *Landing on Water* failed to convince fans or critics that it was anything more than "wires and knobs." The album languished at number forty-six on the charts.

> ## "I'm just me. There are other songwriters who do it a different way. Some other guys might lock themselves in a hotel room with amphetamines and a thesaurus and try to find words that rhyme and go nuts! And write a great album."
>
> ### — NY, 1990

Left: Backstage at the Spectrum, Philadelphia, September 17, 1986.

Opposite main photo: Bryan Bell at the mixing desk, 1986.

Opposite background and inset: Instruction manual for the Human Clock, one of numerous cutting-edge devices Neil used in the recording and touring of his high-tech, low-selling *Landing on Water* album.

While Neil was searching for innovative ways to make music, he and Pegi were also trying to find a new way to care for their son, Ben, and other children with similar conditions. In 1986, Pegi, Jim Forderer, and speech and language pathologist Dr. Marilyn Buzolich cofounded the Bridge School, a non-profit organization designed to provide individualized treatment and life-long educational strategies for those with severe speech and physical impairments. Neil would now put his considerable weight into raising money for the project.

Tucked serenely in the tony, bucolic Northern Californian town of Mountain View, the 30,000-capacity Shoreline Amphitheatre was built by legendary local music promoter Bill Graham in the summer of 1986. Neil thought it would be the perfect place to stage his first Bridge School benefit concert in October of that same year. He put together an impressive lineup: a reunited CSNY, Bruce Springsteen, Don Henley, Tom Petty, Nils Lofgren. The host was Robin Williams.

The event reportedly raised in the neighborhood of $250,000 and has gone on to become an annual fixture in the music calendar: To date there have been twenty-nine Bridge School concerts, with performances from major acts such as David Bowie,

Pearl Jam, REM, Brian Wilson, Beck, Tom Waits, and countless others.

Bryan Bell: When they decided to do the Bridge School, they put in a technical advisory board. I had a discount with Apple, and actually bought all the hardware and helped them find the switches that worked. So I'm involved on the tech side of the school, not the music side.

The school was born of Pegi's frustration at not being able to find the right program for Ben. She met with the experts and she met with the schools. "There's no one who can help not just our son but people like our son. There isn't an answer." Basically, Elliot Roberts said, "Start your own school." And Pegi came back a week later and said, "We'll do a concert. Do a fundraiser first and then build the school and start with the intent of making a place people like Ben could get the help they needed."

The way Neil recounts, a week later, Bruce Springsteen said yes and they were doing it. Neil is really good at knowing what role he wants to play. "I'm the fundraiser and I'm the out of box thinker about the experience of the kids. Having them feel and learn and do more."

The show is a love fest. Everything about the Bridge School is. The way we raise the money, the

way we treat the kids, the way we treat the intellectual property, it's all a love fest. This whole thing is about "How can we serve these children better?" It's very important to Neil. Very important that the artists feel the children and the children feel the artists. *(2015)*

Perhaps energized by his Bridge School fundraising, Neil decided to take Crazy Horse on the road again—a decision he'd soon regret. The 1980s had not been kind to him: Lawsuits, poor album sales, a confused audience, and laughable videos all contributed to what some critics were already dubbing his "lost decade." Not only were Neil's audiences confused about his musical ambiguity for the past few years—but Crazy Horse was, too. Set up alongside giant mechanized cockroaches, the band flailed in recreating the sound of the *Landing on Water* songs, and tensions grew into full-out backstage knockdown fights.

This was the inauspicious backdrop for Neil's final album for Geffen. *Life* was recorded at a pair of shows at the Universal Amphitheatre in Los Angeles just before the end of the tour in November 1986. Upon its release in July 1987, the album fared even less well than *Landing on Water*. But things were about to get better—much better.

Opposite: A jubilant singalong at the first Bridge School benefit concert, October 13, 1986. Left to right, Graham Nash, Tom Petty, Don Henley, J. D. Souther, Neil Young, Bruce Springsteen, David Crosby, and host Robin Williams.

Above: Having cofounded the Bridge School, Pegi Young also plays an active role in the benefit concerts, including this 2004 appearance.

KEEP ON ROCKIN'

1987–1996

"The Chili Peppers get offers
all the time to sell songs for commercials.
Maybe we could whore ourselves out
for the right price someday.
But I always think, 'Would Neil Young
do this?' And the answer is no.
Neil Young wouldn't fuckin' do it."

— Flea, 2010

Timeline

ROCKIN' IN THE FREE WORLD

NEIL YOUNG

1987

November–January 1988:
Records *This Note's for You* as Neil Young and the Bluenotes.

1988

February–July:
Reunites with Crosby, Stills & Nash to record *American Dream*.

April 11:
Release of *This Note's for You*, back on the Reprise label.

August 12–September 8:
Sponsored by Nobody tour of the US with the Bluenotes.

November 17:
Receives the annual Silver Clef award given by the Nordoff-Robbins music therapy charity.

November 22:
Release of *American Dream*.

December 13–15:
Records hard rock–influenced tracks at New York's Hit Factory with a band he calls the Restless.

September 5–6:
Films at the Jones Beach Theater and the Palladium in New York City for the video *Freedom: A Live Acoustic Concert*.

Summer:
Finalizes tracks for *Freedom*.

July 28:
Release of *The Bridge: A Tribute to Neil Young*.

June 14:
Records the live acoustic version of "Rockin' in the Free World" (at the Jones Beach Theater in Wantagh, NY) that is used as the opening track of his next album, *Freedom*.

April 17:
Release of the *Eldorado* EP in Japan and Australia only.

April 5–May 5:
Tour of Japan, Australia, and New Zealand, with his band now renamed the Lost Dogs.

February 21:
First live performance of "Rockin' in the Free World," in Seattle.

January 11–February 23:
US tour with the Restless.

1989

September 30:
Memorable appearance on *Saturday Night Live*, performing "Rockin' in the Free World."

October 2:
Release of *Freedom*.

November 14:
Release of the "Rockin' in the Free World" single, which hits #2 in the *Billboard* Mainstream Rock chart.

1990

April 16:
Performs at the Nelson Mandela tribute concert at Wembley Stadium, London.

April 24–30:
Recording of *Ragged Glory* with Crazy Horse.

September 9:
Release of *Ragged Glory*.

October 15:
Mother, Rassy, dies from cancer, a day before her seventy-third birthday.

1991

February:
Harvest Moon goes platinum in the US.

January 6:
Release of *Lucky Thirteen*, a compilation drawn from his Geffen years.

1993

November 2:
Release of *Harvest Moon*.

October 16:
Plays Bob Dylan's thirtieth-anniversary concert, at Madison Square Garden, New York City, backed by Booker T. & the M.G.s.

January 20–November 22:
Plays four solo tours of US theater venues, comprising nearly fifty dates in total.

1992

November 3:
CSNY play at a memorial concert in San Francisco for pivotal Bay Area promoter Bill Graham.

October 23:
Release of two-disc live album *Weld*, featuring recordings made on the Smell the Horse tour.

September–February 1992:
Recording of *Harvest Moon*.

January 22–April 27:
Smell the Horse tour of the US and Canada with Crazy Horse.

February 7:
Appears on MTV's *Unplugged* show.

June 8:
Release of the *Unplugged* album.

June 26–September 19:
Tour of Europe and the US with Booker T. & the M.G.s.

November–April 1994:
Recording of *Sleeps with Angels*, the last of his albums to be produced by David Briggs.

1994

February:
Receives an Oscar nomination for Best Original Song for "Philadelphia," from the Jonathan Demme movie of the same name.

March 20:
Harvest Moon wins Canadian critics' Juno Award for Album of the Year.

April 5:
Death of Nirvana vocalist, Kurt Cobain, inspiring the title track for *Sleeps with Angels*.

February 27:
Release of the *Dead Man* soundtrack album.

1996

November 26:
Longtime producer and collaborator David Briggs dies after a yearlong battle with lung cancer.

August 12–27:
Tour of Europe backed by Pearl Jam.

June 27:
Release of *Mirror Ball*.

March 27:
Records soundtrack music for Jim Jarmusch film *Dead Man*.

March 26:
Wins Juno Award for Male Vocalist of the Year.

January–February:
Records "live" studio album *Mirror Ball* with Pearl Jam.

January 12:
Inducted into the Rock and Roll Hall of Fame.

1995

August 16:
Release of *Sleeps with Angels*.

August 2:
Release of tribute album *Borrowed Tunes: A Tribute to Neil Young*.

"Neil is the best at being true to himself of anyone
I've ever worked with. Neil does not argue.
All of a sudden if it's not going his way, he'll go out
for coffee or he's on the plane back to his ranch.
He's been true to himself and I really admire that."

— Bill Halverson, 2014

The 1980s may have been tough for Neil, but they also showed that you can go home again—and get sweet revenge. Whether he was dropped by or whether he quit Geffen Records is a matter of dispute, but by January 1988 Neil was back with his old label, Reprise. Almost immediately he delivered the hit that Geffen couldn't coax out of him, and, in a twist of fate, his 1980s nemesis MTV unwittingly enabled him to do it.

"This Note's for You," the title track of Neil's first studio album since returning to Reprise, finally had a nice budget for a video. Julien Temple, an English filmmaker who directed the 1980 Sex Pistols mockumentary *The Great Rock 'n' Roll Swindle*, as well as videos for David Bowie and the Rolling Stones, was to be the director of this now infamous promo, which took the 1980s sell-out product culture to task with an anti-corporate satire.

Fred Goodman:
The spoofs—which sometimes take a malevolent turn, as when a Michael Jackson lookalike's hair catches fire, the famed Budweiser booze hound slobbers on a trio of female models or a woman in the Obsession segment licks spilled perfume off the floor—proved too much for MTV. *(1988)*

Of course, MTV initially banned the video—but not because they were offended by the video spoofing their network, they claimed, but because of the

satirical corporate product placement laced throughout the video. Tom Freston, the President and CEO of MTV at the time, listened to his ad sales staff who reasoned that if the channel began allowing products in their videos why would those companies then pay for advertising.

Tom Freston: I went along with that sentiment, and Neil Young made a big stink about us banning the video in the press. We looked like a bunch of pussies. We were a bunch of pussies. That's a fact. Not playing "This Note's for You" was the biggest mistake I made at MTV. *(2011)*

In a delicious irony, once MTV finally came around and began playing the video in heavy rotation, the channel named it Best Video of the Year for 1989 *and* it was nominated for a Grammy as Best Concept Video. Apparently, revenge is best served with a gold trophy of an astronaut. Neil had gone from claiming, "I guess I don't fit in with them" to accepting an award broadcast on *their* channel—and, more importantly, with all the exposure around the

controversy, he began to sell records again. Of course, the audio of his acceptance speech mysteriously went silent halfway in, so we'll never know exactly what he had to say about it all.

The first of numerous collaborations with co-producer Niko Bolas, the bluesy album *This Note's for You* did not make quite as big a splash as its title song but was nonetheless regarded as a return to form. Neil recruited a mixture of trusted henchmen like Frank Sampedro and Ben Keith and seasoned R&B session players including Rick Rosas and Chad Cromwell and called the band the Bluenotes. Reviewing the album for Melody Maker, Allan Jones described it as "urgent" and "wildly animated."

Opposite: An impromptu jam with Buckwheat Zydeco, Robert Plant, and Curt Smith from Tears for Fears at the Silver Clef award dinner, New York, November 17, 1988.

Above: "Ten Men Workin'." Back with Reprise, Neil recorded the soulful *This Note's for You* with a brass-heavy band he called the Bluenotes (until Harold Melvin took out an injunction to protect the name of *his* band, the Blue Notes).

"When the Bluenotes started, I was talking to Neil and I said, 'I really want to try something with some horns.' And the next thing I knew, we had a horn section. He had written all these tunes, these Jimmy Reed–style songs. You give Neil an inch and he will claim a mile. And do it better than anybody. It's really scary."

— Niko Bolas, 2015

Although Neil had been clandestinely noodling around on songs with Crosby, Stills & Nash over the years, they hadn't released an album as a quartet since *Déjà Vu* in 1970. After the CSNY reunion at the first Bridge School benefit in 1986, Neil made it clear he was open to working again with them. However, the album that followed two years later proved to be a very difficult undertaking and not a particularly rewarding listener experience. Recorded throughout much of 1988, *American Dream* was very much Neil's show; he selected Niko Bolas as producer against the others' wishes and subsequently managed most of the sessions as a very sick David Crosby struggled to even stand to sing his parts. Needless to say, the sessions, at times, were train wrecks, occasionally punctuated with a few moments of the old magic.

Bill Halverson: I was hired for a week when they were doing the *American Dream* album to do some vocals in LA. And then I stayed for another week. Somehow Stephen had played on one of Neil's tunes as a favor and Neil was coming down, drove up in the old Buick, and repaid the favor. And then Neil started sticking around. Just him and me in the studio. No roadies.

So the three of them come in with "old 1969 Crosby, Stills & Nash blend." And Neil looks at 'em and says, "You make the whole album sound like that and I'll stay." From then on we spent another six months putting up with each other while they, as older guys, sang together. They also nicknamed it "air vocals" and they started having fun with each other. *(2014)*

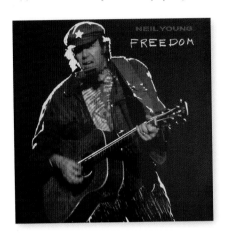

Opposite: Portrait by Aaron Rapoport, 1988.

"One thing I can tell you about recording with Neil. You put the machine on record and then you plug in the microphones in that order. Because there is just no way to predict when Neil's muse hits him. And, when it does, it does. It's up to you to get it right by instinct. Because the music is not gonna wait. You just gotta be ready. And get it right before Neil even gets there."

— Niko Bolas, 2015

Back with his solo work, Neil was capping off this tumultuous decade in raucous style. Glen Boyd attended his February 21, 1989 show in Seattle at the Paramount Theater. Nothing could have prepared the crowd for a seismic moment after the usual first-half acoustic set.

Glen Boyd: I never expected to see Neil Young blast the roof off of that building. For an hour and a half everyone in the place saw one of the loudest, most jaw-dropping performances I have ever seen before or since. It was the first time Neil played "Rockin' in the Free World" live.

I went in there and, at that point, almost had written Neil Young off. After ten years of all the genre-hopping he did, *Everybody's Rockin'* and *Old Ways*. I went to the show thinking it was gonna be nostalgic and fun and he'd do some of his old hits on the acoustic guitar.

Neil did that for the first half of the show. After the intermission I hear feedback. "What the hell?" For the second half of the show he came out with bassist Rick Rosas, drummer Chad Cromwell, and some other people and he proceeded to blow the roof off a 3,000-seat theater with these loud, abrasive songs I'd never heard before like "El Dorado," "Don't Cry," "Heavy Love," and "Rockin' in the Free World." I walked out of there, "Oh my God! I can't wait for his next album." *(2015)*

Released in October 1989 and again co-produced by Niko Bolas, *Freedom* was heavy on hot feedback, fuzzy distortion, and a certain "scuzziness" that some see as Ground Zero for the grunge movement of the 1990s.

Though it was only a modest hit at the time, it may well be Neil's most cutting-edge and influential album since *Rust Never Sleeps*; it would set him up for the next decade, a decade that would see him reach both critical and commercial heights that a few years previously were unimaginable.

Niko Bolas: I love *Freedom* like everything we've done. It was one of my favorite things at the time. There was a lot of exploration and the result was pretty basic. But I think that if there is one thing that happens with that record, it makes you feel the title. There's so much abandon on that record, and there's so much message in the lyrics of each song. I know where a lot of those lyrics came from. So it's very important to me.

Neil calls me the Volume Dealer. It's a name that Neil gave to me, gave to us, that's our partnership. In the late 1980s, I just listened really loud. That's where I live. When we got done with the record we had blown eighty-three woofers in total. I listen on big speakers and live up there. And we were having so much fun. Which is the essence of what Neil gets out of everybody. *(2015)*

neil young

rockin' in the free world

Kevin Chong: I think *Freedom* inaugurated the second generation of Neil Young fans, a recruiting process that was preceded by the "This Note's for You" video (which highlighted Young's attention-nabbing skill but still stunk of his 1980s-era dilettantism) and reached its highest point with *Harvest Moon*—which looped young fans with the first wave. The album is a grab bag: electric and acoustic, ballads and biting satire, songs written in the past and more. But the quality is consistent. Songs like "Crime in the City" and "Someday" have got a cinematic scope. The echoey screech of Young's guitar, as opposed to the more full-on grunge of his 1990s work, still holds up well. The highlight is "Rockin' in the Free World," acoustic and electric versions of which open and close the album like "My My, Hey Hey" on *Rust Never Sleeps*. *(2015)*

NY: The song ["Rockin' in the Free World"] is a lot of images of the destruction in our streets, the homeless and drugs and war and all these Muslims hating us, Americans and Europeans alike. I just write what I think I see and I change my own mind about it every day. *(1989)*

To direct the video for "Rockin' in the Free World," Neil tapped Julien Temple again. The pair came up with the ghostly concept together. Neil plays a spectral vagabond, a sort of bug-shade-wearing homeless messiah waving a staff while prowling the streets of an unforgiving metropolis, interspersed with a flannel- and leather-jacket-clad Neil Young and his band performing on a post-apocalyptic soundstage, thrashing about like an angry garage—grunge?—band, spittle forming around his mouth during the second chorus. The video is considered by many to be Neil's best.

Spurred on by a blistering performance on *Saturday Night Live*, the song reached number two on the US rock singles chart and, more importantly, a smattering of embryonic garage bands in Seattle took special notice of it. A potent tribute album appeared: *The Bridge: A Tribute to Neil Young*. On it Sonic Youth dismantle and refashion "Computer Age" into a punk-tech blaze, Pixies deliver a sweetly cool version of "Winterlong," and Soul Asylum rip up the booze-tinged "Barstool Blues." Neil was on a roll, and grunge bands, like the punk bands of the 1970s, were about to turn the music industry on its head—claiming Neil Young, whether he liked it or not, as their own "godfather."

Above left: Muziektheater Stopera, Amsterdam, December 10, 1989.

Opposite: To bring himself up to a concert level of intensity, Neil worked with a trainer lifting weights and doing calisthenics just before this scorching performance of "Rockin' in the Free World" on *Saturday Night Live*, September 30, 1989.

In late 1990, a mutual friend of Kurt Cobain and Krist Novoselic introduced drummer Dave Grohl to them; two minutes into the audition they had hired him to be the drummer of Nirvana, grunge music's version of the Sex Pistols on commercial steroids.

A year later the band's single "Smells Like Teen Spirit" played in heavy rotation on MTV, becoming a massive hit, and the album from which it was taken, *Nevermind*, replaced Michael Jackson's *Dangerous* at the top of the charts. Grunge had rolled over the King of Pop's reign; and Neil was there at the intersection of it all.

Steve Martin: Despite what some Nirvana fans might say, *Freedom* is the album that started it all. That's when Neil Young became the godfather of grunge. *Freedom*, which Young released in 1989, was the first true alternative album. It seems a stretch to call an album by someone Young's age alternative but the label is applied to the music, not the artist. *(1991)*

Riding high on the success of "This Note's for You" and "Rockin' in the Free World," turns out that Neil had no intention of burning out *or* fading away. In the spring of 1990, he quickly put Crazy Horse back together for the first time since the acrimonious Life tour, and they recorded *Ragged Glory*. The band somehow found it in them to mostly put their troubles behind them—with Neil even apologizing to the others about how he had treated them—and made an album that was hailed by fans, critics, and new devotees.

Billy Talbot: We know each other so well now that we don't have to be together all the time. That spirit that we managed to create in the early years just carries on and on and on. It's like a family: You might not see your uncle for a few years but when you get together you have a lot to talk about and you're happy. *(2001)*

Recorded in the joyous, chance-taking spirit of the best Neil Young and Crazy Horse albums, *Ragged Glory* rocked with some of the same intensity of the loudest tracks on *Rust Never Sleeps*.

Kevin Chong: I was learning to play guitar during the *Ragged Glory* era, and I appreciated the simplicity of the songs and how the mistakes could be washed over through distortion. A lot of the songs were in G or E-minor, like "Mansion on the Hill" and "Country Home." I get a muscle memory of pulling down the down-tuned E-string to play the "F*!#in' Up" riff (which is in D-minor) when I hear it. My favorite is "Over and Over Again," whose riff and tempo match the thematic circularity of the song. I love this album. For me it means warmth: the guitar tones, the group vocals, the barn-inspired reverb. It sounds like a bunch of old friends playing together. *(2015)*

Neil's people instantly recognized the virility of the album and cleverly marketed it with a slogan that would capture the hearts and minds of the new generation: FEEDBACK IS BACK.

Even MTV became a strange bedfellow, cultishly hopping on the *Ragged Glory* bandwagon immediately when Kurt Loder pronounced on air: "I guess Neil Young is the king of rock 'n' roll. I don't see anybody else on the scene standing anywhere *near* this tall nowadays."

The king of rock 'n' roll! The nightmare of the last decade had a new wrinkle: a sort of rock 'n' roll Lazarus rising from the dead—but it was no painless, dreamy metempsychosis.

Ragged Glory's effect on the next generation of musicians was seismic. Bands such as Everclear, Smashing Pumpkins, Dinosaur Jr., Sparklehorse, Son Volt, Wilco, and the Red Hot Chili Peppers all worshipped *Ragged*—and Neil.

Flea: There's a rare contradiction in Neil's work. He works so hard as a songwriter, and he's written

"When I was younger I got pissed off. But as I get older I recognize the fact that Neil always comes back to us and all these other bands he doesn't go back to. We are the one and only Neil Young band that's survived all the cuts, so you get a certain sense of good feeling and security from that."

— Frank Sampedro, 2001

a phenomenal number of perfect songs. And, at the same time, he doesn't give a fuck. That comes from caring about essence. There can be things out of tune and all wild-sounding and not recorded meticulously. And he doesn't care. He's made whole albums that aren't great, and instead of going back to a formula that he knows works, he would rather represent where he is at the time. That's what's so awesome: watching his career wax and wane according to the truth of his character at the moment. It's never phony. It's always real. The truth is not always perfect. *(2010)*

Jeff Tweedy: He's right up there in terms of a constant in my musical life as an influence and as a mentor. He's kind of just a force of nature. And I take him for granted sometimes like I take the sun for granted ... I'm really happy the sun comes up everyday and I'm happy Neil Young keeps making records. *(2010)*

With his career riding high, Neil suffered a major low. His beloved mother, Rassy, the woman who had done

so much to support his early ventures in music, died on October 15, 1990. Rehearsing with Crazy Horse for that year's Bridge School benefit a week or so later, it suddenly struck him that this was the first thing he had done without her.

The following year Neil took Crazy Horse on tour. The Smell the Horse tour began in January; the opening acts included indie-favorites Social Distortion and alt-rock deities Sonic Youth. It was to be a good-time old school/new school traipse through jam-packed arenas.

The live album of the tour, *Weld*, which set out to capture this flash of carefree forcefulness, is an uncanny snapshot of a tumultuous band at its apogee.

Opposite: "Smells like Teen Spirit," sounds like Neil Young. A new generation of bands such as Nirvana acknowledged their debt to the so-called "godfather of grunge." After nearly a decade of stylistic floundering, he was back in the game.

Above: Smell the Horse tour, Brendan Byrne Arena, East Rutherford, New Jersey, February 24, 1991.

With grunge at its height, the movement's so-called godfather stood down Crazy Horse, picked up his acoustic guitar, and spent much of 1992 touring the US solo. He played almost fifty dates from January to November, punctuated in October with an appearance at Bob Dylan's thirtieth-anniversary show in New York City at Madison Square Garden—an event Neil dubbed "Bobfest." The band onstage with him, however, surprised everyone: Booker T. and the M.G.s. An instrumental R&B group that cut its teeth playing the late-night bars of Memphis in the early 1960s, the M.G.s became synonymous with Southern soul music, a smoky hybrid of gospel, country, blues, and pure groove.

Neil, the M.G.s, and drummer Jim Keltner grooved their way through Dylan's "All Along the Watchtower" and "Just Like Tom Thumb's Blues." Neil also joined George Harrison, Tom Petty, Eric Clapton, Roger McGuinn, and Dylan himself for a sing-along of "My Back Pages," which found Neil's phrasing of the lines revealing; he wasn't trying to sing like Dylan, but kept his own counsel. Everyone on the stage was clearly all over the map, but their "Kumbayah" gathering was one of the most interesting points of the night.

Jim Keltner: The first time I ever played drums with Neil, it was on a couple of my favorite Bob Dylan songs at the thirtieth-anniversary concert. Playing "All Along the Watchtower" with Neil was fun, because of the way he made it sound. Big, wide, and foreboding. The song just allowed him to soar, completely fly and it allows for a big beat. It has so many powerful elements.

Later in 1992, I toured with Neil. It was really good. It was cool watching Neil play with guys like Steve Cropper and Donald "Duck" Dunn. They couldn't have been more different from Crazy Horse but Neil made it work so well that *Rolling Stone* magazine called it the best tour of that year. *(2015)*

"What's cool about Neil is that he never hesitates to try whatever it takes to get his point across musically. Whether it's just him on an acoustic guitar, him solo on piano, or with Crazy Horse, it seems that he will find the best way to play the song, whether its grungy or doo-wop ... he always finds the best way to serve his music."

— Kirk Hammett

"What this album is about is this feeling, this ability to survive and continue and grow and get higher than you were before. Not just maintain, not just feel well. Not just 'I'm still alive at forty-five.' You can be more alive."

— NY, 1992

On November 2, 1992, Neil released *Harvest Moon*. Always one to keep everyone—including himself—on their toes, he assembled an ad-hoc version of the Stray Gators: Tim Drummond on bass, Ben Keith on steel, Kenny Buttrey on drums, with special appearances by James Taylor and Linda Ronstadt. He also brought back his longtime collaborator Jack Nitzsche to arrange the strings on one of the tracks ("Such a Woman").

Although he insisted it wasn't a sequel to *Harvest*, it was hard not to see the parallels. Perhaps due to tinnitus, a persistent ringing sensation in the ears like an opera of frogs in your head, or perhaps, well, because he felt like it, *Harvest*'s acoustic and piano heart seemed an obvious ode to early-1970s Neil Young. Was country Neil back for good?

"I always thought the first time I heard Harvest Moon it sounded more like a follow-up to Comes a Time than a sequel to Harvest. It's one of a handful of Neil Young albums where every cut is good for radio."

— Mike Grant, 2014

Acoustic or not, his old—and new—fans loved *Harvest Moon*, making it his first million-selling album in the US since *Rust Never Sleeps*. The title track is one of Neil's most covered songs, with everyone from Pearl Jam and Elliott Smith to jazz singer Cassandra Wilson, and even Scott Matthew, doing versions. *Rolling Stone* hailed it as a "delicate beauty that tipped its hat to the Everly Brothers' 'Walk Right Back.'"

As *Harvest Moon* went platinum in early 1993, and with his popularity at an all-time high, Neil reluctantly agreed to do MTV's new show *Unplugged*. Although he may have had a hard time adapting to the MTV culture at first, the rationale behind *Unplugged* seemed a lot closer to his DNA. Inspired by the pivotal rock 'n' roll performances on TV—especially Elvis's *1968 Comeback Special*—the show was intended to mimic a gig in your living room: cozy, introspective, down-home, and ... unplugged. By the time of Neil's performance on February 7, 1993 (it aired on March 10), contemporaries such as Eric Clapton, whose album of the show went on to sell over ten million units, had already popularized the series. And Neil did not disappoint.

Rob Hill: Any Gen Xer who had not been tuned into Neil Young before the show was going to be when it was over. I remember he was wearing a black leather jacket, Harley Davidson T-shirt, jeans, and boots and was sitting on a stool, head bowed. Then a haunting harmonica chirped for a few seconds and then that voice, so soulful and melancholic, just oozed through the dark studio. But it was when he played "Like a Hurricane" that I really began to understand why the rock stars of my generation, Eddie Vedder and Kurt Cobain, were worshipping Young. He ambled over to the organ and began doing his thing and I was just transfixed. He had a presence that was timeless and a demeanor that was rumpled yet almost regal in a reluctant way. Then after "Helpless" I decided that I had to head to the record store after the show and buy most of his earlier albums. I didn't do that after I saw Eric Clapton or Rod Stewart on *Unplugged*. *(2015)*

To anyone who was watching, the show was a huge success—but backstage things were somewhat different. From note one of the rehearsals Neil was ornery, chastising the Stray Gators for not knowing their parts; and then to kill the vibe completely members of the Gators began demanding more money. Feeling held hostage and betrayed, he would never work with them again.

Opposite: Never slow to give a name to things like cars and backing bands, Neil called Bob Dylan's thirtieth-anniversary celebration concert "Bobfest." October 16, 1992.

Overleaf: Recording his show for MTV's *Unplugged* series with the Stray Gators and Nils Lofgren (far right), February 7, 1993.

The year 1994 started on a positive note with Neil receiving an Oscar nomination for Best Original Song for "Philadelphia." A few months later, however, tragedy hit the music world, with Neil being more affected than most.

On a gloomy spring Seattle day in April 1994, Kurt Cobain killed himself. At the end of his suicide note, Cobain quoted Neil Young as his epitaph: "It's better to burn out, than to fade away." To add an eerie irony to the events, Neil admitted that he had been trying to contact Cobain for weeks before his untimely death to assure him of his talents and offer some advice.

Although Neil had finished recording his next album before Cobain's death, he wrote an extra song, "Sleeps with Angels," immediately after he had heard about the tragedy and included it as the title track of the album. Beginning with a brooding, funereal guitar, "Sleeps with Angels" is a moving tribute to Cobain. Neil finally enters, his voice subdued, fatigued, and monotone, before the song somberly settles into a kind of hypnotic prayer, clocking in at a terse 2:44. It may have been the shortest song on the album, but not only did it set the tone for the entire piece, it bled with a heartfelt sentiment up there with anything in Neil's oeuvre.

Rob Hill: *Sleeps with Angels* in particular really affected me. It had a dewy atmosphere of delicate beauty and a sort of whispered fragility; it could be a haunting tale with its bleak guitars and prosaic vulnerability but also soothing ... like a psalm or something: dreamy, matter-of-fact, and romantically subdued. *(2015)*

To be sure, Neil had a deep respect for the Nirvana front man. It was unusual for him to praise another musician so effusively.

NY: He really, really inspired me. He was so great. Wonderful. One of the best, but more than that. Kurt was one of the absolute best of all time for me. I really could hear his music. There's not that many absolutely great performers. In that sense, he was a gem. *(1994)*

As a reminder of how many musicians Neil had himself inspired, August 1994 saw the release of *Borrowed Tunes: A Tribute to Neil Young*, a two-CD set. Mirroring the format of *Rust Never Sleeps*, one disc was acoustic and the other electric. Included on the album were renditions of "Tired Eyes" by the Cowboy Junkies, "Transformer Man" by David Wilcox, "Harvest" by Jeff Healey, and a version of "The Loner" by Neil's old Winnipeg compadre Randy Bachman.

The tributes continued the following year. On January 12, 1995, Neil was inducted by Pearl Jam's Eddie Vedder into the Rock and Roll Hall of Fame.

Eddie Vedder: And when I hear, you know, the speeches and inducting Janis Joplin and Frank Zappa, I get, uh, I'm just really glad he's still here. And I think I'm gonna have to say that I don't know if there's been another artist that has been inducted into the Rock and Roll Hall of Fame that is still as vital as he is today. Some of his best songs were on his last record. *(1995)*

A few weeks later, Neil and Pearl Jam convened at Bad Animals Studios in Seattle. The downtown studio was synonymous with grunge—Alice in Chains, Nirvana, Soundgarden, and Pearl Jam all recorded there—and was the perfect lab for this cross-generational collaboration.

Rob Hill: By combining Young's sixties brand of idealism and Pearl Jam's more nineties Gen X

Above: The untimely death of Nirvana singer Kurt Cobain in April 1994 moved Neil to write the song "Sleeps with Angels," which became the title track of his next album.

Left: Performing "Rockin' in the Free World" with Pearl Jam at the 1993 MTV Awards.

Far left: Neil entered the Rock and Roll Hall of Fame on January 12, 1995. Pearl Jam's Eddie Vedder gave the induction speech.

Below: With longtime producer and confidant David Briggs, 1980s.

cynicism, both in melodies and lyrics, *Mirror Ball* simultaneously sounds retro and modern. As always, Young's lyrics emanate conscious harangues about the dichotomy of love and hate, political correctness, abortion, utopian ideas, and the reality of broken dreams. The buzzwords for the album were clear: big, booming, live, and robust. *(2015)*

Soon after completing *Mirror Ball*, Neil recorded music for Jim Jarmusch's indie western *Dead Man* starring Johnny Depp—his first full movie soundtrack. The eccentric filmmaker had always been a big Neil Young fan and claimed he had been listening constantly to Neil Young and Crazy Horse records while writing the script for *Dead Man*. He felt Neil's music had the perfect haunting etherealness for his atmospheric film set in the nineteenth-century American West. Almost exclusively using an organ and some piano blended with delicate doses of electric guitar, the purely improvised songs were minimalistic, poetic, and beautifully enigmatic. Neil called the album "kind of a hippie-beatnik New Age record."

A two-week summer tour of Europe with Pearl Jam—minus Vedder—was triumphant, bordering on ecstatic; it seemed to catch everybody off guard.

Then another tragedy struck. On November 26, 1995, two weeks after Neil's fiftieth birthday, longtime producer David Briggs died of lung cancer.

Neil's faithful musical partner, with whom he fought like a brother and conspired like a master criminal, was now gone, at just the moment when Neil's vitality as a creative force was at its apex.

"David Briggs used to say, 'Life is a shit sandwich. Eat it or starve.'"
— NY, 2012

A LONG ROAD BEHIND ME

A LONG ROAD AHEAD 1996-2006

"Neil has loyal fans because he never fails to deliver a quality product. It's his pursuit of excellence. If you're gonna do anything, do it with all of your spirit, all of your heart, all of your mind."

— Bryan Bell, 2015

Timeline

EIN FILM VON JIM JARMUSCH

A TALE OF 4 GUYS WHO LIKE TO ROCK

1996

March–April:
Recording of *Broken Arrow* with Crazy Horse.

March 18–June 9:
Tour of unannounced club gigs in California with Crazy Horse (as the Echoes).

May 10:
Dead Man movie released in the US.

June 20–July 22:
Broken Arrow tour of Europe with Crazy Horse.

July 2:
Release of *Broken Arrow*.

August 9–November 17:
Broken Arrow tour of the US with Crazy Horse.

1999

November 18:
Release of *The Bridge School Concerts Vol. I*.

July 11–August 24:
Headlines the 1997 HORDE festival tour.

June 17:
Release of live album *Year of the Horse*, also featuring recordings from the Broken Arrow tour but with a different track listing from the movie.

May 9:
Release of *Year of the Horse*, Jim Jarmusch's concert film of the Broken Arrow tour.

1997

October 19-20:
Tenth-anniversary Bridge School annual fundraiser.

March 2–June 2:
An Evening with Neil Young solo tour of the US and Canada.

October 26:
Release of CSNY's *Looking Forward*, featuring songs recorded between 1996 and 1999.

2000

January 24–April 19:
CSNY2K North American tour, which grosses over $41 million.

April 25:
Release of *Silver & Gold*, featuring tracks recorded between August 1997 and May 1999.

August 8–October 1:
Music in Head tour of the US, backed by Friends and Relatives, a band including "Duck" Dunn on bass, Spooner Oldham on keyboards, Jim Keltner on drums, and wife Pegi and half-sister Astrid on vocals.

Opposite main photo: The finale of the Canadian Live 8 show, Park Place, Barrie, Ontario, July 2, 2005.

Page 142: Portrait by Mark Humphrey to promote the 2005 album *Prairie Wind*.

April 9:
Release of *Are You Passionate?*, an excursion into soul music with a lineup including Booker T. & the M.G.s.

February 6–April 29:
Another blockbuster CSNY tour of US and Canada.

2002

September 21:
Takes part in *America: A Tribute to Heroes* TV benefit show in response to 9/11 attacks.

June 9–July 24:
Eurotour '01 with Crazy Horse.

April 4:
Wins a Juno Award for Best Male Artist.

January 18–20:
Plays two festivals in Buenos Aires and Rio de Janeiro with Crazy Horse, his first shows in South America.

2001

December 5:
Release of concert album *Road Rock Vol. I: Friends and Relatives*, recorded during the Music in Head tour.

May 18–21:
A handful of dates in Germany and the UK backed by Frank Sampedro and the M.G.s.

2003

July–September:
Recording of ten-song "rock opera" Greendale, chronicling events in a small California town. The Greendale concept also gives rise to a movie, a book, and a graphic novel.

April 22–May 24:
European solo acoustic tour.

June 8–September 20:
Greendale tour of the US with Crazy Horse.

August 19:
Release of *Greendale* album.

October 9:
Release of *Greendale* movie, directed by Neil.

November 6–22:
Greendale tour of Hong Kong, Japan, and Australia with Crazy Horse.

2004

February 19–March 21:
Winter Greendale tour of the US and Canada with Crazy Horse.

February 10
Release of Jonathan Demme film *Neil Young: Heart of Gold*, featuring the Ryman Auditorium Prairie Wind concerts.

2006

September 27:
Release of *Prairie Wind*.

August 18–19:
Premieres *Prairie Wind* during two concerts at the Ryman Auditorium in Nashville.

July 2:
Performs at the Live 8 concert in Barrie, Ontario.

June 12:
Father, Scott, dies at the age of eighty-seven.

March 29:
Undergoes surgery after potentially fatal brain aneurism.

March:
Recording of *Prairie Wind* in Nashville.

2005

November 16:
Release of *Greatest Hits*.

October 2–6:
Joins the Vote for Change tour in support of Democratic candidate John Kerry's presidential campaign.

"I asked myself: What does this album mean to me? To me it represents the fun, the frankness, and the liberty of people who played together, like we did thirty years ago, when I wrote 'Broken Arrow' and I was just twenty years old."

— NY, 1996

Still reeling from the loss of David Briggs, in spring 1996 Neil summoned Crazy Horse to make their eighth album together and their first without their straight-talking producer. *Broken Arrow*, recorded in just over three weeks, is heavy with long-form tunes finely balancing blues and folk. Although the album has since been reappraised, at the time it was generally seen as a failure. Most critics dismissed it as a sloppy throwaway work, with only a minority hailing its raw take on the Crazy Horse sound. *People* called it the worst album of the year and *Spin* magazine chimed, "It makes you wonder whether Young has grown so confident in his complacency that he could play out his career as solidly and unceremoniously as, say, Muddy Waters—never dismissed, but taken for granted." Reviewers tended to agree, though, that the highlight of the album was the almost-ten-minute "Loose Change," a classic Crazy Horse E-chord-driven jam that would have made Briggs proud.

Sharry Wilson: *Broken Arrow* deserves more praise than it originally received. It has aged well and even though not every song is a gem, it has a great Crazy Horse feel to it. "Interstate" ranks right up there with the best. Mysteriously, this song is included on the LP version only, in addition to the "Big Time" CD single from 1990. "Big Time," "Slip Away," "Music Arcade," and "Loose Change" are all solid numbers and worthy of attention. The cover art reinforces Neil's continuing fascination with Native American culture, which is also evident in the cover design of later releases such as *Americana* and *Psychedelic Pill*. (2015)

Scott Atkin: By 1996 Young had had an impressive streak of positively received albums. He was really in a groove by the time he released *Broken Arrow*. As good as this album is, it's just too much listening for the average ear. There's only one obvious single ("Changing Highways") and plenty of longer songs to have to learn to appreciate. That didn't bode well for sales, but like other poorly received Neil Young albums it resonated more strongly when reassessed a few years later. It has something for every kind of Neil Young fan—great melodies, great guitar, and great lyrics. (2015)

Main photo: Broken Arrow tour with Crazy Horse, Phoenix Festival, Stratford-upon-Avon, UK, July 19, 2006.

As well as spending much of the summer and fall touring *Broken Arrow* with the Horse, Neil lined up a standout bill for the tenth-anniversary Bridge School fundraiser: Patti Smith, Cowboy Junkies, Pearl Jam, and David Bowie—not to mention Neil Young and Crazy Horse.

Dead Man director, Jim Jarmusch, returned the favor of Neil's soundtrack recordings with an intimate documentary focusing on Crazy Horse. Released in summer 1997, *Year of the Horse* spans the band's long history, using footage from tours in 1976, 1986, and the previous year's Broken Arrow tour.

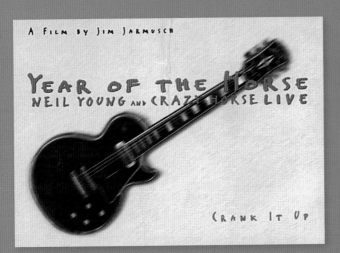

Jim Jarmusch: Neil and the band liked the results of the video I did for the song "Big Time," which was shot entirely on Super-8 film in and around Half Moon Bay in California. Neil particularly liked the rough look of the Super-8. He called me up a little while later and said, "Listen, we should do a longer film that looks and feels like the 'Big Time' video!" *(1996)*

"**Crazy Horse have become more pure and more loose at the same time. They are more open to letting something take them away into the sky without knowing the destination necessarily. I think they're more courageous in that way.**"
— Jim Jarmusch, 1996

Above: Hanging out with Jim Jarmusch, director of the 1996 *Year of the Horse* documentary.

"Neil's guitar playing is unlike any other guitar player. Sound is his palate. A big canvas with a lot of paint. The actual guitar sound from Neil is based on such complex stuff but, like everything else in Neil's life, he makes it look like it's simple and organic."

— Jim Keltner, 2015

The image of the American Indian has always been strongly associated with Neil Young—recent tours have even featured a large wooden Indian totem on stage. His work has also consciously drawn from images of the West (Winnipeg itself was called the "Gateway to the Golden West"); his early iconic buckskinned costuming signified a deep alliance with a pioneering spirit, a perfect accompaniment to his prairie-parched voice and folkloric song craft.

NY: There I was making 120 bucks a week at the Whisky as a musician. I wore them [fringe jackets] on TV shows and whenever we worked. Then I went to this place on Santa Monica Boulevard near La Cienega. I saw this great Comanche war shirt, the best jacket I've ever seen. I had two more made. The group was western, the name Buffalo Springfield came off a tractor, so it all fit. I was the Indian. That's when it was cool to be an Indian. *(1992)*

Sharry Wilson: A photo taken in 1955 that appears in the booklet accompanying *The Archives Vol. 1* shows nine-year-old Neil holding a bow and arrow while his elder brother, Bob, is holding a rifle—the Indian vs. the Cowboy. During Neil's time in Buffalo Springfield he wore a fringed leather jacket with beads around

his neck; his band mates called him "the Indian of the group." Neil has often written songs with specific references to Native peoples, including "Broken Arrow," "Cortez the Killer," and "Pocahontas." The cover of *Broken Arrow* features an image of teepees and Native warriors with a symbolic broken arrow at the top. "Broken Arrow" is also the name he gave to his ranch. And, of course, Crazy Horse took its name from the famous Oglala Lakota leader. *(2015)*

Another essential element of Neil's iconography is Old Black, his famous Gibson Les Paul guitar. For those who have not seen him live, watch *Year of the Horse*, the *Live Rust* movie, or the riveting 1989 appearance on *Saturday Night Live* to see how he uses Old Black like Paul Bunyan used a hatchet; Neil clears a swath onstage that leaves band mates and the audience bloodied and bowed. It never sounds pretty because it's never meant to.

Opposite, clockwise from top left: Press conference to promote that evening's Honour the Treaties benefit show at Toronto's Massey Hall, January 12, 2014; the iconic Crazy Horse logo on Ralph Molina's bass drum; "I was the Indian"—portrait, 1967; the original Crazy Horse, chief of the Oglala Sioux, 1870.

Above: Painting pictures with Old Black on tour in 1986.

Left and opposite: Performing with Crazy Horse at the opening show of the HORDE festival tour, Shoreline Amphitheatre, Mountain View, California, July 11, 1997.

Neil elected to spend most of the summer of 1997 headlining the HORDE festival, a sort of jam-band road show that also featured the piano-driven Ben Folds Five. The eponymous leader of the group was another of Neil's Gen X acolytes.

Ben Folds: I must have done forty dates with Neil, and he taught me something just by my being able to sit side-stage and watch his shows. All us whippersnappers were trying to make small clubs feel like a coliseum, and there he was making these coliseums and the big, Blockbuster Pavilion kind of places into living rooms. There's a vibration about what he does that's so pure and has so much integrity that I think it just transcends. He can write a bad song and it's OK. It's like an old blues artist or something; they're not sitting there going through every lyric and every note. It's more about the bigger picture. *(2005)*

The HORDE trek was a tipping point for Neil Young, expanding his audience demographic as his catalog received additional airplay on Americana and college radio channels.

After over thirty years on that hard road, he continued to fascinate and inspire his fans; and not just the geeks but pony-tailed university professors, rack jobbers, and retail vendors, jaded artist managers, and even those woe-begotten second engineers who still crowded the stage or worked with him

behind the scenes. You'd think they would have become tired by now, but Neil Young remained an artist of endless fascination.

The decade ended with the release of a third CSNY studio album, *Looking Forward*, a collection of tracks recorded between 1996 and 1999 after Neil had offered to play guitar on a Stephen Stills song he liked. The resulting album, though, was a letdown to just about everyone and is probably the least-heard CSNY release. Younger music fans tended to dismiss it as a bunch of rich hippies looking back on their magic carpet ride. If the music had lived up to the title, this might not have been the last CSNY album to date.

Scott Atkin: With these volatile musicians in each other's company once again, what would we the listening public get? A fine follow-up to the legend that is *Déjà Vu*—or the final nail in the coffin after the disappointing *American Dream*? Upon its release back in 1999, I didn't give *Looking Forward* much of a chance to make an impression on me. I knew it was going to be bad, so why waste my time? I just checked out the Neil cuts and moved on.

Now in 2015, upon further review, this album is actually quite enjoyable! All the songs cover the usual CSNY ground, but the memorable harmonies are marvelously still intact. The title track is just another great Neil Young song. *(2015)*

The forty-one-show CSNY2K tour of the US called at the San Jose Arena, San Jose, California on February 4, 2000 (below).

Neil began the new century by hitting the road with CSNY. Dubbed CSNY2K, it was their first official tour since 1974, and judging from the $41 million gross, the fans' appetite for the group hadn't diminished over the years.

Graham Nash: We knew we had the magic. We've always known our music speaks to people's hearts. We've always known it's been as real as possible. On tour I fell back in love with who David and Stephen and Neil were. It was very emotional. I think one of the things very obvious to me was listening to Neil Young play on other people's songs. How generous he was. *(2014)*

On the heels of the mega-successful tour, Neil's much anticipated *Silver and Gold* album finally was released four years after *Broken Arrow*, his longest hiatus to date. Billed as a return to his folksy style, the meditative record, which had been under construction one way or another for the previous three years, showed Neil at his most introspective. At times it almost feels more like reading his bedside diary than listening to his music. It began as a solo acoustic project, but was eventually fleshed out with trusted collaborators like Ben Keith, Spooner Oldham, and Jim Keltner, and Emmylou Harris and Linda Ronstadt on backing vocals.

Glen Boyd: It is certainly a quieter, moodier-sounding record than either of its more obvious commercial predecessors. What really makes *Silver and Gold* stand out, though, is the fact that Young has never sounded more, dare we say it, *contented* than he does on this album. The easy, back-porch vibe of the music certainly reinforces the album's overall laid-back mood. But the lyrics of the songs also seem to reveal a far more relaxed and less restless side of Young's typically more relentless nature. *(2012)*

Feeling "contented," Neil then took the band on the road, with Pegi even joining here and there to sing backing vocals. The shows were subsequently taped and quickly released as *Road Rocks VI: Friends and Relatives*.

Jim Keltner: I did Neil's tour with the Friends and Relatives, a kind of *Harvest Moon* tour. You could feel the audience involvement in every part of every song. And that really propelled everybody forward. Some of my friends tell me they are the best shows they've ever seen. Neil inhabits these different worlds with all these different players.

But, to me, Crazy Horse is still the best. Crazy Horse is the best Neil Young you will hear. They don't play his music like anybody else would. I played "Cowgirl in the Sand" with Neil many times. And all I could ever think was how I wished it had that wide, slow-motion glide that Ralph, Billy, and Poncho bring to it.

The times I've played on stage with Neil, I wanted so badly to create that big loose but tight feel that the Horse was all about but I realized it was a different musical situation I was in. And Neil didn't expect us to try to be Crazy Horse.

I have a few live performances and rehearsals that I've taped along the way, and especially a version of his song "Words" from a gig somewhere out on the road that is one of my favorite things I've ever been a part of. Like Dylan's harp solos, Neil's guitar playing can make you feel as though you're playing with a great jazz artist instead of who the world thinks they are. (2015)

After spending the early part of 2001 noodling around in the studio with the Horse, and doing a handful of gigs in South America and Europe, Neil was as shaken as the rest of the world by 9/11. And with his musical antennae as sensitive as ever, he wrote passionately about it.

In the fashion of "Ohio," his response to the 1970 Kent State killings, Neil wrote and recorded "Let's Roll" just a few weeks after the attacks. The song was specifically inspired by the passengers who took on the hijackers of United Airlines Flight 93.

On September 21, Neil participated in the *America: A Tribute to Heroes* telethon, which was organized by George Clooney. Sitting somberly at a piano on a darkened stage crowded with hundreds of flickering candles, wearing a worn straw cowboy hat, Neil soulfully tinkered his way through John Lennon's "Imagine." He was then joined by Pearl Jam's Eddie Vedder and Mike McCready for the melancholy "Long Road." And he also helped to man the phone banks taking pledges; the event raised more than $200 million.

For now, the world had stopped spinning. But business as usual isn't quieted for long. The cash machine of CSNY continued in the first part of 2002, with a sold-out tour of the United States and Canada.

Then came Neil's unique take on soul music. Released on April 9, *Are You Passionate?* was ostensibly a love letter to Pegi; if you were listening to it in the dark, however, you'd never guess it was a Neil Young album. With backing from Booker T. & the M.G.s, it's a wistful, breezy love-dance of guitar solos, touching lyrics, and aching countertenor vocals.

The album delves into some familiar themes, too: love gone wrong, keeping the faith, and a smattering of Youngian guitar solos. *Passionate?* seemed to pass all the groove requirements; it's clear his recruits were not going to let Neil fall into any clichés here. While most of the balmy love songs were dedicated to Pegi, Neil doesn't pull any punches when he hauls out Old Black to give a jolt to such heavy songs as "Let's Roll" and "Goin' Home," which were recorded with Crazy Horse and not Booker and the soul gang.

Sharry Wilson: I think *Are You Passionate?* is an underappreciated album. Although there is certainly a lot to admire, it is not without its faults. Neil's soaring guitar line on the title track is sublime and other tracks, written obviously with his wife, Pegi, in mind, are truly soulful. However, "Let's Roll" and "Goin' Home," both recorded with Crazy Horse, feel out of place. Their inclusion is actually quite jarring, with "Goin' Home" ending abruptly and a heavy curtain of doom overshadowing "Let's Roll." (2015)

Scott Atkin: If there's a more misunderstood album by Neil Young, I don't know which one it would be. A very easygoing "You're My Girl" doesn't give much away as to how this album will evolve. Next is "Mr. Disappointment." I guess we that like Neil Young so much like his storytelling ways. I know I do. He tells me a story with his songs. Well, I think they're stories. Great melodies. By the end of this album I feel the way I usually feel after another Neil Young album—satisfied that he gave me the best he had to offer, and so authentically. I sense I know Neil Young better and better after each release. To me he's the ultimate conduit between artist and common man. *Are You Passionate?* has several great tracks. One thing, though: I'm glad Neil placed "Let's Roll" in the middle of the album as opposed to at the end. This way he ended positively with "She's a Healer." A spiritual move for the better. (2015)

Feeling the groove, Neil took Booker T. and the gang on the road, playing a few dates in Europe, before getting started on his first, yes, "rock opera."

You're only as Neil Young as you feel.
NEIL YOUNG
SILVER & GOLD
The new album. Featuring: "Razor Love" and "Buffalo Springfield Again" Also available on DVD and VHS: The live concert *Silver & Gold*. The Limited Edition of *Silver & Gold* features special packaging and a poster.
Produced by Ben Keith & Neil Young. Direction: Elliot Roberts at Lookout Management
Join us for an on-line listening party at www.neilyoungmusic.com the week of 4/11 where you can hear songs from Neil's new album *Silver & Gold*.
Album in stores April 25   www.repriserec.com   www.neilyoung.com

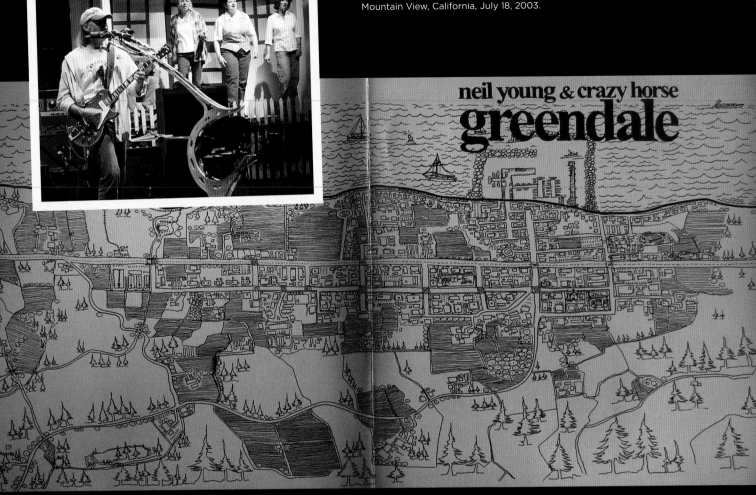

neil young & crazy horse
greendale

Greendale was released in August 2003. The whole album revolved around the fictional murder of a police officer in a sleepy California town. Neil used this horrific event to delve, *à la* John Mellencamp, into small town American issues such as corruption, unemployment, desperation, and environmental blight in one almost freestyle narrative rant. Recorded with Crazy Horse and co-produced by Larry Johnson, the head of Neil's film production company, the album's setting *was* Greendale, a fictional seaside town. Perhaps confused by this first venture into rock opera territory, fans tended to steer clear, whereas critics were split down the middle, hailing *Greendale* either as the best record of 2003 or Neil's least successful work since the unheralded Geffen years.

However, for Neil himself the process and characters of *Greendale* were the driving creative force propelling the project forward.

NY: It came song by song. I didn't really know what I was doing when I started. I just started writing the songs and after two songs I realized the same characters were in the two songs. So I just continued to explore it. I just wrote one song at a time. Kinda like an alcoholic. One day at a time. I thought if they stop coming with these characters then I'm finished. If they don't then I keep going. They're all speaking for me. So I can be all of these people and I don't have to deal with it myself. I'm liberated. *(2003)*

The mixed response didn't bother him as he began the Greendale tour that summer—the high-concept project would also include a movie and graphic novel. Reactions to the tour seemed even more sharply divided than they had been for the album, the venom more poisonous and the praise more lofty.

"The Greendale show at Radio City Music Hall was a true hoot. From my seat at least, you could plainly peer backstage to watch the various backdrops being hoisted shakily back and forth into place, and the chorus ensembles milling and joshing around waiting for their cues. Yep, it was exactly as if Neil & Co. had brought a bit of Earl Grey Junior High onto the Avenue of the Americas for the night. Perfect!"
— Gary Pig Gold, 2015

"The aneurysm gave me more faith ... I know there are a lot of stories. There is the Bible. There is the Koran. There are all these things. Everybody's got one. Everybody has a faith. And there are stories that have gone through the ages, and I respect all of them. But I don't know where I fit in. I just have faith."

— NY, 2008

A well-wisher outside the 2005 Juno Awards held in Winnipeg on April 3, less than a month after Neil underwent surgery on a brain aneurysm.

Although the ambitious Greendale tour extended into spring 2004, the rest of that year was unusually quiet save for some campaigning in the fall on behalf of Democratic presidential candidate John Kerry. However, the following year would more than make up for this fallow period. Within months of each other, Neil would suffer two major challenges: First, in March 2005, he would undergo surgery for a potentially fatal brain aneurysm; and then, in June, his father, Scott, suffering from Alzheimer's disease would pass away at the age of eighty-seven. Ignoring doctor's orders, Neil decamped to Nashville just weeks after his operation to record another album.

John Metzger: What binds the pieces of *Prairie Wind* together are Young's strikingly emotional lyrics, which arguably are the most revealing and intimate that he has penned since *Tonight's the Night*.

Full of bittersweet reflection, *Prairie Wind* finds Young bidding farewell to his Canadian homeland, his father, his family, his guitar, and Elvis, and the end result is a spiritual journey that encapsulates the fragile and fleeting nature of life itself. *(2005)*

Moving adroitly from the introspective to the retrospective, Neil's next project was a documentary collaboration with Academy Award–winning film director Jonathan Demme. The pair had first worked together more than a decade earlier, when Neil provided the theme song to Demme's acclaimed 1993 drama *Philadelphia*.

Released in February 2006, *Neil Young: Heart of Gold* centered around a pair of August 2005 shows at the historic Ryman Auditorium in Nashville. The first set premiered songs from *Prairie Wind*, and then, at the director's suggestion, the second set featured songs from throughout Neil's career, from "I Am a Child" to "Harvest Moon," which are interspersed with commentaries and insights. Demme deftly captures Neil at his most emotional and vulnerable.

NY: You want the people in the theaters to be engrossed in the songs and the presentation, and in the story, the instruments, and the musicians. That's a music film. There's no reason to see the audience, unless you're trying to impress people with how many tickets you sold." *(2006)*

Jonathan Demme: It looks like some kind of weird, human lava lamp back there. I wish I could say that Neil and I told Ellen [Kuras, director of photography] to put a 300 mm lens on, so that the backdrop would be blurry like that. But whatever the lens was, it was perfect. And that helped all the dissolves in that song ["It's a Dream"] to make the cinematic version of the song be as visually dreamy as it sounds. This was made for moviegoers. We took all the best seats for the cameras. *(2006)*

It seemed that *Prairie Wind* and *Heart of Gold*, forged in Neil's heart of darkness, were, indeed, cathartic experiences—even, perversely, enjoyable ones. But Neil, never one to stay still or repeat himself, was to look *out* at the mess of the world again with his next album—and what a scathing look it was!

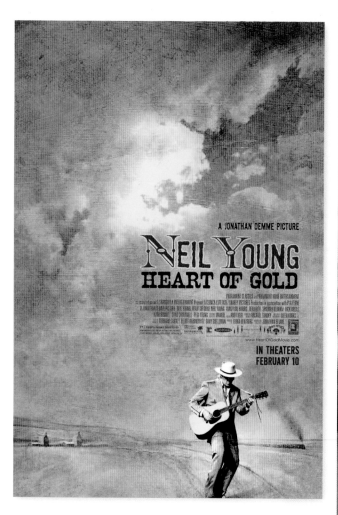

Director Jonathan Demme oversees filming of Neil's August 2005 shows at Nashville's Ryman Auditorium for the *Heart of Gold* documentary.

WAR AND HEAVY PEACE

2006-2012

"Look: You either love the guy
or you don't love the guy.
He marches to his
own drum and that's him."

— Richie Furay, 2015

Timeline

Page 158: Marching on during the Continental tour, Madison Square Garden, New York, December 15, 2008.

October 14–December 16:
Continental tour of the US and Canada.

Fall–Spring 2009:
Recording of *Fork in the Road*.

June 22–September 20:
Continental tour of Europe.

December 2:
Release of *Sugar Mountain: Live at Canterbury House 1968*.

2006

March–April:
Recording of *Living with War*.

February 11–March 15:
Chrome Dreams Continental Tour of Europe.

2009

April 2:
Wins the Adult Alternative Album of the Year Award at the Juno Awards for *Prairie Wind*, as well as the Jack Richardson Producer of the Year Award for "The Painter," the opening track on the album.

Devotes much of his time to the LincVolt eco-car project.

January 16–February 1:
The Continental tour kicks off the year in Australia and New Zealand …

2008

April 6–May 3:
… and returns to the US and Canada.

May 8:
Release of *Living with War*.

November 6:
Release of *Borrowed Tunes II: A Tribute to Neil Young*, a sequel to the 1994 tribute album.

April 7:
Release of *Fork in the Road*.

July 6–September 10:
CSNY Freedom of Speech tour of the US and Canada.

October 23:
Release of *Chrome Dreams II*.

May 30–June 27
The Continental tour finishes with another European leg, including headline UK festival appearances.

October 21–22:
Twentieth Bridge School benefit.

October 18–December 19:
Chrome Dreams Continental tour of the US and Canada.

November 14:
Release of *Live at the Fillmore East*.

June 2:
Release of *The Archives Vol. 1: 1963–1972*.

March 13:
Release of *Live at Massey Hall 1971*.

December 19:
Release of *Living with War: "In the Beginning"*.

2007

December 8:
Release of *Dreamin' Man Live '92*.

June:
Publication of *Neil Young's Greendale*, a graphic novel by Josh Dysart, Cliff Chiang, and Dave Stewart.

May 18–September 28:
Twisted Road solo tour of the US and Canada.

May:
Announces recording of a new album with eminent Canadian producer Daniel Lanois.

March 19:
Release of *Neil Young: Trunk Show*, a documentary and concert film by Jonathan Demme.

February 28:
Performs at the closing ceremony of the Winter Olympic Games in Vancouver.

February 19–20:
The Neil Young Project, a pair of tribute concerts organized by music producer Hal Willner, takes place in Vancouver.

January 29:
Receives the MusiCares Person of the Year Award.

January 22:
Appears on the *Hope for Haiti Now* telethon.

2010

September 28:
Release of *Le Noise*.

October 2:
Twenty-fifth-anniversary Farm Aid concert.

October 23–24:
Plays with a reformed Buffalo Springfield at the twenty-fourth Bridge School benefit.

2011

February 13:
Wins Grammy Award for Best Rock Song with "Angry World" from *Le Noise*.

March 27:
Wins Artist of the Year, Adult Alternative Album of the Year (for *Le Noise*), and the Allan Waters Humanitarian Award at the Juno Awards.

April 15–May 11:
The Twisted Road solo tour of the US and Canada winds its way to a conclusion.

June 1–11:
Buffalo Springfield Reunion tour.

June 11:
Release of *A Treasure*, comprising unreleased live recordings from the 1984 and 1985 tours with the International Harvesters.

October 30:
Release of *Psychedelic Pill*.

September 25:
Publication of *Waging Heavy Peace: A Hippie Dream*, the first volume of his autobiography.

August 3–December 6:
Alchemy tour of the US and Canada with Crazy Horse.

June 5:
Release of *Americana*.

February 10:
Plays live with Crazy Horse for the first time since 1997, at a Paul McCartney tribute gala at the Los Angeles Convention Center.

January:
Recording of *Psychedelic Pill* with Crazy Horse.

2012

October–December:
Recording of *Americana* with Crazy Horse.

September:
Premiere of *Neil Young Journeys*, a third Jonathan Demme documentary, at the Toronto Film Festival.

"I was at Neil's ranch doing something in the studio. Neil called and said, 'Come over for dinner.' So I finished what I was doing, drove across, we had some supper, and he asked me, 'How come nobody does protest records? There's all this war happening and none of these kids bands are doin' it.'"

— Niko Bolas, 2015

By the spring of 2006 the United States had been at war in Iraq for three years and in Afghanistan for more than four years, with no end to either conflict in sight. Neil was jolted into action when he happened to see a newspaper front page showing injured soldiers laid out on operating tables. Haunted by the suffering of the wounded servicemen and women and their families, he responded in the way he knows best—by writing about it.

Niko Bolas: Neil had one song written that became the first track on *Living with War*. Then, about five days later, he said, "I've got three. Let's start." So I got the guys and we cut the first three songs. And, in the process of that he wrote the next three. Then we cut the next three and he wrote two more. And then he needed one more song and said, "I'm outta ideas."

And I knew there was a new Martin guitar on the premises. "There's gotta be a song in this new guitar. You haven't played it yet. I've got editing to do. Get over there, write a song, come back and we'll do it tonight." He did and we did. It was really fun. We did the whole record and then Neil said, "I want a hundred voices singing this with me."

So we booked them inside Capitol Studio A and we got a projector and screened the lyrics up the wall. We put up three microphones and everyone sang along with Neil for every song. Ten songs. Capitol Studios. It's gonna sound really Californian. But there's a vibration there. When you walk into a room at Capitol you want to be great and there's no such thing as a demo at Capitol. *(2015)*

Neil had not made an overtly political album since *Freedom* in 1989, but he'd seen enough of war,

deceit, and death—and he had his sights set on the commander-in-chief, George W. Bush, whose impeachment he controversially called for in one of the tracks on the album.

Working again with Niko Bolas, Neil recorded *Living with War* in a creative flash lasting an astonishing ten days. The result was as strong an antiwar album as perhaps has ever been made.

Roy Trakin: Neil Young's fierce antiwar missive strives to be, like hip-hop, the CNN of its culture. But if, just post-9/11, he was urging everyone, "Let's Roll," that's known as the kind of "flip-flop" he so self-righteously attributes to Dubya in the notorious "Let's Impeach the President."

And how is a Canadian dictating what the United States should do, even one so intimately wrapped up in our country? That said, you don't have to dig Neil's politics to appreciate the garage-rock fury of the title track. More effective still is Young's blast at "The Restless Consumer," a barrage that draws an unbroken line between the lies of Madison Avenue and those of our government. *(2015)*

There was no denying the potency of the album, and it also sold surprisingly well. It peaked at number fifteen on the *Billboard* charts even though there was nary an antiwar protest or march on a college campus to speak of.

It seemed Neil was almost the only one making a stand. He even turned his website into a virtual war portal, including links to other protest songs and videos throughout the ages. This was a man on a mission and he needed to figure out how to get these songs into everyone's heads. Well, what better way than to tour the album with CSNY?

"I was a nervous wreck by the end of that tour.
[There were] death threats and bomb-sniffing dogs
and everything every night, and people were glaring
at you and standing up and giving you the finger."

— NY, 2008

The CSNY Freedom of Speech
tour showcased songs from
Neil's *Living with War* album.
Sleep Train Pavilion, Concord,
California, July 25, 2006.

The Freedom of Speech tour began in Camden, New Jersey on July 6, 2006 and ended in Burgettstown, Pennsylvania, on September 10. The set list would usually begin with the *Living with War* song "Flags of Freedom" and end with "Rockin' in the Free World."

It was what was in between that seemed to puzzle everyone. Moving back and forth, literally song to song, between mellow CSNY classics and acidic anti-combat tunes from *Living with War*, the shows lacked any cohesive feel—and provoked hostility, particularly in Republican states. The movie of the tour, *CSNY/Déjà Vu*, candidly caught the chafing up close.

In October, Neil hosted his twentieth Bridge School benefit. The mood for the frigid night in Northern California was clear from the start. Pearl Jam took the stage and played a stinging cover of Dylan's antiwar anthem "Masters of War." Neil then joined them for the acerbic "Throw Your Hatred Down." War was on everyone's mind—on stage at least.

Toward the end of the year came the first release under the umbrella of Neil's ambitious Archives project. *Live at the Fillmore East* was culled from two March 1970 shows with the original Crazy Horse at the historic New York venue.

Produced by Paul Rothchild, renowned for his work with Love, the Doors, the Paul Butterfield Blues Band, and Janis Joplin, and complete with facsimiles of reviews and original handwritten lyrics, *Fillmore East* is historically important for two reasons: It was the first live recording featuring original Horse

guitarist Danny Whitten, who died just two years later; and it also showcases keyboardist Jack Nitzsche as a fully fledged member of the band.

Barney Hoskyns: Live seventies rock doesn't come much better than NY in NYC. An album of rough beauty and electric density, *Fillmore East* captures the formerly frail troubadour at his most fired up. *(2007)*

Subsequent Archives releases would include live recordings from throughout Neil's career, including the epochal *Live at Massey Hall 1971*, which was greeted enthusiastically upon its release in March 2007.

Michael Fremer: Chris Bellman's astonishingly transparent cut of a magnificent piece of engineering and mixing by Young's longtime producing and engineering cohort David Briggs adds up to a musical and sonic treat Young fans would be foolish to pass up. Surely this won't be in print forever, so get it while you can! Live recordings don't get much better than this. *(2007)*

Another release from late 2006, *Living with War: "In the Beginning"*, was harder to grapple with. Essentially a bare-bones version of *Living with War* with an added video for each song, this was clearly for rabid Neil Young fans only. The awkward collection of rough first mixes and in-studio horsing around fell flat and never found an audience.

"When I'm recording and I don't have that many new songs, I'll start by recording some old songs, not expecting to use them. There's no pressure. It just gets everybody going. But these came out well."

— NY, 2007

ore than a year having passed since the Freedom of Speech tour with CSNY, Neil hit the road again in October 2007 to promote his latest album. Released a few days after the start of the tour, *Chrome Dreams II* was conceived as a sequel to his fabled mid-1970s *Chrome Dreams* album, which was mysteriously put in the cellar and replaced by *American Stars 'n Bars.*

Co-produced again by Niko Bolas, and featuring stalwarts such as Ralph Molina, Ben Keith, and Rick Rosas, *Chrome Dreams II* was mostly recorded without overdubs, giving it a live feel. It featured a combination of old, unreleased material—"Beautiful Bluebird" from 1985 and the eighteen-minute "Ordinary People" from the late 1980s—and newer, more piano-based songs like "The Way," which includes the Young People's Chorus of New York City. The album was another hit, peaking just outside the Top Ten.

Sharry Wilson: *Chrome Dreams II* is a mishmash of old, unreleased material and newer tunes. Somehow it all works and the overall vibe is positive. Neil seems to be exploring his spirituality on tracks such as "The Way," "Shining Light," "Spirit Road," and "No Hidden Path." The power of love and communication is also featured at the forefront of many of the songs. After suffering in isolation since the late 1980s, the epic "Ordinary People" finally found a home. It works well with the other numbers and is enhanced by the Bluenotes' horns. *(2015)*

Scott Atkin: Neil seems to conjure up his outlaw image on *Chrome Dreams II.* Paradoxically, the album seems to evolve along a spiritual path with titles like "Spirit Road," "The Believer," "Shining Light," and "Ever After." Only good listening is all I can say about this album. *(2015)*

Neil's star seemed to be on the rise again. Not only were his own records selling, but a pair of tribute albums released in 2008 provided further evidence of the esteem in which his peers held him. The first

of these, *The Loner: Nils Sings Neil,* was a collection of cover versions by longtime friend and collaborator Nils Lofgren.

Nils Lofgren: Somebody suggested that I do an album of Neil Young covers. I initially thought, why? He's done them all very well. But to honor the idea and his songs, I thought I would sing some favorites and see where it leads with no commitment. It's completely live with a piano or guitar, with no production or fixes. Just a live snapshot of these songs. *(2014)*

Later that year *Borrowed Tunes II,* a follow-up to the original 1994 *Borrowed Tunes* tribute, gave various Canadian musicians such as the Barenaked Ladies, Ron Sexsmith, and Jeremy Fisher an opportunity to express their admiration. One of the contributors was Neil's own half-sister, Astrid, who sang a version of "Sleeps with Angels."

The mammoth Continental world tour rounded off its 2008 dates in New York on December 16.

Gary Pig Gold: I braved the masses at Madison Square Garden to check in on Neil in 2008. It was a great big pre-Christmas Young-a-thon with Wilco opening, but long before he got to the hits—with the natives in their two-hundred-dollar-seats getting increasingly restless—Neil decided to plow into what seemed to some like an eternity's worth of new material from his not-even-released-yet *Fork in the Road.* "We're just auditioning for the record company," Neil (possibly) joked. "So cheer for the new songs even if you don't like them." To which the *Village Voice* immediately replied, "Let's Avoid Neil Young's Next Record." *(2015)*

Above: United Palace, New York, December 12, 2007.

Opposite: Toward the end of 2008, Neil tried out songs from his unreleased *Fork in the Road* album. Madison Square Garden, New York, December 15, 2008.

When he wasn't on the road in 2008, Neil was focusing on his LincVolt eco-car project. Always on the cutting edge, and one of the first artists to express concerns about the environment, he set out with motorcar messiah Jonathan Goodwin to develop a viable electric power system in his own 1959 Mark IV Lincoln Continental. The project has been costly and suffered many setbacks, including a fire in the car, but Neil is pressing on undeterred.

NY: The car was plugged in to charge and left unattended. The wall charging system was not completely tested and had never been left unattended. A mistake was made. It was not the fault of the car. The reason we started this project has not changed. As a nation we are still excessively burning fossil fuels, doing damage to our planet that will hurt our children's lives and future generations as well … On a project like this, setbacks happen for a reason and we can see that very well from here. *(2010)*

Neil had something else—another first—up his sleeve: a LincVolt concept album called *Fork in the Road*, which he had been trying out on unreceptive audiences on tour. Upon its eventual release in April 2009, this ambitious creative endeavor was met with mostly lackluster reviews which more often than not centered around a common complaint: The idea was great but the songs were not. Writing for the online popular culture magazine *PopMatters*, Michael Metivier was one of the unconvinced reviewers.

Michael Metivier: Young's latest is a concept album about his LincVolt project, a zero-emissions auto technology that will reduce dependency on oil, and by extension war, environmental destruction, etc. Worthy? Yes. Interesting in theory? Sure. Unfortunately, with a few notable exceptions, the ten-song record comes off as enthusiastic but hasty, and the pretext for writing most songs far more involved and involving than the songs themselves. *(2009)*

"I was writing and performing a lot of songs about LincVolt and the subject of electric-powered cars … A lot of people were pissed that I made an album about that subject and I got bad reviews, but it was what was on my mind and I can be obsessive. Being obsessive is not such a bad thing for creativity."

— NY, 2014

Introducing LincVolt at the SEMA auto show in Las Vegas, November 2, 2010.

The mammoth Continental tour rolled on into 2009, visiting Australia, New Zealand, and Europe. It climaxed in June with headline slots at three large UK festivals: Isle of Wight, Glastonbury, and Hard Rock Calling in London's Hyde Park.

Closing the Isle of Wight festival, Neil delivered a memorable set which spanned his entire career. Wearing his usual garb of flannel shirt and jeans, he opened with "From Hank to Hendrix" and closed with a torching feedback version of the Beatles' "A Day in the Life," breaking his guitar strings with a diabolical grin on his face. Glastonbury focused mainly on the Horse years, interspersed with a few acoustic numbers, including "Heart of Gold," and once again concluded with a string-busting "A Day in the Life."

The real highlight, however, came a few nights later at Hard Rock Calling when Neil was joined onstage by an actual Beatle, Paul McCartney, who helped finish his song before giving the godfather of grunge a peck on the cheek.

The year also saw by far the most ambitious release in Neil's Archives series. Twenty or so years in the making, the nine-disc *Archives Vol. 1: 1963–1972* contains a staggering 128 tracks, as well as a first home release for the 1972 film *Journey through the Past*. As if that were not enough, the Blu-ray took you further deep into the Youngian catacombs with its pioneering interactive experience. Even when he was looking back, Neil was still state of the art.

Main photo: Closing the Isle of Wight Festival in style, June 14, 2009.

Inset: Paul McCartney joined Neil for an encore of the Beatles' "A Day in the Life" at Hard Rock Calling, Hyde Park, London, June 27, 2009.

Left: Twisted Road tour, DAR Constitution Hall, Washington, DC, May 24, 2010.

Opposite: Performing "Long May You Run" at the closing ceremony of the Winter Olympic Games, BC Place, Vancouver, February 28, 2010.

Another year, another line of fellow artists paying tribute. On January 29, 2010, Neil became the twentieth recipient of the MusiCares Person of the Year award, which recognizes the philanthropic contribution of members of the music community. The event featured performances of his songs by a galaxy of artists, including Elton John, the Red Hot Chili Peppers, Sheryl Crow, and Crosby, Stills & Nash, as well as a somewhat embarrassed yet gracious speech by the man himself. A week earlier he had illustrated yet again why he had been chosen for the award, participating in the *Hope for Haiti* telethon to raise money for the earthquake victims in the poverty-stricken Caribbean republic. Neil teamed up with Dave Matthews for a sentimental rendition of Hank Williams's impassioned plea "Alone and Forsaken."

The Queen Elizabeth Theatre in Vancouver is the home of the Vancouver Opera and British Columbia Ballet; in mid-February 2010 it also hosted the Neil Young Project, a pair of concerts celebrating Neil's songs. The shows had an impressive lineup, including Elvis Costello launching a full-out attack on "Cowgirl in the Sand" and "Cinnamon Girl" and Lou Reed giving a poignant performance of "Helpless," but Neil himself did not attend.

However, Neil *was* in Vancouver for the closing ceremony of the Winter Olympic Games on February 28. Clad in his best Johnny Cash ensemble, complete with black cowboy hat, he delivered on his promise to close the Games with spirit. As if on cue, when he took the stage with his harmonica and Hank Williams's Martin D-28 guitar to play "Long May You Run," a resplendent snow began falling, dusting the man in black's jacket.

The following month saw the release of *Neil Young: Trunk Show*, another concert movie and documentary directed by Jonathan Demme. Shot with handheld cameras, and wobbly Super-8 during the 2007 Chrome Dreams Continental tour, *Trunk* captured two particularly energized nights in Philadelphia. Demme's acute auteur eye puts you in the front row and Neil always knows when to turn it up a level, making *Trunk* a thrilling two hours of him doing his best whirling-dervish rock star pantomime, jamming, bashing and obliterating his guitar like a boy in his teens.

The *Hollywood Reporter* applauded the film: "Young's raw energy is evident in his tremendous power chords and fierce delivery on electric tunes, balanced by a high, plaintive croon on unplugged numbers. The performances are intense and often emotional, backed by a group of musicians who know Young's songs almost as well as he does and are able to interpret them anew with successive iterations."

Neil also found time to help out Beach Boys' cofounder Al Jardine with his 2010 debut solo album, *A Postcard from California*.

Al Jardine: Neil Young and I share lead vocals and have a duet together on "California Saga," describing that wonderful West Coast vibe we have when we're driving Highway 1.

I first met Neil when we did a tour with Buffalo Springfield in 1968. I wanted Neil to be on the album. I kept bugging him. "Al, just keep bugging me." He was in Big Sur producing his wife, Pegi. My wife and I went to see them performing; Pegi has got such a great country thing going. After the show I went backstage and asked Neil if he would play on the album. "Yes, but we have to record together and be in the same room together. None of this ProTools stuff. You have to come up to the ranch and do it."

So I brought the music with me and recorded at his studio between his tours. And he laid it down. Neil, like Brian Wilson, is a total professional and does it until he gets it right. It's like watching and being with Brian, where he gets to a point where you have to sit back and just let it happen. It was great. *(2010)*

Meanwhile, Neil was working on a new album of his own and had enlisted the services of a notable new producer. Daniel Lanois, the sonic voodooist, Grammy-winning Canadian record producer, guitarist, and songwriter, who had famously worked with Brian Eno and U2, Bob Dylan, Peter Gabriel, Willie Nelson, and Emmylou Harris, is known for his beguiling, atmospheric style deliciously brushed with myriad peculiar textures. With a punning title in honor of its producer, *Le Noise* certainly did not disappoint. Heavy on loops, sonic fabrics, and faint inflections, blunt, bare, and obsessive, the album is vintage Lanois-meets-Young.

David Gassman: It's fantastic. It's his best in decades, at least since *Ragged Glory*. It's also without a clear precedent in Young's catalogue. Sidestepping the mellow acoustic/barnstorming electric dichotomy that characterizes nearly everything Young has done, *Le Noise* is solo electric—just Young and his crushing guitar. It's loud and heavy enough to satisfy adrenaline junkies and Crazy Horse fans, but retains a starkness and immediacy that would be difficult to replicate in a full-band setting. Its relatively concise thirty-eight-minute runtime keeps the admittedly limited sonic palette from wearing thin, and the swirling echoes of Young's voice and guitar (presumably courtesy of producer Daniel Lanois) fill out the sound, and add an air of psychedelic mystery. *(2010)*

"Le Noise is amazing. Basically, it's solo stripped-down Neil. Except rather than doing the acoustic thing, it's pretty loud and electric. And there's the Daniel Lanois influence with the ambient sounds in there. There's a lot on that record from Neil's past that had been lying around forever."
— Glen Boyd, 2015

A busy year ended with two memorable live appearances. In early October Neil played the twenty-fifth Farm Aid concert in Milwaukee. The lineup included Dave Matthews, Norah Jones, and the other two cofounders, John Mellencamp and Willie Nelson. Neil opened his set with "Down by the River," followed up with "Ohio" and a couple of songs from *Le Noise*, "Hitchhiker" and "Sign of Love," before Pegi and two backing singers joined him for a harmonica-romp through classics "Mother Earth" and "Long May You Run."

But it was the *other* performance that really had people buzzing. At the twenty-fourth Bridge School benefit on October 23 and 24, Neil re-teamed with Buffalo Springfield for the first time since 1968.

Though there had long been rumors of a reunion, none had come to fruition, until now. (Neil even declined to join the other members for a jam when the band was inducted into the Rock and Roll Hall of Fame in 1997.) Sadly, it was not the original lineup, as bassist Bruce Palmer had died in 2004 and drummer Dewey Martin in 2009, but the reunion did not disappoint.

Richie Furay: There was as much excitement about the band now as there had been back in the day because we hadn't done it for forty years. Buffalo Springfield was a unique situation that worked. We didn't plan it. We started playing. "OK. Here's our band. Here's our sound."

We tried to get together in the 1980s. That was a train wreck. Just awful. We tried three times. This time, when Neil called, it was simply, "What would you think about doin' the Bridge School?" And I thought, "That would be really cool. I'd love to." And Neil said, "Well, I think if you want to do it, Stephen would do it." That was the way Neil went about it.

So we hooked up together with Rick Rosas on bass and Joe Vitale on drums, and you know, when we started to play it was like putting a hand into a glove. It had to be fresh for all of us. We hadn't been on stage together for forty years! The three-guitar thing works for us. Because you've got two dynamic electric lead guitar players who play two different styles, and I'm the guy giving them some rhythm to kind of work on. It worked!

There was no tension. It just fit and it was so easy. Joey and Rick covered the bases perfectly for Bruce

and Dewey. It was Neil's decision to have Rick, and Stephen's decision to have Joey.

Look, the original five members of Buffalo Springfield couldn't be replaced. But when we put the reunion together, Rick and Joey were so tuned in. *(2015)*

"I got the phone call to be in the reformed Buffalo Springfield. Probably one of the most exciting moments in my life."
— Rick Rosas, 2009

Rick Rosas: All during my tours and recording with Neil, he and I would talk about Buffalo Springfield. I never hid my excitement about Buffalo Springfield and loved to talk to him about that band, sometimes over a couple of glasses of wine. He embraced the band. He loved it. Neil would talk about it as much as he could remember. He probably knew I went to the last Buffalo Springfield concert. And I was already a graduate of Neil Young University. That gave me a tremendous amount of confidence to take on this job. The shows were magic. *(2014)*

Opposite: Taking producer Daniel Lanois for a spin in LincVolt, September 2010.

Above: Willie Nelson salutes the audience at the twenty-fifth-anniversary Farm Aid concert, Miller Park, Milwaukee, October 2, 2010.

Overleaf: Rediscovering the old magic with Stephen Stills and Richie Furay during the Buffalo Springfield Reunion tour, Bonnaroo Festival, Manchester, Tennessee, June 11, 2011.

It was clear that everyone involved in the Bridge School reunion had a blast. Rumors of a Buffalo Springfield tour refused to go away. However, as usual, Neil kept everyone on their toes: One day it was on, one day it was off. Then, finally, it was on.

The first date was set for June 1, 2011 in Oakland, California, followed by six other dates, ending June 11 at the Bonnaroo music festival in Tennessee.

Richie Furay: Bonnaroo was our only date away from the West Coast. Stephen came up to me in front of thousands of people and we finally saw the impact and legacy of Buffalo Springfield's music as everyone out there mouthed every word on every song. *(2015)*

An additional thirty dates were called off with little further explanation. Though most fans were happy for any Springfield shows, some closer to the Buffalo family felt the reunion deserved more scale.

Stephen Stills: We were supposed to work for most of the summer. It left me in a lurch and ruined my financial planning. Also, 150 people got laid off who were supposed to work on the tour ... We didn't go to all that trouble for seven shows. That's what impetuosity will do for you. You can't go off half-cocked. When Neil is involved with anything you need a seatbelt ... Working with Neil is a privilege, not a right. *(2012)*

In June 2012, Neil had remarked to Andy Greene in *Rolling Stone*, "I'd be on a tour of my past for the rest of fucking time. I have to be able to move forward, I can't be relegated. I did enough of it right then, but there is this seed of something great still there. It's worth exploring again."

Peter Lewis: This encapsulates the entire Neil Young and Stephen Stills relationship. Buffalo Springfield had a beach house in Malibu in 1967. Moby Grape had one in Malibu at the same time. We were renting Rod Steiger's beach house. One day I remember Neil and Stephen walked in and they wanted to borrow this boat that Rod Steiger had. It was a dinghy. They wanted to grab this boat and go out and get it beyond the shore break. They both climb in there and then they spend a half an hour on who is going to get to row. And then here comes this wave and sinks the whole thing, you know. I don't remember if the boat ever got recovered. Nobody from the band went out and got it. But today Neil Young is rowing the boat. *(2014)*

Neil closed out the year with another reunion of sorts. *Americana* was the first album he had cut with Crazy Horse since *Greendale* in 2003. A collection of classic folk songs reworked with a certain electric darkness and cynicism for the modern age, the album went down a storm when it was released in June 2012.

Stuart Henderson: *Americana* is, finally, Neil Young's best and most complete record since 1994's *Sleeps with Angels*. It is a swirling confusion of noise, grooves, darkness, joy, and horror.

It is an album, ultimately, of *folk music* (which is how most of these nineteenth-century-era songs would have been categorized by the 1950s), a music

that wallows in murder, sex, danger, fear, but also political turbulence and workingman's blues, a music that studies the textures of daily dread, of the ongoing reality of a world in which death is swift, meaning is elusive, and real justice is rare. Equal parts Nick Cave's *Murder Ballads* and Bob Dylan's *World Gone Wrong*, this is Neil Young's blissful evocation of a past that nevertheless haunts him, haunts us still. Americana, indeed. *(2012)*

In another evocation of the past, Neil teamed up again with Jonathan Demme to make a third documentary, *Neil Young Journeys*. Part travelogue, part historical document peppered with performance footage from Toronto's Massey Hall in May 2011, the film is the least dynamic of Demme's trilogy, but it does contain some revealing personal moments: Neil cruising around his childhood neighborhood in Omemee, Ontario, in a 1956 Crown Vic; giving a play-by-play with his brother, Bob, of the different places they lived when they were young; and reminiscing about one Goof Whitney, a boy who offered him a nickel if he would eat some tar.

Premiered in Toronto in September 2011, the movie was largely overlooked when it went on general release the following summer. However, Neil's next offering was *not* to be ignored.

Opposite and above: The opening show of the Buffalo Springfield Reunion tour, Fox Theater, Oakland, California, June 1, 2011.

Above right: Premiere of *Neil Young Journeys*, Toronto International Film Festival, September 12, 2011.

eil began recording *Psychedelic Pill* with Crazy Horse in January 2012 at Broken Arrow. There, they would jam for hours on end, thrashing about looking for the kernels of songs—and, boy, did they find them. Released in October 2012, the two-disc album would contain some of his strongest work in a decade. *Rolling Stone* listed *Psychedelic Pill* as one of the ten best albums of the year; *New Musical Express* claimed that the tracks "Ramada Inn" and "Walk Like a Giant" could "sit among Young's best." This was the Horse at full gallop.

John Mulvey: *Psychedelic Pill* is the work of a man still preoccupied with concepts of liberty, who still feels the need—both spiritually and, it seems, financially—to work, but who has engineered himself into a position where he can carry out his business with extraordinary freedom. Jonathan Demme, the director who has now collaborated on three films with Young, told Jaan Uhelszki, "Before Neil had the aneurysm [in 2005] he told me he used to feel like a giant, and now he feels like a leaf in the stream ... It was a watershed moment. It's allowed him to take bigger risks." *(2012)*

James Cushing: I think *Psychedelic Pill* is one of Neil's best records ever. Just the outrageousness of having the first cut being twenty-eight minutes. The courage of that. The audacity of that. The willingness to be criticized as boring and indulgent. The belief in one's own work. And the guitar playing ... Oh man!

The album's wedded to a very spacious Jimi Hendrix–informed jam session sensibility. So it's all the right notes but they jam on them as chords. And everything is kind of crystalline.

When we heard Neil for the first time, particularly when he embarked on a solo career, his voice was a rather high alto tenor with that distinct Canadian accent. And so a lot of people didn't like his voice because it sounded to them whiny and irritating. But it stood out at the time because so many alpha males were trying to rock and be macho. And Neil gets extra points for never trying to sound like anybody except his Ontario Prairie self. *(2015)*

A month before the release of *Psychedelic Pill*, Neil published his first autobiography, *Waging Heavy Peace: A Hippie Dream*. Unlike most rock bios, the book was written by Neil himself, without any assistance from a ghostwriter. Neil starts his account in 2011 and proceeds to jump backward and forward through the ups and downs of his personal and professional life.

David Carr: "*Waging Heavy Peace* eschews chronology and skips the score-settling and titillation of other rocker biographies. But as the book progresses, the operatics of the rock life give way to signal family events, deconstructions of his musical partnerships, and musings on the natural world. It is less a chronicle than a journal of self-appraisal. *(2012)*

Waging Heavy Peace was well received critically and sold well. It would not be the last time he would follow his father's path. But Neil wasn't ready to give up making music just yet either. The hippie dream was far from finished.

"I don't think I'm going to be able to continue to mainly be a musician forever, because physically I think it's going to take its toll on me— it's already starting to show up here and there. Writing a book allows me to do what I want the way I want to do it."

— NY, 2012

Above: Brothers in arms, Frank Sampedro, Billy Talbot, Neil Young, and Ralph Molina. Alchemy tour with Crazy Horse, United Center, Chicago, October 11, 2012.

LONG MAY YOU RUN

2013 AND ON

"At this point, it's interesting to try and ... make some sort of a difference because I've attained a certain level that I feel a responsibility to use for positive things rather than just getting my name in People magazine."

— NY, 2015

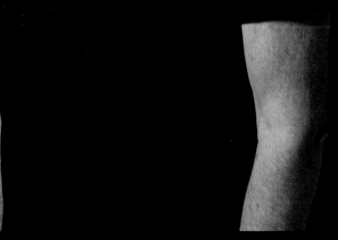

Timeline

2013

February 8:
Performs "Born in the U.S.A." with Crazy Horse at the Bruce Springsteen MusiCares Person of the Year gala.

March 2–21:
Alchemy tour of Australia and New Zealand with Crazy Horse.

September:
Travels to Fort McMurray, Alberta to support opposition to proposed Keystone XL oil pipeline.

June 2–August 7:
Alchemy tour of Europe with Crazy Horse.

September:
Records *A Letter Home* at Jack White's Third Man Records in Nashville using a 1947 Voice-O-Graph vinyl recording booth.

October 30:
Performs at a fundraiser for the Silverlake Conservatory of Music in Los Angeles.

July 7-August 8:
Tour of Europe with Crazy Horse.

July 29:
Files for divorce from Pegi after nearly thirty-six years of marriage.

July 3-24:
Rebel Content tour of the US and Canada with Promise of the Real.

April 14:
Release of *A Letter Home*, on Record Store Day.

August-September:
Main recording phase of double album *Storytone*, which features the same ten songs performed solo and with a full orchestra led by composer and arranger Chris Walden.

June 30:
Release of *The Monsanto Years*.

March 29-April 22:
Solo tour of the US.

April 25:
Performs with Stephen Stills at the Light Up the Blues concert in aid of autism research.

October 5-9:
Short solo tour of the US.

March:
Announces launch of Pono, a high-resolution digital download service.

October 14:
Publication of *Special Deluxe: A Memoir of Life & Cars*, the second installment of his memoirs.

February 6:
Performs "Blowin' in the Wind" at the Bob Dylan MusiCares Person of the Year event.

January 12-19:
Honour the Treaties solo tour of Canada to raise awareness of issues facing indigenous communities and to raise money for anti-oilsands organizations.

January:
Official launch of the Pono music player.

January 6-10:
Plays four solo dates at the Carnegie Hall in New York City.

January-February:
Records *The Monsanto Years* with Promise of the Real, a band featuring Willie Nelson's sons Lukas and Micah.

2014

2015

December 10:
Release of *Live at the Cellar Door*.

November 4:
Release of *Storytone*.

November 9:
Guests at environmentalist David Suzuki's Blue Dot speaking tour appearance in Vancouver.

"My boss is my muse. If I had an idea for a song, I'd get up right now and go. I've learned if I don't get it, it's gone. It's a gift. If you don't pick it up, what kind of respect are you giving it? Whatever it is, I'll go do that first. I just follow the idea to where it leads me."

— NY, 2012

In February 2013, Neil found himself in Los Angeles on stage with the Horse playing the Bruce Springsteen MusiCares Person of the Year gala. The Horse stumbled through a wildly off-key version of "Born in the U.S.A." but no one noticed. This was a night to celebrate, not pick holes.

The band spent the bulk of the spring and summer touring Europe, Australia, and New Zealand before Neil traveled down to Nashville to record a new album with Jack White at the former White Stripes frontman's Third Man Studios. *A Letter Home* is about as contrarian and kooky as anything he has ever done.

It is not the songs—a batch of acoustic covers including Dylan's "Girl from the North Country," Springsteen's "My Hometown," and Bert Jansch's "Needle of Death"—that are unconventional; it is the way in which they were recorded, using a 1940s contraption called a Voice-O-Graph, a long-forgotten curio used to send voice postcards to friends and family. In this spirit, Neil opens the album with a touching spoken message to his mother in which he urges her to speak to his father.

Although undoubtedly a head-scratcher, *A Letter Home* did resonate with many reviewers. Simon Vozick-Levinson in *Rolling Stone* described the album "in its perverse way" as "one of the most enjoyable records Young has made this century."

The year 2014 would be one of Neil's busiest and most turbulent. An on-and-off solo acoustic tour took up much of the period, including dates at Carnegie Hall in New York City in January. His four-night stay at Carnegie has become legendary: Fans were treated to acoustic sets of his early work, especially from *Harvest* and *After the Gold Rush*.

Mark Guerrero: Neil is a real artist playing the acoustic guitar to accompany his singing. He comes up with great guitar parts like the ones on "Tell Me Why," "Old Man," and "The Needle and the Damage Done." Neil usually plays acoustic without a pick which creates a fatter, more organic sound. He often uses D modal tuning on acoustic and electric. Examples of songs using this tuning on electric songs are "Ohio," Cinnamon Girl," and "When You Dance." On acoustic he uses it on "Don't Let It Bring You Down," his acoustic version of "Mr. Soul," and "The Old Laughing Lady." Bringing the high and low E strings down a step to D gives the guitar a droning sound because they ring through most of the chord changes. *(2014)*

Immediately after his stint at Carnegie Hall, Neil played four "Honour the Treaties" benefit concerts in Canada in support of the Athabasca Chipewyan First Nations' legal fund to defend their land rights against incursions by oil companies and the government.

Sharry Wilson: I was at the show in Toronto where Neil was very vocal in his support of the First Nations people. Some members of the First Nations gathered outside Massey Hall in a drum circle while others danced in a circle on the street. Time was also allotted to their cause at the beginning of the evening, with a drum circle formed on stage. Neil felt so strongly about this issue that, in September 2013, he drove hundreds and hundreds of miles to Fort McMurray, Alberta in LincVolt, his 1959 Lincoln Continental hybrid electric car, to see the damage wrought by the oil companies on Native lands.

He had some strong words to describe what he witnessed and his remarks were reported in the press. He did not endear himself to some of the residents of Fort McMurray when he equated what he had seen to the devastation of Hiroshima. *(2015)*

In another engagement inspired by his strong environmental convictions, Neil joined award-winning Canadian scientist/environmentalist David Suzuki's Blue Dot speaking tour of Canada during the fall of 2014 when it stopped in Vancouver.

Sharry Wilson: The aim of the speaking series was to engage citizens to demand a change to Canada's Charter of Rights and Freedoms with the ultimate goal of "having the right to breathe fresh air, drink clean water, and eat healthy food" added to the charter. Neil has long been an environmentalist and has lobbied for many years in support of family farms vs. corporate operations. His participation in Farm Aid since its inception in 1985 demonstrates his strong support and devotion to the cause. "Mother Earth," his plea to keep the earth sustainable for future generations, was included on *Ragged Glory*.

During his most recent tour with Crazy Horse in Europe during the summer of 2014, Neil wore a black T-shirt with the word EARTH in big block letters on the front. A new song, "Who's Gonna Stand Up (and Save the Earth)?," was featured prominently at each performance. *(2015)*

Longtime Crazy Horse bassist Billy Talbot suffered a mild stroke shortly before the summer tour of Europe and was replaced by Rick Rosas, making him the only musician other than Neil himself to have played with Buffalo Springfield, CSNY, and Crazy Horse. Sadly, this was to be Rosas's last tour, as he succumbed to lung disease the following November.

During the tour, Neil's personal life unraveled: In July he filed for divorce from his wife, Pegi, after thirty-six years of marriage. Their long run had come to an end.

To promote *A Letter Home*, Neil and Jack White brought the Voice-O-Graph booth to the studio of NBC's *Tonight Show* and Neil performed two songs from the album. May 12, 2014.

"It's gonna be very confusing to people because it's retro-tech. Retro-tech means recorded in a 1940s recording booth. A phone booth. It's all acoustic with a harmonica inside a closed space, with one mic to vinyl. Directly to vinyl."

"An ideal session for me is when Neil never even comes into the control room. He doesn't have to. He does live vocals. Delivering the message is what matters."

— Niko Bolas, 2015

Delivering his message to producer Niko Bolas during the *Storytone* sessions, September 2014.

Promoting his second book, *Special Deluxe*, in a public conversation with *New Yorker* writer Nick Paumgarten, October 12, 2014.

Through all the turmoil in his personal life, current climate navigator Neil Young in 2014 did what he always does: He was recording and working.

Neil began recording the double album *Storytone* in early summer. The album, recorded with a big band orchestra, was released in two formats—one with the orchestra and one with stripped-down versions of the tunes. The orchestral version was, typically, a big departure from his previous lo-fi affair, *A Letter Home*.

Niko Bolas: The *Storytone* album happened when Neil called me at the beginning of the summer and said "I wrote ten songs and I don't know what to do with them and I want to get started. And I'm really intrigued by the idea of singing with an orchestra."

Neil came to Capitol Studios. The idea was to have him stand in a room with a big band and sing these tunes really old school. But we had to get the essence of the song down.

So I got Al Schmitt booked to engineer and Neil showed up. And on the first night, we cut just about everything.

What we did was not let him bring any of his own instruments. I called Lonn Cohen and asked him to build me "Neil Young's Pawn Shop." He brought about a dozen old weird instruments from a mandolin, cello, to ukulele to old guitars to a storytelling piano itself. And then Neil wandered around the room and sat down with all the instruments he never played. Banjos, weird instruments. And when he picked one up and it kind of felt like whatever that song was, that's when we recorded.

Then Neil went on the road with Crazy Horse and I took the recordings to my two arranger buddies Michael Bearden and Chris Walden. And when Neil came back, we then went into Sony Studios and cut everything with the orchestra.

Neil had never stood in the middle of the room and sung live before. And that was the big difference. I put him up in between the piano and the conductor. So he had something for pitch reference facing the orchestra and we basically just picked takes based on the best vocal. *(2015)*

Jim Beviglia: Often overlooked amidst Young's different genre forays is his skill as a tunesmith. *Storytone* features some of his most ingratiating melodies in years, songs that don't even need the orchestration to reveal their beauty. Rarely do the arrangements get showy, with the possible exception of the one for the environmental plea "Who's Gonna Stand Up?" *(2014)*

Neil found time to publish his second memoir, *Special Deluxe: A Memoir of Life & Cars*, in October 2014.

Sharry Wilson: In *Special Deluxe*, Neil talks about his Ontario years. I really love the book, more than *Waging Heavy Peace*. It's special. I like the way it's set out. Neil has done tracings and water colors of all of his cars that mean the most to him. So the whole book is framed around these different cars and why they were special to him, what was happening at the time, and what he was thinking. It was done in chronological order. His childhood, Buffalo Springfield years, and his own solo career.

For each car he also includes a notation about how much carbon fuel the car emitted. Neil is thinking about how much damage he did with his earlier cars. *(2015)*

Now, the future was beckoning again. Pono, Neil's own high-resolution digital download player, was launched in January 2015.

NY: We're going make this technology public. We would like to be more open about it. We want to start a community of music lovers worldwide so future generations will be able to hear today's classics in a way that's representative of what music is, instead of having a museum of MP3 files. *(2015)*

Neil hired engineer and sound consultant Bruce Botnick as VP of Content Acquisitions at Pono. Botnick had worked with Buffalo Springfield decades previously at Sunset Sound in Hollywood.

Bruce Botnick: I went to go see a reunited Buffalo Springfield concert three years ago and I went backstage. Neil then showed me Pono. At that time it was in LincVolt, his hybrid Lincoln convertible, but it was an astonishingly great speaker system and amplifiers, and he had a prototype—not the one we hold in our hands today, but electronically, the concept—in place, and he was able to demonstrate it. Neil Young, in his own way, is a visionary. *(2015)*

Neil Young's career clearly does have its highs and lows. But the highs and lows are there because he has consistently shown a pattern of wanting to experiment and wanting to try new things and wanting to remain in a state of becoming. Rather than a state of being.

Graham Nash: I don't know what goes on in Neil's head. I'm not even sure Neil knows half the time. When Neil's heart moves, he has to move. Will there be any more CSNY? Right now it looks pretty bleak. Neil is a little upset with me because of my book, *Wild Tales*. Neil's packed every second. We're getting older, how long can this go on? Rick Rosas has died. It is very sad. But I'm never surprised by anything Neil does. He's been very dedicated to his music, he has always thought to explore new ways of doing it and God bless him. *(2015)*

By remaining a very active and innovative recording artist, he avoids the nostalgia label that is pinned to many of his contemporaries.

Gary Stewart: At Rhino/Warner Music Group, we were involved only peripherally with the release of the Buffalo Springfield box set and rarely were able to use his tracks on our other compilations, but Neil Young was somebody we always talked about as the gold standard for how to be a veteran artist without falling into the "classic rock coffin" that engulfed so many of his peers.

I remember when *The Bridge* came out in 1989. It was one of the first serious tribute albums, before they became a predictable trend. That in itself was an indication of both how much he mattered and how long he had mattered for.

Then I noticed the lineup, which didn't consist of legacy acts, or sensitive singer-songwriter types, but of the then-cream of post punk and indie rock: Pixies, Nick Cave, Sonic Youth—the kind of artists you'd expect to see on a Velvet Underground tribute. But then I realized that the punks got him because he always got the punks. That was made explicit on *Rust Never Sleeps*, but you can even hear it on some of the earliest edgier Springfield recordings.

If you look at that elite group, the veteran artists who started in the rock 'n' roll idiom, but who are still making diverse music that matters by looking forward and telling the truth—Elvis Costello, Patti Smith, Tom Waits chief among them—it's hard not to think of Neil as the first person to set the example for having perspective and legacy without losing his edge. He was built for speed *and* distance. *(2015)*

The late, great songwriter, record producer, author, and maverick music man Kim Fowley, in one of his last interviews, also recognized Neil's longevity.

Kim Fowley: I give Neil Young kudos for having a lifetime career like Bing Crosby and Frank Sinatra. Good for him. He worked hard and deserves all the good things that happened. He started in Hollywood with Greene and Stone. They were like Hy Weiss, founder of Old Town Records, minus the humility. They had connections. Neil was then fortunate to work with record men like Ahmet Ertegun at Atlantic and Mo Ostin at Reprise. *(2014)*

Peter Lewis was a member of the influential West Coast band Moby Grape, which shared a residency with Buffalo Springfield at the Ark in Sausalito (near San Francisco) in November 1966.

Peter Lewis: Maybe the person who Neil reminds me of is Gregory Peck. *The Guns of Navarone*. He had a remoteness about him. An unreachable quality. I mean the guy who can survive that way. When I talk about Gregory Peck and Neil Young in the same breath, I see a lot of control. I think that is their religion and that is what they are selling.

Neil teamed up with Willie Nelson's sons Lukas and Micah and Lukas's band, Promise of the Real, to record his 2015 album *The Monsanto Years*. Lukas (left) and Micah (right) also guested during his set at Farm Aid in Raleigh, North Carolina on September 13, 2014.

Neil is one year older than me. Away from Buffalo Springfield and Moby Grape, what we wanted to do was change the script. If we could do that it would be a great example to people. That's what people in show business are supposed to do. That's what they are getting paid for. To not get overwhelmed by people's preconception of them. What people really like about Neil would be the idea that he's isolated what it means to be free. Being free means you are free to do anything you want. Whether anyone likes it or not.

In 2015, Neil is still doing it. That's the point. I think Neil understands that life is a metaphor. Kind of like surfing. If you are at Mavericks and the Pacific Ocean waves are big, you got three choices. You can get stuck inside and die. Or you can paddle like crazy and try to get over that next one. Or, if you're at the right place in the lineup, you can get a ride. That's life.

I think Neil Young has been smart enough to either get outside or get a ride. It's about the choices you make and what you want to do. And it's not about being perfect. I know he's not perfect. That's not what I'm talking about. I'm talking about survival. And I think Neil is a survivor. You gotta stay ahead of the curve so you'll survive. *(2015)*

Still other collaborators, chroniclers, tour veterans, poets, and pundits give their thoughts on this unique and enduring talent.

Dickie Davis: Neil's longevity? This comes from way outside, but Neil plays well with others. You know, he connected with bands, had a lot of younger bands open for him in the nineties. Did shows and collaborated in a studio with them. Neil remained an important guitar player to a bunch of people who were coming along. And they buoyed him up, in terms of reputation. *(2014)*

"Neil is a truly authentic poet in the classic sense of the word. Think Shakespeare. He writes stories set to music, takes them from town to town to share them, the tales delight and move us, and we can't wait for the next time he passes through. But Neil's got a slight edge on William S.— that wicked guitar."

— Jonathan Demme, 2005

Peter Goddard: I think to understand Neil Young you have to think of him as a performance artist, like Lady Gaga. No one has ever applied this term to him. That's the kind of space he occupies. The fringe. John Lennon, after meeting Yoko Ono, understood this about himself. John and I talked a lot about this. It freed him up enormously. From being the commercial guy that he thought he was.

The real thing about Neil Young is he's very quirky, very idiosyncratic. You see this with artists who, right from the get go, sort of take a vision and the vision, of course, creates its own complications, its own needs and demands. So you have to follow them. And I think that's what Neil did. *(2014)*

In *MOJO* magazine's March 2002 "Hero" issue, Oasis cofounder Noel Gallagher picked Neil Young to writer Jon Bennett. "'Cause he's still relevant, still got his voice, and he's still got his enthusiasm, and he still looks like he means it."

Before drummer Clem Burke joined Blondie, as a teenager he saw Neil Young and Crazy Horse opening for Deep Purple at the Felt Forum in New York in 1969. More than forty years on, Burke has some observations about Neil Young's influence on today's recording artists.

Clem Burke: The whole sound of Oasis, to my mind, I would go as far as to say, besides the Beatles, it's kind of based on Neil Young and Crazy Horse. I mean, the guitars are really loud, the bass playing and the drumming is very minimal. I saw Oasis in Las Vegas at the Hard Rock and for an encore they did "Hey Hey My My." Brilliant. I really rate Noel Gallagher as a writer, performer, guitar player, and singer. And it was just phenomenal when they came out and did that.

Aside from Neil's songwriting and solo career, CSNY, you hear his tremendous influence on rock bands. The sound of Crazy Horse, the guitar playing have a big influence on contemporary rock music. Pearl Jam, Oasis. Neil kind of goes on both sides of the street: He's a phenomenal folk singer and a phenomenal rocker. *(2014)*

Stuart Henderson: To borrow from Paul Williams, Neil Young has always understood that "slick is sloppy." His live shows have never, in my quarter century of seeing them, followed any specific path. They may follow a set list, and they may involve some scripted elements night after night, but it has always seemed to me that Neil Young couldn't fake it if he tried. He isn't a professional in the classic sense. He's ornery, he's self-centered, he's loquacious, he's aloof, he's on, he's off … you're going to get what he gives. No bullshit, no showboating, just the songs. When he

plays with Crazy Horse, he gets a band that has the same basic live profile: Play the songs, see what happens. Let's try this, now that. *(2015)*

"You want to stay relevant onstage after fifty years, even as your material waxes and wanes in terms of quality? Be real. If that means shambling your way through some off nights every once in a while, or taking a ten-minute guitar solo just to see where it goes, or playing acoustic ballads to a restless arena, or staging a quixotic rock opera … just trust yourself that it'll be good if it's real. Resist the temptation to paint it in some slick gloss. Slick is sloppy."
— Stuart Henderson, 2015

Glen Boyd: Why do people still go to his shows? Because it's such great shit. I mean, that's the best way I can put it. I think there is a percentage of his audience who are like I am and they buy everything.

At every Neil show you get the hardcore "Rusties" there. They're always the guys out on the rail. They gather before the show in the parking lot and do their own tailgate parties. They're not as celebrated as Dead heads and Springsteen fans. But they're every bit as dedicated.

But, there's this larger group of people that are divided right down the middle. There are the guys who go to an acoustic show and they will sit in the fifth row and yell out "Rockin' in the Free World." They can't really separate the acoustic Neil from the electric Neil.

And then, you've got the other group of people who are more the Starbucks sort of crowd who, you know, love *Harvest Moon*, but when Neil comes out and does something like the Alchemy tour for *Psychedelic Pill*, they don't understand that. Neil's fan base is really strange, but the one thing that is common between all of these different camps is that they are very loyal to him. *(2015)*

Don Randi: Neil was smart enough to know what he wanted and knew how to get it. And he had Ahmet Ertegun in his corner.

Jack Nitzsche and I never judged artists by their voices. To me it didn't matter 'cause I loved the music so much. And Neil was able to sell it. There are some people you can't stand them on record until you see them live. And once you see them live you can understand their records. That doesn't happen a lot. But it does happen. *(2014)*

James Cushing: I marvel at Neil Young's career. His songs are so powerfully and simply constructed. They seem to have been discovered rather than written. Neil's guitar playing has that marvelously rough-hewn rock-out quality that nothing else quite has. His voice is unique. Even though he's not a blues guy, the interiority and the momentum of his best music is everything that rock music was designed to deliver. And his calm and beautiful folk songs are emotionally affecting on an almost pre-verbally deep level. Neil is just like Bob Dylan and nothing like Bob Dylan. *(2014)*

Above: Anatomy of a Neil Young audience. Paleo Festival, Nyon, Switzerland, July 23, 2013.

Opposite: Guesting at Stephen Stills's Light Up the Blues benefit for Autism Speaks, Pantages Theatre, Los Angeles, April 25, 2015.

Overleaf: MusiCares Person of the Year event in honor of Bob Dylan, Los Angeles Convention Center, February 6, 2015.

The sheer range of Neil Young's activities has always been astounding, and if anything is becoming increasingly diverse as he approaches the start of his eighth decade. Just since the turn of the century, he has given us thirteen studio albums, including a concept rock opera, a journey into the supernatural world of Daniel Lanois, a first foray into the big band sound, and, most recently, a polemic against biotechnology corporation Monsanto. But in between these releases, he has also managed to write two memoirs, turn a 1959 Lincoln Continental into a hybrid electric car, direct one movie and collaborate on another three with Jonathan Demme, develop his Pono device, win multiple Grammys, execute an improbable Buffalo Springfield reunion, and compile dozens and dozens of hours from deep inside the Youngville vaults. (Volume two of *The Neil Young Archives* is being readied, although the release date is yet to be confirmed.)

And presiding over each of these quixotic moves is Neil's long-serving manager, Elliot Roberts.

Bryan Bell: Neil has said, "I'm a musician. And I would be a musician whether I could eat or not. The reason I'm a professional musician is because of Elliot Roberts. He's the one who has learned how to monetize me." *(2015)*

Brian Stone: I saw Neil with CSNY earlier this century. As far as the career Neil Young has created, I am not surprised at all. Neil is a genius and Elliot is a sensational manager. There aren't many people who can sustain a career this long. I think Neil is a goddamn genius and always tries to keep himself fresh. He's brilliant. I feel proud that I contributed in some way. *(2014)*

Andrew Loog Oldham: I think for a suburbanite from Toronto who lived next door to a chicken farm, Neil Young did remarkably well. Neil Young knows how it all works. OK. And people like me or people like Charlie Greene and Brian Stone only get to Mount Etna when the chariot we're driving knows as much as people like Neil Young know.

Because Neil Young also had adversity in his life. Polio and epilepsy. Adversity either buries you, like it did Brian Jones and so many others, or like Roman Polanski and others, drives you on and gives you a common touch with the public that your talent can seize upon and multiply.

The Neil Young and Elliot Roberts team. It's a gift to still stay engaged. But what you really have to say is thank God for the songs. *(2014)*

The Neil Young 2015 model seems to be a very happy person. I've seen him a couple of times cruising around Mulholland Drive near Malibu State Park in LincVolt.

But don't look for Neil to take part in any topping-off ceremonies just yet. So what could be next? Well, anything. Especially in Neil Young's down-to-the-wire universe.

"I don't know much about the future.
I want to [focus on Pono] and I want
to continue playing music. Those two
things should keep me pretty busy.
I have some film editing and things
to do on the side. I'll probably be
writing some more books. I want
to keep doing what I do. I'd like
to continue doing it for a long time."

— NY, 2015

Contributors

Kerwin Dean Abramovitch is an audio archivist and recording engineer. He first saw Neil Young in concert in 1982 at the Universal Amphitheatre in Southern California.

Scott Atkin is a dedicated and long-standing Neil Young fan who has gone so far as to give a rating to each album and all of his nearly 500 songs.

Randy Bachman cofounded iconic bands the Guess Who and Bachman-Turner Overdrive. Widely regarded as the "architect of Canadian rock 'n' roll," his most recent album is *Heavy Blues* (2015).

Bryan Bell is a multi-instrumentalist, technician, and sound innovation pioneer and programmer. He worked closely with Neil Young in the mid-1980s and is on the Board of Directors of the Bridge School.

Tosh Berman is a writer, poet, and publisher/editor for TamTam Books. Among his most recent publications are *Sparks-Tastic* (Rare Bird, 2013) and *The Plum in Mr. Blum's Pudding* (Penny Ante, 2014).

Rodney Bingenheimer is a radio DJ who has presented his world-famous weekly show, *Rodney on the ROQ*, on KROQ-FM (106.7) since 1976.

Niko Bolas is a record producer and engineer. As well as working with artists such as Herbie Hancock, Keith Richards, Melissa Etheridge, and KISS, he has produced numerous Neil Young albums, from *This Note's for You* (1988) to *Storytone* (2014).

Richard Bosworth is a record producer, mixer, and recording engineer. He worked as an engineer on Neil Young's 1986 album *Landing on Water*, and has also collaborated with Don Henley, Roy Orbison, Santana, Dolly Parton, and Warren Zevon.

Bruce Botnick is a sound engineer and record producer. He worked extensively with the Doors and Love, as well as engineering tracks on the second Buffalo Springfield album, *Buffalo Springfield Again* (1967).

Glen Boyd is the author of *Neil Young FAQ* (Backbeat Books, 2012). You can also check out his work at his website (www.therockologist.com).

David Briggs (1944–1995) was a record producer best known for his work with Neil Young. He produced Neil's debut album in 1968 and the pair continued to work closely together until his death in 1995. He also produced albums for Alice Cooper, Spirit, and Nick Cave and the Bad Seeds.

Denny Bruce played drums with the pre-*Freak Out* Frank Zappa's Mothers of Invention before moving on to personal management and producing. His clients have included Leo Kottke, the Fabulous Thunderbirds, T-Bone Burnett, and John Hiatt. He became the owner of Takoma Records and presently owns Benchmark Recordings.

Clem Burke is best known as the drummer for Blondie, but has also played with a number of other artists and bands, including Pete Townshend, Iggy Pop, the Ramones, Nancy Sinatra, and Bob Dylan.

Johnny Cash (1932–2003) was a giant of twentieth-century popular music. He was inducted into both the Country Music Hall of Fame and the Rock and Roll Hall of Fame, and received a Grammy Lifetime Achievement Award and a Kennedy Center Honor.

Kevin Chong is the author of five books, including the fan memoir *Neil Young Nation* (Greystone, 2005).

Merry Clayton is a renowned support singer, who featured in the Oscar-winning documentary *20 Feet From Stardom* (2013). As well as singing on Neil Young's debut solo album, she has contributed to recordings by artists such as Ray Charles, Bobby Womack, Carole King, the Rolling Stones, and Elvis Presley.

David Crosby found fame as a member of the Byrds before cofounding Crosby, Stills & Nash.

Iris Cushing is the author of *Wyoming* (Furniture Press Books, 2014). Her poems and criticism have appeared in the *Boston Review* and numerous other publications.

James Cushing is a poet and has taught literature and creative writing at Cal Poly, San Luis Obispo, since 1989. He also hosts a weekly jazz and rock program on the college's radio station, KCPR-FM. He was Poet Laureate of San Luis Obispo from 2008 to 2010.

Chris Darrow is a multi-instrumentalist and veteran recording artist and producer/music publisher. As a member of Kaleidoscope, he played on the debut Leonard Cohen album. He was also a member of the Nitty Gritty Dirt Band. His 1972 solo album *Artist Proof* was recently rereleased, and in 2013 he brought out *Island Girl* in collaboration with his former Kaleidoscope band mate Max Buda.

Richard "Dickie" Davis cofounded the Monday Night Hoots at the Troubadour. He became a managing partner of Buffalo Springfield in 1966. Following

the breakup of the group, he went on to manage Poco. He currently works in the film industry in Los Angeles.

Jonathan Demme is an Academy Award–winning filmmaker. His films include *The Silence of the Lambs* (1991), *Philadelphia* (1993), and the Talking Heads concert film *Stop Making Sense* (1984). A longtime fan of Neil Young, he has made a trilogy of documentaries about the musician: *Neil Young: Heart of Gold* (2006), *Neil Young Trunk Show* (2009), and *Neil Young Journeys* (2011).

Henry Diltz cofounded the folk group the MFQ before taking up photography during a 1965 tour. He has taken cover shots for *Rolling Stone*, *LIFE*, and *MOJO*, as well as publishing a number of books including *California Dreaming* (Genesis, 2007) and *Unpainted Faces* (Morrison Hotel, 2011). He is also a partner in the Morrison Hotel Gallery (www.morrisonhotelgallery.com).

Stanley Dorfman is a British film director and producer. He was the original co-producer/director of the long-running BBC music show *Top of the Pops* and later directed the *In Concert* series. His long-form shows on Neil Young, Laura Nyro, and Cat Stevens, among others, helped to introduce their music to British and European viewers.

John Einarson is a Canadian music history writer with more than a dozen critically acclaimed biographies to his credit including works on Buffalo Springfield, Randy Bachman, Ian & Sylvia, Gene Clark, Arthur Lee, and the Flying Burrito Brothers. His 1992 book *Don't Be Denied: The Canadian Years* was the first to chronicle in detail Neil Young's early music years in Canada with Neil's cooperation.

Flea (born Michael Peter Balzary) is a founding member of the Red Hot Chili Peppers. His funk-influenced bass playing is a crucial element of the band's sound.

Ben Folds formed the alt-rock band Ben Folds Five in the mid-1990s. Though best known for his piano playing, he is also a singer, guitarist, composer, bassist, and drummer. In 2013, he became a founding member of the Independent Music Awards' judging panel.

Kim Fowley (1939–2015) was an influential force in rock 'n' roll music for more than half a century, garnering well over a hundred gold and platinum records for his songwriting, music publishing, and record production skills. This decade he was heard as a DJ on Little Steven's Underground Garage via the SiriusXM satellite radio network.

Tom Freston cofounded MTV in 1981. In 1987, he became the President and CEO of MTV Networks, where he remained for almost twenty years. He is now a board member of the ONE Campaign, the advocacy organization for extreme poverty issues founded by U2 lead singer, Bono.

Richie Furay is best known for forming the bands Buffalo Springfield with Stephen Stills, Neil Young, Bruce Palmer, and Dewey Martin, and Poco with Jim Messina, Rusty Young, George Grantham, and Randy Meisner.

David Geffen is an entertainment industry magnate. Having managed Crosby, Stills & Nash in the late 1960s, he founded Asylum Records in 1970. He then created Geffen Records in 1980 and sold it to MCA in 1990. He also cofounded the DreamWorks film studio in 1994 along with Jeffrey Katzenberg and Steven Spielberg.

Peter Goddard is an award-winning journalist and a bestselling Canadian publisher, musician and writer/producer for radio and television. He has written books on a variety of recording artists including Frank Sinatra, David Bowie, the Who, Bruce Springsteen, Cyndi Lauper, Michael Jackson, and the Police.

Gary Pig Gold, like Neil Young himself, fell under the spell of the almighty 1050 CHUM-AM Toronto at a most impressionable age, and has spent the half century since playing and writing about music wherever and whenever possible. (www.garypiggold.com)

Bill Graham (1931–1991) was a rock impresario and game-changing concert promoter who launched the careers of countless rock 'n' roll legends in the 1960s and early 1970s at his famed Fillmore venues in New York and San Francisco. He worked with or managed the Grateful Dead, Jefferson Airplane, Santana, Jimi Hendrix, Led Zeppelin, CSNY, and the Rolling Stones.

Mike Grant is the host of *The California Music Show* heard weekly on BigglesFM (www.bigglesfm.com) in the UK. He is the former editor of the *Beach Boys Stomp* magazine.

Mark Guerrero is a singer-songwriter whose songs have been recorded by Herb Alpert, Trini Lopez, Chan Romero, and his late father, Lalo Guerrero. Mark's website (www.markguerrero.com) is a leading source of information on Chicano and East Los Angeles music.

Bill Halverson started his music career in jazz big bands as a trombone player with Allyn Ferguson and Tex Beneke. In 1965 he began working with studio owner Wally Heider as an engineer on remote live recordings. He engineered the debut Crosby, Stills & Nash album (1969) and also worked on CSNY's first album, *Déjà Vu* (1970).

Kirk Hammett has been lead guitarist in Metallica since 1983. He is credited with the riff on the band's biggest hit, "Enter Sandman." He is also the creator of *Kirk Hammett's Fear FestEvil*, an annual horror convention.

Stuart Henderson is a culture critic and historian. He is the author of *Making the Scene: Yorkville and Hip Toronto in the 1960s* (University of Toronto Press, 2011).

Rob Hill is a magazine journalist and editor who has worked for *Ray Gun*, *Bikini*, *FHM*, *Giant*, *Hollywood Life*, *THC Expose*, and *Treats!*, as well as contributing to *Playboy*, *Uncut*, *LA Weekly*, *Black Book*, and *Rolling Stone*.

Ian Hunter was the vocalist, songwriter, and bandleader of 1970s British rock legends Mott the Hoople. He has gone on to forge a highly regarded solo career.

Al Jardine is a founding member of the Beach Boys. In 2010, he released his long-awaited debut solo album, *A Postcard From California*.

Jim Jarmusch has been a filmmaker since 1980. His acclaimed feature films include *Mystery Train* (1989), *Night on Earth* (1991), *Dead Man* (1995), and *Only Lovers Left Alive* (2013), and he also directed *Year of the Horse* (1997), a documentary on Neil Young and Crazy Horse.

Howard Kaylan founded the Turtles and Flo & Eddie, both with his longtime partner Mark Volman. He has written an autobiography called *Shell Shocked: My Life with the Turtles, Flo & Eddie, and Frank Zappa, etc.* (Backbeat Books, 2013).

Jim Keltner is a drummer best known for his session work with John Lennon, George Harrison, and Ringo Starr. He has recorded and toured with Bob Dylan and Neil Young, and was the drummer for the Traveling Wilburys. His studio credits also include Leon Russell, Leonard Cohen, Joni Mitchell, Laura Marling, Elvis Costello, and the Rolling Stones.

Dan Kessel has charted globally as a producer, recording artist, songwriter, and publisher. A latter-day member of the Wrecking Crew, he performed on guitar, bass, keyboards, and backing vocals with John Lennon, Cher, Dion DiMucci, Darlene Love, Leonard Cohen, the Ramones, and Celine Dion, and was production coordinator for Phil Spector.

Kenneth Kubernik is the co-author of *Big Shots: The Photography of Guy Webster* (Insight Editions, 2014) and *A Perfect Haze: The Illustrated History of the Monterey International Pop Festival* (Santa Monica Press, 2011). He is currently writing a history of the iconic jazz group Weather Report.

Larry LeBlanc is a Canadian music journalist, broadcaster, and archivist, described by BBC Radio 2 DJ Bob Harris as "the glue that holds the Canadian music industry together." He was the recipient of the 2013 Walt Grealis Special Achievement Award, recognizing individuals who have made an outstanding contribution to the Canadian music industry.

Peter Lewis is perhaps best known as one of the founders of the influential band Moby Grape. The singer-songwriter and guitarist is the youngest of two sons by award-winning actress Loretta Young and producer Thomas Lewis. He has released three solo albums on the Taxim label and is still an active performer and recording artist.

Nils Lofgren formed his first band, Grin, in 1968, and then contributed to Neil Young's landmark albums *After the Gold Rush* (1970) and *Tonight's the Night* (1975). In 1984, he joined Bruce Springsteen's E Street Band. He has also performed with Ringo Starr's All-Starr Band and released a number of well-received solo albums.

Dewey Martin (1940–2009) played drums for Buffalo Springfield. He held the rhythm together while that formidable frontline reinvented the wheel.

Elliot Mazer is best known for his engineering, mixing, and record productions with Neil Young, Bob Dylan, the Band, and Linda Ronstadt. He also designed the world's first all-digital recording studio.

Jim Messina was a second engineer at Sunset Sound where he worked behind the console for the Doors, Lee Michaels and Buffalo Springfield, a band he joined as bassist. He went on to cofound the pioneering country rock outfit Poco and later teamed with Kenny Loggins as the duo Loggins and Messina. Messina has continued to release solo albums.

Ralph Molina is best known as the drummer for Crazy Horse. In his 2012 memoir *Waging Heavy Peace: A Hippie Dream*, Neil Young praised Molina's "sympathy to improvisation," which, along with Billy Talbot's "simplicity, soul, and aggression," gives Crazy Horse a rock-solid rhythm section.

Bill Mumy is an actor/songwriter/writer/producer/musician who has been making music for even longer than Neil Young. His latest album is *Ten Days* (2015), and he is currently completing a group project with Vicki Peterson and John Cowsill, which also features the late Rick Rosas on bass.

Bill Munson, a researcher of and authority on Canadian popular music and culture, served as an advisor on the acclaimed *Yonge Street: Toronto Rock & Roll Stories* documentary.

Graham Nash is a two-time Rock and Roll Hall of Fame inductee—with Crosby, Stills & Nash and with the Hollies. He was also inducted into the Songwriter's Hall of Fame twice, as a solo artist and with CSN. In 2013, he published his autobiography *Wild Tales: A Rock & Roll Life* (Crown/Archetype).

Jack Nitzsche (1937–2000) was a multi-instrumentalist, arranger, songwriter, producer, and movie composer. He became known as Phil Spector's arranger and conductor and also contributed to recordings by artists such as the Rolling Stones, the Monkees, Ricky Nelson, Marianne Faithfull, Barbra Streisand, Sonny & Cher, the Neville Brothers, Captain Beefheart, and, of course, Neil Young.

Andrew Loog Oldham is a record producer, music manager, and author. In 1963 he discovered the Rolling Stones, whom he managed and produced from 1963 to 1967. He is the author of several acclaimed memoirs and in 2014 he was inducted into the Rock and Roll Hall of Fame in the non-performer category.

Bruce Palmer (1946–2004) was the bassist in Buffalo Springfield. His playing was, according to Neil Young, the signature voice in the band. Like a Duck Dunn or Jim Fielder, he provided the ballast that kept the band in focus.

Don Randi is a keyboardist/arranger and longtime member of the famed Wrecking Crew studio musicians, known particularly for working with producer Phil Spector. He recorded with Buffalo Springfield and on Neil Young's debut solo album.

Robbie Robertson was the lead guitarist and main songwriter for the Band. He has gone on to a successful career as a solo artist, actor, and composer of film music, including for Martin Scorsese's *Raging Bull* (1980).

Johnny Rogan has written more than twenty books including biographies of Neil Young, the Byrds, CSNY, the Smiths, Van Morrison, and Ray Davies. He is currently completing the second volume of his Byrds biography, *Requiem for the Timeless*.

Linda Ronstadt began her singing career in the mid-1960s with the folk-rock group the Stone Poneys. Over the last five decades she has sold millions of albums, toured the world, and appeared on stage and screen. She has sung on several Neil Young albums, including *Harvest* (1972) and *Harvest Moon* (1992).

Rick Rosas (1949–2014) worked extensively with Neil Young, Johnny Rivers, CSNY, the reformed Buffalo Springfield, and Pegi Young. He was the owner of Smartso Digital Studio.

Stan Ross (1928–2011) was the cofounder, with David S. Gold, of the legendary Gold Star Studios in Los Angeles.

Lorne Saifer is a Canadian music manager and label executive. Having managed Neil Young's early band the Squires, he went on to hold positions at Portrait and Alfa Records, as well as managing the solo career of Guess Who lead singer, Burton Cummings.

Frank Sampedro has been a member of Crazy Horse since 1975. Known for his thick-stringed Gibson Les Paul, he has been seen as a catalyst in Crazy Horse's transition from a jam band into a more heavy-rocking unit. He also worked for many years on the *Tonight Show with Jay Leno* under bandleader Kevin Ubanks, running the ensemble MIDI board.

Kirk Silsbee writes about jazz and culture from Southern California. Some of his music writing is archived on the Rock's Back Pages website, and he can be read in *Downbeat*, the *Glendale News-Press*, *Jewish Journal*, *Los Angeles Downtown News*, *Treats!* and the Artsmeme website.

Gary Stewart is a former senior Vice President of Rhino Records. Later he worked in catalogue and repertoire development at iTunes from 2004 to 2007. He subsequently cofounded the Trunkworthy website—shining a much-deserved spotlight on relevant popular culture.

Stephen Stills is a true "Southern Man," born in the Lone Star state. This gifted guitarist, singer, and songwriter was a driving force behind Buffalo Springfield and Crosby, Stills & Nash (and occasionally Young).

Brian Stone, with former partner, Charlie Greene, has been a publicist, talent scout, music publisher, artist manager, and occasional record producer. The pair's discoveries and stable of recording artists include Sonny & Cher, Buffalo Springfield, Dr. John, and Iron Butterfly.

Billy Talbot has been Crazy Horse's bassist since the band was founded in the late 1960s. In 2004, he formed the Billy Talbot Band before joining forces with Ralph Molina, George Whitsell, and Ryan Holzer to form the band Wolves.

Roy Trakin is a pop culture critic, pop and rock music aficionado, published author (having written biographies of Tom Hanks, Jim Carrey, and Sting), and former online talk-show host.

He writes for Grammy.com, Addicted to Noise, and his own weekly Trakin Care of Business blog.

Jeff Tweedy is an American songwriter, singer and producer, who has fronted various alt country bands including Uncle Tupelo, Loose Fur, Golden Smog, Tweedy, and, most notably, Wilco.

Ian Tyson is a Canadian singer-songwriter whose "Four Strong Winds" has reached anthem status in that country. He was inducted into the Canadian Country Music Hall of Fame in 1989. In 2015, he released the album *Carnero Vaquero*.

Eddie Vedder is the front man of Pearl Jam. The band's debut album, *Ten* (1991), helped to trigger Seattle's grunge movement and Pearl Jam are still touring and recording today.

Daniel Weizmann is a writer whose work has appeared in the *Jewish Journal*, *Guardian*, *Glendale News-Press*, and several books including *Drinking with Bukowski* (2000), *Israel Short Stories* (2011), and Harvey Kubernik's *Turn Up the Radio!* (2014).

Jerry Wexler (1917–2008) was an inspirational record producer, A&R genius, and co-head of Atlantic Records. A former reporter for *Billboard*, he invented the term "rhythm and blues" during his stint at the trade magazine.

Nurit Wilde is a Los Angeles–based photographer whose music photography has been featured in many books and magazines.

Jonathan Wilson is a producer and singer-songwriter. As well as producing Father John Misty, Conor Oberst, and Dawes, he has also released two critically acclaimed records of his own, *Gentle Spirit* (2011) and *Fanfare* (2013). He owns and operates Fivestar Studios in Los Angeles.

Sharry Wilson is a lifelong Neil Young fan who has contributed numerous articles to *Broken Arrow*, the quarterly magazine of the Neil Young Appreciation Society. Published in 2014, *Young Neil: The Sugar Mountain Years* (www.youngneil.com) is her first book.

Steve Wynn began his recording career in 1982 as a founding member of the Dream Syndicate. He has since released more than twenty-five records and played more than 3,000 shows. (www.stevewynn.net)

Ritchie Yorke has been a widely syndicated rock music commentator and broadcaster for more than fifty years. He has written books on Led Zeppelin, Van Morrison, John Lennon, the history of rock 'n' roll, and the Canadian rock music scene. (www.ritchieyorke.com)

Discography

By John Einarson

THE SQUIRES

SINGLES

September 1963: "The Sultan"/"Aurora"

BUFFALO SPRINGFIELD

STUDIO ALBUMS

Buffalo Springfield 1966

Recorded at Gold Star Recording Studio and Columbia Recording Studio in Hollywood

Produced by Charlie Greene and Brian Stone

Personnel
- Neil Young: guitar, piano, harmonica, vocals
- Stephen Stills: guitar, piano, vocals
- Richie Furay: guitar, vocals
- Bruce Palmer: bass
- Dewey Martin: drums, vocals

Cover art
- Design: Sandy Dvore
- Photography: Ivan Nagy

Tracks
"Go and Say Goodbye" (Stills)
"Sit Down, I Think I Love You" (Stills)
"Leave" (Stills)
"Nowadays Clancy Can't Even Sing" (Young)
"Hot Dusty Roads" (Stills)
"Everybody's Wrong" (Stills)
"Flying on the Ground Is Wrong" (Young)
"Burned" (Young)
"Do I Have to Come Right Out and Say It" (Young)
"Baby Don't Scold Me" (Stills)
"Out of My Mind" (Young)
"Pay the Price" (Stills)

Release dates
December 5, 1966 (US/Canada)/
January 1967 (UK)

Label and catalogue numbers
US/Canada: ATCO 33-200
UK: Atlantic 587070

Highest chart position on release
US 80

Notes
"Baby Don't Scold Me" was replaced by "For What It's Worth" for the April 1967 rerelease of the album following the success of the hit single.

The album was reissued in the UK in 1973 under the title *The Beginning* (Atlantic K30028).

The contract signed with managers Greene and Stone stipulated that the pair should also produce the group's recordings; however, they were not experienced producers. Consequently, the overall sound of the album was flat and muddy with the bass in particular barely audible, a result that disappointed the group. The album boasted all original material, Stills providing seven songs and Young five. Furay's lone track, "My Kind of Love," was cut in favor of Young's "Flying on the Ground Is Wrong." Furay sang three of Young's compositions on the album because the latter lacked confidence in his voice.

With the addition of "For What It's Worth" in the spring of 1967, the album sold some 150,000 copies.

Buffalo Springfield Again 1967

Recorded at Atlantic Studios, New York and in Hollywood at Gold Star Recording Studio, United Recording, Sunset Sound, and Columbia Recording Studios

Produced by Charlie Greene, Brian Stone, Neil Young, Stephen Stills, Richie Furay, Dewey Martin, Ahmet Ertegun, and Jack Nitzsche

Personnel
- Neil Young: guitar, harmonica, vocals
- Stephen Stills: guitar, piano, vocals
- Richie Furay: guitar, vocals
- Bruce Palmer: bass
- Dewey Martin: drums, vocals

Additional credits
The American Soul Train from Louisiana, horns; James Burton, dobro; Charlie Chin, banjo; Merry Clayton, vocals; David Crosby, guitar, vocals; Jim Fielder, bass; Jim Gordon, drums; Brenda Holloway, vocals; Gloria Jones, vocals; Carol Kaye, bass; Shirley Matthew, vocals; Gracia Nitzsche, vocals; Jack Nitzsche, piano; Don Randi, piano & harpsichord; Chris Sarns, guitar; Russ Titelman, guitar; Bobby West, bass

Cover art
- Design: Loring Eutemey
- Illustration: Eve Babitz

Tracks
"Mr. Soul" (Young)
"A Child's Claim to Fame" (Furay)
"Everydays" (Stills)
"Expecting to Fly" (Young)
"Bluebird" (Stills)
"Hung Upside Down" (Stills)
"Sad Memory" (Furay)
"Good Time Boy" (Furay)
"Rock & Roll Woman" (Stills)
"Broken Arrow" (Young)

Release dates
November 1, 1967 (US/Canada)/
February 1968 (UK)

Label and catalogue numbers
US/Canada: ATCO 33-226-2
UK: Atlantic 588070

Highest chart position on release
US 44

Notes
The album emerged from a period of instability with Palmer busted and deported in January, replaced by several bass players before returning in late May, and Young quitting in June only to return in August. Sessions for the album began in earnest after Young's return. He brought with him an almost completed "Expecting to Fly" from solo sessions with Jack Nitzsche.

Young's "Mr. Soul" was the last production by Greene and Stone, recorded in New York in January 1967. The band subsequently fired the two as producers and later bought out their management contract. "Mr. Soul" was rejected by ATCO as a follow-up single to "For What It's Worth" because the label viewed Stills as the voice of the band. In the end it was relegated to the B-side of Stills's "Bluebird."

Last Time Around 1968

Compiled from tracks recorded between February 1967 and May 1968 at Atlantic Studios, New York and Sunset Sound and Columbia Studios in Hollywood

Produced by Jimmy Messina, Neil Young, Stephen Stills, and Richie Furay

Personnel
- Neil Young: guitar, harmonica, vocals
- Stephen Stills: guitar, piano, organ, vocals
- Richie Furay: guitar, vocals
- Bruce Palmer: bass
- Jimmy Messina: bass
- Dewey Martin: drums, vocals

Additional credits
Jimmy Carstein, drums; Stephen Davis, bass; Gary Marker, bass; Buddy Miles, drums; Jeremy Stuart, harpsichord, calliope; Rusty Young, pedal steel guitar

Cover art
– Design: Jimini Productions
– Photography: Derinda Christiansen

Tracks
"On the Way Home" (Young)
"It's So Hard to Wait" (Furay, Young)
"Pretty Girl Why" (Stills)
"Four Days Gone" (Stills)
"Carefree Country Day" (Messina)
"Special Care" (Stills)
"The Hour of Not Quite Rain"
  (Furay, Callen)
"Questions" (Stills)
"I Am a Child" (Young)
"Merry-Go-Round" (Furay)
"Uno Mundo" (Stills)
"Kind Woman" (Furay)

Release dates
July 18, 1968 (US/Canada)/
January 1969 (UK)

Label and catalogue numbers
US/Canada: ATCO 33-256
UK: ATCO 228 024

Highest chart position on release
US 42

Notes
Young had left the band in March
1968 during sessions for a third album,
recording "I Am a Child" separately
from the other members. He rejoined
in time for a final tour in April. He later
dismissed *Last Time Around*, claiming
Messina's production efforts had ruined
several tracks, particularly "On the Way
Home." Even before the album came
out he had already been formulating
a solo career.

COMPILATIONS

Retrospective

Released February 1969 (US/Canada)/
March 1969 (UK)
US/Canada: ATCO SD 33-283
UK: ATCO 228 012
Chart: US 42

Tracks
"For What It's Worth" (Stills)
"Mr. Soul" (Young)
"Sit Down, I Think I Love You"
  (Stills)
"Kind Woman" (Furay)
"Bluebird" (Stills)
"On the Way Home" (Young)
"Nowadays Clancy Can't Even Sing"
  (Young)
"Broken Arrow" (Young)
"Rock & Roll Woman" (Stills)
"I Am a Child" (Young)
"Go and Say Goodbye" (Stills)
"Expecting to Fly" (Young)

Buffalo Springfield

Released November 1973
US/Canada: ATCO SD 2-806
UK: Atlantic K 70001
Chart: DNC

Tracks
"For What It's Worth" (Stills)
"Sit Down, I Think I Love You" (Stills)
"Nowadays Clancy Can't Even Sing"
  (Young)
"Go and Say Goodbye" (Stills)
"Pay the Price" (Stills)
"Burned" (Young)
"Out of My Mind" (Young)
"Mr. Soul" (Young)
"Bluebird" (Stills)
"Broken Arrow" (Young)
"Rock & Roll Woman" (Stills)
"Expecting to Fly" (Young)
"Hung Upside Down" (Stills)
"A Child's Claim to Fame (Furay)
"Kind Woman" (Furay)
"On the Way Home" (Young)
"I Am a Child" (Young)
"Pretty Girl Why" (Stills)
"Special Care" (Stills)
"Uno Mundo" (Stills)
"In the Hour of Not Quite Rain"
  (Furay, Callen)
"Four Days Gone" (Stills)
"Questions" (Stills)

Notes
A double-album compilation notable
for including a nine-minute jam version
of "Bluebird" not to be found on any
other releases.

Buffalo Springfield (box set)

Released July 17, 2001 (US/Canada)
US/Canada: ATCO/Electra/Rhino 74324
Chart: US 194

Tracks
Disc 1
"There Goes My Babe" (Young) – (demo)
"Come On" (Stills) – (demo)
"Hello, I've Returned" (Stills, Parks)
  – (demo)
"Out of My Mind" (Young) – (demo)
"Flying on the Ground Is Wrong"
  (Young) – (demo)
"I'm Your Kind of Guy" (Young) – (demo)
"Baby Don't Scold Me" (Stills) – (demo)
"Neighbor Don't You Worry" (Stills)
  – (demo)
"We'll See" (Stills) – (demo)
"Sad Memory" (Furay) – (demo)
"Can't Keep Me Down" (Furay) – (demo)
"Nowadays Clancy Can't Even Sing"
  (Young)
"Go and Say Goodbye" (Stills)
"Sit Down, I Think I Love You" (Stills)
"Leave" (Stills)

"Hot Dusty Roads" (Stills)
"Everybody's Wrong" (Stills)
"Burned" (Young)
"Do I Have to Come Right Out and
  Say It" (Young)
"Out of My Mind" (Young)
"Pay the Price" (Stills)
"Down Down Down" (Young) – (demo)
"Flying on the Ground Is Wrong" (Young)
"Neighbor Don't You Worry" (Stills)
  – (remix)

Disc 2
"Down Down Down" (Young) – (remix)
"Kahuna Sunset" (Stills, Young)
"Buffalo Stomp (Raga)" (Furay, Kunkel,
  Stills, Young)
"Baby Don't Scold Me" (Stills) –
  (previously unreleased version)
"For What It's Worth" (Stills)
"Mr. Soul" (Young) – (previously
  unreleased version)
"We'll See" (Stills)
"My Kind of Love" (Furay)
"Pretty Girl Why" (Stills) – (remix)
"Words I Must Say" (Furay) – (demo)
"Nobody's Fool" (Furay) – (demo)
"So You've Got a Lover" (Stills) – (demo)
"My Angel" (Stills) – (demo)
"No Sun Today" (Eisner)
"Everydays" (Stills)
"Down to the Wire" (Young) –
  (previously unreleased version)
"Bluebird" (Stills)
"Expecting to Fly" (Young)
"Hung Upside Down" (Stills) – (demo)
"A Child's Claim to Fame" (Furay)
"Rock & Roll Woman" (Stills)

Disc 3
"Hung Upside Down" (Stills)
"Good Time Boy" (Furay)
"One More Sign" (Young) – (demo)
"The Rent Is Always Due" (Young)
  – (demo)
"Round and Round and Round"
  (Young) – (demo)
"Old Laughing Lady" (Young) – (demo)
"Broken Arrow" (Young)
"Sad Memory" (Furay)
"On the Way Home" (Young) – (remix)
"Whatever Happened to Saturday
  Night?" (Young) – (remix)
"Special Care" (Stills)
"Falcon Lake (Ash on the Floor)"
  (Young) – (remix)
"What a Day" (Furay)
"I Am a Child" (Young)
"Questions" (Stills)
"Merry-Go-Round" (Furay)
"Uno Mundo" (Stills)
"Kind Woman" (Furay)
"It's So Hard to Wait" (Furay, Young)
"Four Days Gone" (Stills) – (demo)

Disc 4
"For What It's Worth" (Stills)
"Go and Say Goodbye" (Stills)

"Sit Down, I Think I Love You" (Stills)
"Nowadays Clancy Can't Even Sing"
 (Young)
"Hot Dusty Roads" (Stills)
"Everybody's Wrong" (Stills)
"Flying on the Ground Is Wrong"
 (Young)
"Burned" (Young)
"Do I Have to Come Right Out and
 Say It" (Young)
"Leave" (Stills)
"Out of My Mind" (Young)
"Pay the Price" (Stills)
"Baby Don't Scold Me" (Stills)
"Mr. Soul" (Young)
"A Child's Claim to Fame" (Furay)
"Everydays" (Stills)
"Expecting to Fly" (Young)
"Bluebird" (Stills)
"Hung Upside Down" (Stills)
"Sad Memory" (Furay)
"Good Time Boy" (Furay)
"Rock & Roll Woman" (Stills)
"Broken Arrow" (Young)

Notes
Compiled by Young and his archivist
Joel Bernstein over the course of ten
years, this box set was eagerly received
by longtime fans. It offered a treasure
trove of unreleased tracks and came
with a detailed booklet. The fourth CD
contains the band's first two albums in
track order, and repeats tracks from the
first three CDs.

SINGLES

US releases unless otherwise stated.

– *July 1966*: "Nowadays Clancy Can't
 Even Sing"/"Go and Say Goodbye"
– *October 1966*: "Burned"/"Everybody's
 Wrong"
– *January 1967*: "For What It's Worth"/
 "Do I Have to Come Right Out and
 Say It"
– *June 1967*: "Bluebird"/"Mr. Soul"
– *November 1967*: "Rock & Roll
 Woman"/"A Child's Claim to Fame"
– *February 1968*: "Expecting to Fly"/
 "Everydays"
– *March 1968*: "Uno Mundo"/
 "Merry-Go-Round"
– *July 1968*: "Kind Woman"/
 "Special Care"
– *September 1968*: "On the Way
 Home"/ "Four Days Gone"
– *October 1972 (UK)*: "Bluebird"/
 "Mr. Soul"/"Rock & Roll
 Woman"/"Expecting to Fly"

NEIL YOUNG

STUDIO ALBUMS

Neil Young 1968

Recorded at Wally Heider Recording,
Sunset Sound, Sunwest Recording,
and TTG Recording, Los Angeles

Produced by David Briggs, Neil Young,
Ry Cooder, and Jack Nitzsche

Personnel
– Neil Young: guitar, piano, organ, vocals
– Merry Clayton: vocals
– Ry Cooder: guitar
– George Grantham: drums
– Brenda Holloway: vocals
– Patrice Holloway: vocals
– Gloria Jones: vocals
– Shirley Matthews: vocals
– Jimmy Messina: bass
– Jack Nitzsche: electric piano
– Gracia Nitzsche: vocals

Cover art
– Art direction: Ed Thrasher
– Portrait: Roland Diehl
– Apple Girl drawing: Lance Sterling
– Photography: Danny Kelly

Tracks
"The Emperor of Wyoming"
"The Loner"
"If I Could Have Her Tonight"
"I've Been Waiting for You"
"The Old Laughing Lady"
"String Quartet from Whiskey Boot Hill"
"Here We Are in the Years"
"What Did You Do to My Life"
"I've Loved Her So Long"
"The Last Trip to Tulsa"

Release dates
November 12, 1968 (US/Canada)/
September 1969 (UK)

Label and catalogue numbers
US/Canada: Reprise RS 6317
UK: Reprise RSLP 6317

Highest chart position on release
Did not chart (DNC)

Notes
All songs written by Neil Young except
"String Quartet from Whiskey Boot Hill"
composed by Young and Jack Nitzsche.
 Young failed to acknowledge Messina
and Grantham's playing on the album.
Both were rehearsing with Richie Furay's
post-Springfield group Poco. He later
corrected the error on his 1977 *Decade*
album notes. Young was still a reluctant
vocalist and much of his singing was
recorded line by line. The first pressing
of the album buried his vocals within

the music. In January 1969 a remixed
version of the album was released with
the vocals brought up in the mix.

Everybody Knows This Is Nowhere 1969

Recorded at Wally Heider Recording,
Los Angeles

Produced by David Briggs and Neil Young

Credited to Neil Young & Crazy Horse

Personnel
– Neil Young: vocals, guitar
Crazy Horse
– Ralph Molina: drums, vocals
– Billy Talbot: bass, vocals
– Danny Whitten: guitar, vocals

Additional credits
Robin Lane, guitar & vocals;
Bobby Notkoff, violin

Cover art
– Direction: Ed Thrasher
– Photography: Frank Bez

Tracks
"Cinnamon Girl"
"Everybody Knows This Is Nowhere"
"Round & Round (It Won't Be Long)"
"Down by the River"
"The Losing End (When You're On)"
"Running Dry (Requiem for the Rockets)"
"Cowgirl in the Sand"

Release dates
May 14, 1969 (US/Canada)/
July 1969 (UK)

Label and catalogue numbers
US/Canada: Reprise RS 6349
UK: Reprise RSLP 6349

Highest chart position on release
US 34

Notes
Young first met Crazy Horse back in
1967 when they were the Rockets.
Much of the album was recorded live
in the studio with Neil and Crazy Horse
jamming together. Extended jam songs
like "Down by the River" and "Cowgirl
in the Sand" defined Neil's sound and
style for years to come.

After the Gold Rush 1970

Recorded at Sunset Sound, Los Angeles;
Sound City, Los Angeles; and Neil's
house on Summit Drive, Topanga Canyon

Produced by David Briggs, Neil Young,
and Kendall Pacios

NEIL YOUNG: HEART OF GOLD

Personnel
- Neil Young: vocals, guitar, piano, harmonica, vibraphone
- Nils Lofgren: vocals, piano, guitar
- Ralph Molina: vocals, drums
- Jack Nitzsche: piano
- Bill Peterson: flugelhorn ("After The Gold Rush")
- Greg Reeves: bass
- Stephen Stills: vocals
- Billy Talbot: vocals, bass
- Danny Whitten: vocals, guitar

Cover art
- Design: Gary Burden
- Photography: Joel Bernstein

Additional credit
- Patches: Susan Young

Tracks
"Tell Me Why"
"After the Gold Rush"
"Only Love Can Break Your Heart"
"Southern Man"
"Till the Morning Comes"
"Oh Lonesome Me"
"Don't Let It Bring You Down"
"Birds"
"When You Dance I Can Really Love"
"I Believe in You"
"Cripple Creek Ferry"

Release date
September 19, 1970

Label and catalogue numbers
US/Canada: Reprise RS 6383
UK: Reprise RS 6383

Highest chart position on release
US 8

Notes
All songs written by Neil Young except "Oh Lonesome Me" by Don Gibson. The title song and several others were inspired by a screenplay by Dean Stockwell and Herb Berman entitled *After the Gold Rush*. The film was never made but Young kept the music. The cover photo of Young was taken outside the New York University (NYU) School of Law. His face is a reverse of the negative, a process known as solarizing. "Birds" dates back to the final months of the Buffalo Springfield and was performed by Young with the band on their last tour in April 1968. Although credited for sewing the many patches on Young's jeans on the back cover photo, wife Susan left Young the same month the album was released and filed for divorce the following month. "Southern Man" prompted Florida band Lynyrd Skynyrd to include a reference to Young in their 1974 song "Sweet Home Alabama."

The album was certified gold in November 1970 and ranked third on the *The Top 100 Canadian Albums*.

Harvest 1972

Recorded at Quadrafonic Studios, Nashville; Barking Town Hall, London; Broken Arrow Studio #2, Woodside, CA; and UCLA's Royce Hall, Los Angeles

Produced by Elliot Mazer, Neil Young, Jack Nitzsche, and Henry Lewy

Personnel
- Neil Young: vocals, guitar, piano, harmonica
The Stray Gators
- Ken Buttrey: drums
- Tim Drummond: bass
- Ben Keith: pedal steel guitar
- Jack Nitzsche: piano, slide guitar

Additional credits
David Crosby, vocals; John Harris, piano; Teddy Irwin, guitar; London Symphony Orchestra conducted by David Meecham; James McMahon, piano; Graham Nash, vocals; Linda Ronstadt, vocals; Stephen Stills, vocals; James Taylor, banjo, guitar & vocals

Cover art
- Design: Tom Wilkes
- Photography: Joel Bernstein

Tracks
"Out on the Weekend"
"Harvest"
"A Man Needs a Maid"
"Heart of Gold"
"Are You Ready for the Country?"
"Old Man"
"There's a World"
"Alabama"
"The Needle and the Damage Done"
"Words (Between the Lines of Age)"

Release date
February 1, 1972

Label and catalogue numbers
US/Canada: Reprise MS 2032
UK: Reprise K 54005

Highest chart position on release
US 1

Notes
All songs by Neil Young. *Harvest* mixed solo acoustic tracks with orchestrated tracks and had a country music leaning. Ben Keith had never heard of Young when he was invited to play on sessions in Nashville. He would go on to become a close friend, stalwart sideman, and collaborator for the next four decades.

On the Beach 1974

Recorded at Broken Arrow Ranch, Redwood City, CA and Sunset Sound, Hollywood

Produced by Neil Young, David Briggs, Mark Harman, and Al Schmidt

Personnel
- Neil Young: vocals, guitar, banjo, piano, harmonica, bass (as Joe Yankee)
- Tim Drummond: bass
- Ben Keith: pedal steel guitar, slide guitar, piano, organ, percussion, bass, vocals
- Ralph Molina: drums, vocals

Additional credits
David Crosby, guitar; Rick Danko, bass; Levon Helm; drums; Rusty Kershaw, slide guitar & fiddle; Graham Nash, electric piano; Billy Talbot, bass; George Whitsell, guitar

Cover art
- Design: Gary Burden for R. Twerk
- Photography: Bob Seideman
- Lettering: Rick Griffin

Tracks
"Walk On"
"See the Sky About to Rain"
"Revolution Blues"
"For the Turnstiles"
"Vampire Blues"
"On the Beach"
"Motion Pictures"
"Ambulance Blues"

Release date
July 19, 1974

Label and catalogue numbers
US/Canada: Reprise R 2180
UK: Reprise K 54014

Highest chart position on release
US 16

Notes
All songs by Neil Young. Released just prior to CSNY's massive 1974 stadium tour (the so-called "Doom Tour"), this dark, confessional album underlined Young's status as the most compelling songwriter of the quartet.

The second installment in his so-called "Ditch Trilogy" (after the live album *Time Fades Away*), *On the Beach* was partly inspired by his crumbling relationship with girlfriend Carrie Snodgress. Young addresses his folkie past in "Ambulance Blues," the Manson murders in "Revolution Blues," critics in "Walk On," and greedy concert promoters in "For the Turnstiles."

Tonight's the Night 1975

Recorded at Studio Instrument Rentals (SIR), Hollywood; Fillmore East, New York; Broken Arrow Ranch, Redwood City, CA

Produced by Neil Young, David Briggs, Tim Mulligan, and Elliot Mazer

Personnel
- Neil Young: guitar, harmonica, piano, vibes, vocals
The Santa Monica Flyers
- Ben Keith: pedal steel guitar, slide guitar, vocals
- Nils Lofgren: guitar, piano, vocals
- Ralph Molina: drums, vocals
- Billy Talbot: bass, vocals

Additional credits
Kenny Buttrey, drums; Tim Drummond, bass; Jack Nitzsche, piano; Danny Whitten, guitar & vocals

Cover art
- Design: Gary Burden for R. Twerk

Tracks
"Tonight's the Night"
"Speakin' Out"
"World on a String"
"Borrowed Tune"
"Come On Baby Let's Go Downtown"
"Mellow My Mind"
"Roll Another Number"
"Albuquerque"
"New Mama"
"Lookout Joe"
"Tired Eyes"
"Tonight's the Night – Part II"

Release date
June 20, 1975

Label and catalogue numbers
US/Canada: Reprise R 2180
UK: Reprise K 54014

Highest chart position on release
US 25

Notes
All songs by Neil Young except "Come On Baby Let's Go Downtown" by Danny Whitten. Inspired by the drug deaths of Crazy Horse guitarist Whitten and CSNY roadie Bruce Berry (brother of Jan Berry of Jan & Dean), the album is an aural wake for two fallen comrades. Young and his band would drink excessive amounts of tequila before turning on the tape recorder and several songs are first takes. It's an unpolished gem that Young fans often cite as his crowning achievement. He called the recording style "audio vérité," a warts-and-all approach. "Come On Baby Let's Go Downtown" was recorded back in March 1970 at a Neil Young & Crazy Horse concert at the Fillmore East (a recording of the full concert was later released as part of Young's Archives series) and features Whitten on vocals and guitar with Young. Most of the album was recorded in one long session at SIR on August 26, 1973.

Zuma 1975

Recorded at Broken Arrow Ranch, Redwood City, CA and Point Dume, CA

Produced by Neil Young and David Briggs

Credited to Neil Young & Crazy Horse

Personnel
- Neil Young: guitar, vocals
Crazy Horse
- Ralph Molina: drums, vocals
- Frank Sampedro: guitar, vocals
- Billy Talbot: bass, vocals

Additional credits
David Crosby, vocals; Rick Danko, bass; Tim Drummond, bass; Levon Helm, drums; Russ Kunkel, congas; Graham Nash, electric piano; Stephen Stills, bass, vocals

Cover art
- Design and artwork: James Mazzeo
- Lettering: Rick Griffin

Tracks
"Don't Cry No Tears"
"Danger Bird"
"Pardon My Heart"
"Lookin' for a Love"
"Barstool Blues"
"Stupid Girl"
"Drive Back"
"Cortez the Killer"
"Through My Sails"

Release date
November 10, 1975

Label and catalogue numbers
US/Canada: Reprise MS 2242
UK: Reprise K 54057

Highest chart position on release
US 25

Notes
All songs by Neil Young. A more upbeat offering after the "Ditch Trilogy" of *Time Fades Away*, *On the Beach*, and *Tonight's the Night*. "Don't Cry No Tears" is a rewrite of the old Squires song "I Wonder" which was recorded in Winnipeg in 1964 (and released on *Archives Vol. 1* in 2009). "Cortez the Killer" was banned from airplay in Spain but remains one of Young's most popular live electric songs. "Through My Sails" dates from the aborted 1974 CSNY *Human Highway* album sessions.

American Stars 'n Bars 1977

Recorded at Quadrafonic Studios, Nashville; Wally Heider Recording, Los Angeles; Broken Arrow Ranch, Redwood City, CA; Indigo Recording Studio, Malibu, CA

Produced by Neil Young, David Briggs (with Tim Mulligan), and Elliot Mazer

Personnel
- Neil Young: guitar, harmonica, vocals
- Tim Drummond: bass
- Karl Himmel: drums
- Ben Keith: pedal steel guitar, dobro, vocals
- Carole Mayedo: violin
- Ralph Molina: drums, vocals
- Frank Sampedro: guitar, stringman
- Billy Talbot: bass, vocals
The Saddlebags
- Emmylou Harris: vocals
- Nicolette Larson: vocals
- Linda Ronstadt: vocals

Cover art
- Design: Tom Wilkes

Tracks
"The Old Country Waltz"
"Saddle Up the Palomino"
"Hey Babe"
"Hold Back the Tears"
"Bite the Bullet"
"Star of Bethlehem"
"Will to Love"
"Like a Hurricane"
"Homegrown"

Release date
May 27, 1977

Label and catalogue numbers
US/Canada: Reprise MSK 2261
UK: Reprise K 54088

Highest chart position on release
US 21

Notes
All songs by Neil Young. The five straight out country music tracks (the first five tracks) were recorded in one long session with Linda Ronstadt and Nicolette Larson in Nashville. The rest of the songs run the gamut from a grungy rock jam inspired by a drunken night at a local bar ("Like a Hurricane") to acoustic folk and country rock.

Comes a Time 1978

Recorded at Triad Recording, Fort Lauderdale, FL; Columbia Recording Studio, London; Wally Heider Recording, Los Angeles; Woodland Sound Studios and Sound Shop, Nashville; Broken Arrow Ranch, Redwood City, CA

Produced by Neil Young, Ben Keith, Tim Mulligan, and David Briggs

Personnel
– Neil Young: guitar, harmonica, vocals
Gone with the Wind Orchestra
– Bucky Barret: guitar
– George Binkley: strings
– Grant Boatright: guitar
– J. J. Cale: electric guitar
– Marvin Chantry: strings
– Roy Christensen: strings
– Virginia Christensen: strings
– John Christopher: guitar
– Tim Drummond: bass
– Ray Edenton: guitar
– Rita Fey: autoharp
– Steve Gibson: guitar
– Carl Goroditzky: strings
– Larry Harvin: strings
– Maryanna Harvin: strings
– Karl Himmel: drums
– Vic Jordan: guitar
– Ben Keith: pedal steel guitar
– George Kosmola: strings
– Shelly Kurland: strings
– Nicolette Larson: vocals
– Larry Lasson: strings
– Larrie Londin: drums
– Rebecca Lynch: strings
– Martha McCrory: strings
– Farrell Morris: percussion
– Spooner Oldham: piano
– Joe Osborne: bass
– Dale Sellers: guitar
– Jerry Shook: guitar
– Steve Smith: strings
– Rufus Thibodeaux: fiddle
– Gary Vanosdale: strings
– Carol Walker: strings
– Stephanie Woolf: strings

Additional credits
Ralph Molina, drums, vocals; Tim Mulligan, saxophone; Frank Sampedro, guitar, vocals; Billy Talbot, bass, vocals

Cover art
– Direction: Tom Wilkes
– Photography: Coley Coleman

Tracks
"Goin' Back"
"Comes a Time"
"Look Out for My Love"
"Peace of Mind"
"Lotta Love"
"Human Highway"
"Already One"
"Field of Opportunity"
"Motorcycle Mama"
"Four Strong Winds"

Release date
October 21, 1978

Label and catalogue numbers
US/Canada: Reprise 2266
UK: Reprise K 54099

Highest chart position on release
US 7

Notes
All songs by Neil Young except "Four Strong Winds" by Ian Tyson. "Human Highway" was originally intended as the title for the aborted 1974 CSNY reunion album. Unhappy with the original mix and track order, Young purchased the first pressing, some 200,000 copies, and used them as shingling on one of his barns. He remixed the album for release.

Rust Never Sleeps 1979

Recorded at the Boarding House, San Francisco; Civic Center, St. Paul; Nichols Arena, Denver; Cow Palace, San Francisco; Triad Recording, Fort Lauderdale; Woodland Studios, Nashville; Broken Arrow Ranch, Redwood City, CA

Produced by Neil Young, David Briggs, and Tim Mulligan

Credited to Neil Young & Crazy Horse

Personnel
– Neil Young: guitar, vocals
Crazy Horse
– Ralph Molina: drums, vocals
– Frank Sampedro: guitar, stringman, vocals
– Billy Talbot: bass, vocals

Additional credits
Gone with the Wind Orchestra
Karl Himmel, drums; Nicolette Larson, vocals; Joe Osborne, bass

Cover art
– Design: Tom Wilkes

Tracks
"My My, Hey Hey (Out of the Blue)"
"Thrasher"
"Ride My Llama"
"Pocahontas"
"Sail Away"
"Powderfinger"
"Welfare Mothers"
"Sedan Delivery"
"Hey Hey, My My (Into the Black)"

Release date
June 22, 1979

Label and catalogue numbers
US/Canada: Reprise 2295
UK: Reprise Reprise K 54105

Highest chart position on release
US 8

Notes
All songs by Neil Young except "My My, Hey Hey (Out of the Blue)" co-written with Jeff Blackburn. Technically a live album (minus crowd noise) recorded at several venues and overdubbed later. The first half of the album is mostly Young recorded solo at San Francisco's Boarding House, while the second half is recorded with Crazy Horse. "Sail Away" is a leftover from the *Comes a Time* sessions. Jeff Blackburn was a San Francisco singer-songwriter formerly in Blackburn & Snow. He and Young teamed up in a short-lived Santa Cruz bar band named the Ducks. "Thrasher" is a pointed shot at CSNY.
    Rust Never Sleeps was awarded Album of the Year by *Rolling Stone* magazine, which also named Young as their Male Vocalist of the Year.

Hawks & Doves 1980

Recorded at Quadrafonic Studios, Nashville; Village Recorders, Los Angeles; Indigo Recording, Malibu; Triad Recording, Fort Lauderdale; Gold Star Recording, Los Angeles

Produced by Neil Young, David Briggs, Tim Mulligan, and Elliot Mazer

Personnel
– Neil Young: guitar, piano, vocals
– Dennis Belfield: bass
– Tim Drummond: bass
– Levon Helm: drums
– Ben Keith: pedal steel guitar, dobro, vocals
– Ann Hillary O'Brien: vocals
– Frank Sampedro: guitar, stringman, vocals
– Tom Scribner: saw
– Rufus Thibodeaux: fiddle
– Greg Thomas: drums

Cover art
Uncredited

Tracks
"Little Wing"
"The Old Homestead"
"Lost in Space"
"Captain Kennedy"
"Stayin' Power"
"Coastline"

"Union Man"
"Comin' Apart at Every Nail"
"Hawks & Doves"

Release date
October 29, 1980

Label and catalogue numbers
US/Canada: Reprise 2297
UK: Reprise K 54109

Highest chart position on release
US 30

Notes
All songs by Neil Young. On the original vinyl release, side one, "Doves," was acoustic folk in style, while side two, "Hawks," was country rock with a flag-waving, working man's theme to the tracks.

Misunderstood by fans at the time, *Hawks & Doves* was Young's poorest-selling album to date. In his defense, much of Young's time was spent coming to terms with the diagnosis of his recently born son Ben's severe cerebral palsy.

Re-ac-tor 1981

Recorded at Modern Recorders, Redwood City, CA

Produced by Neil Young, David Briggs, Tim Mulligan, and Jerry Napier

Credited to Neil Young & Crazy Horse

Personnel
– Neil Young: guitar, keyboards, synclavier, vocals
Crazy Horse
– Ralph Molina: drums, vocals
– Frank Sampedro: guitar, keyboards, vocals
– Billy Talbot: bass, vocals

Cover art
– Direction and design: Simon Levy

Tracks
"Opera Star"
"Surfer Joe and Moe the Sleaze"
"T-Bone"
"Get Back on It"
"Southern Pacific"
"Motor City"
"Rapid Transit"
"Shots"

Release date
October 28, 1981

Label and catalogue numbers
US/Canada: Reprise 2304
UK: Reprise K 54116

Highest chart position on release
US 27

Notes
All songs by Neil Young. Young's last album in his first spell with Reprise was again the product of a distracted artist. The 24/7 regimen required for Ben took its toll and the album seemed unfocused, listless, and sloppy. Young's attempts at embracing current sounds and styles was laudable but unsatisfactory. The bizarre Latin inscription on the back cover is the Serenity Prayer used by Alcoholics Anonymous in their Twelve Step program.

Trans 1982

Recorded at Modern Recorders, Redwood City, CA and Commercial Recorders, Honolulu

Produced by Neil Young, David Briggs, and Tim Mulligan

Personnel
– Neil Young: guitar, keyboards, vocoder, vocals
– Ben Keith: pedal steel guitar
– Joe Lala: percussion
– Nils Lofgren: guitar, vocals
– Ralph Molina: drums, vocals
– Bruce Palmer: bass
– Frank Sampedro: guitar, keyboards, vocals
– Billy Talbot: bass, vocals

Cover art
– Design: Tommy Steele/Art Hotel
– Front cover art: Barry Jackson
– Back cover art: Tetsu Nishi
– Photography: Moshe Brakha

Tracks
"Little Thing Called Love"
"Computer Age"
"We R in Control"
"Transformer Man"
"Computer Cowboy (aka Syscrusher)"
"Sample and Hold"
"Mr. Soul"
"Like an Inca"

Release date
December 29, 1982

Label and catalogue numbers
US/Canada: Geffen 2018
UK: Geffen GEF 25019

Highest chart position on release
US 75

Notes
All songs by Neil Young. *Trans* finds Young heavily influenced by the electronic music of German group Kraftwerk. His voice on many of the tracks is processed through a vocal synthesizer known as a vocoder, the idea coming from his attempts to communicate with his son Ben. *Trans* saw Young reuniting with Buffalo Springfield bass player Bruce Palmer.

Everybody's Rockin' 1983

Recorded at Modern Recorders, Redwood City, CA

Produced by Neil Young and Elliot Mazer

Credited to Neil Young & the Shocking Pinks

Personnel
– Neil Young: guitar, piano, harmonica, vocals
The Shocking Pinks
– Larry Byrom: piano, vocals
– Anthony Crawford: vocals
– Tim Drummond: double bass
– Karl Himmel: snare drum
– Ben "King" Keith: alto sax, guitar
– Rick Palombi: vocals

Cover art
– Design: Tommy Steele/Art Hotel
– Photography and hand tinting: Dennis Keeley
– Inner sleeve hand tinting: Rebecca Keeley

Additional credit
Dedicated to Pegi and Alex

Tracks
"Betty Lou's Got a New Pair of Shoes"
"Rainin' in My Heart"
"Payola Blues"
"Wonderin'"
"Kinda Fonda Wanda"
"Jellyroll Man"
"Bright Lights, Big City"
"Cry, Cry, Cry"
"Mystery Train"
"Everybody's Rockin'"

Release date
July 27, 1983

Label and catalogue numbers
US/Canada: Geffen 4013
UK: Geffen GEF 25590

Highest chart position on release
US 46

Notes
All songs by Neil Young except "Betty Lou's Got a New Pair of Shoes" by Bobby Freeman, "Rainin' in My Heart" by James Moore and Jerry West,

"Bright Lights, Big City" by Jimmy Reed, "Mystery Train" by Sam Phillips and Herman Parker Jr., and "Kinda Fonda Wanda," which Young co-wrote with Tim Drummond. Young had planned to release a country-tinged album after the vocoder adventures of *Trans*, but this idea was rejected by label boss David Geffen, who demanded that he come up instead with some "rock 'n' roll." Young took him more literally than he had intended in deciding to record this authentic-sounding rockabilly album. The result is surprisingly good if an odd turn for Young. It bewildered fans and infuriated Geffen, who sued Young for creating "unrepresentative" music.

Old Ways 1985

Recorded at House of David Recorders, Nashville; the Castle, Franklin, TN; Pedernales Recording Studio, Spicewood, TX; and live at the Opry, Austin, TX

Produced by Neil Young, Ben Keith, David Briggs, and Elliot Mazer

Personnel
– Neil Young: guitar, banjo, harmonica, vocals
– Joe Allen: bass
– Grant Boatwright: guitar
– Johnny Christopher: guitar
– Anthony Crawford: mandolin, vocals
– Denise Draper: vocals
– Tim Drummond: bass
– Ray Edenton: guitar
– Bela Fleck: banjo
– Carl Gorodetzky: violin
– Karl Himmel: drums
– Waylon Jennings: guitar, vocals
– Ben Keith: pedal steel guitar, dobro
– David Kirby: guitar
– Terry McMillan: harmonica, Jew's harp
– Ralph Mooney: pedal steel guitar
– Farrell Morris: percussion
– Willie Nelson: guitar, vocals
– Spooner Oldham: piano, vocals, strings
– Joe Osborne: bass
– Hargus "Pig" Robbins: piano
– Gove Scrivenor: autoharp
– Marty Stuart: mandolin
– Gordon Terry: fiddle
– Rufus Thibodeaux: fiddle
– Bobby Thompson: banjo

Additional credits
George Binkley, strings; John Borg, strings; Larry Byrom, vocals; Roy Christensen, strings; Virginia Christensen, strings; Doana Cooper, vocals; Gail Davies, vocals; Charles Everett, strings; Carl Goroditzby, strings; Mark Hambree, strings; Betsy Hammer, vocals; Larry Harvin, strings; Mary Ann Kennedy, vocals; Lee Larrison, strings; Larry Lasson, strings; Betty McDonald, strings; Kristine Oliver-Arnold, vocals; Janis Oliver-Gill, vocals; Rick Palombi, vocals; Pam Rose, vocals; Pamela Sixfin, strings; Mark Tanner, strings; David Vanderkooi, strings; Gary Vanosdale, strings; Carol Walker, strings; Leona Williams, vocals; Stephanie Woolf, strings

Cover art
– Design: Tommy Steele
– Photography: Dennis Keeley

Tracks
"The Wayward Wind"
"Get Back to the Country"
"Are There Any More Real Cowboys?"
"Once an Angel"
"Misfits"
"California Sunset"
"Old Ways"
"My Boy"
"Bound for Glory"
"Where Is the Highway Tonight?"

Release date
August 12, 1985

Label and catalogue numbers
US/Canada: Geffen 24068
UK: Geffen GEF 26377

Highest chart position on release
US 75

Notes
All songs by Neil Young except "The Wayward Wind" by Stan Lebowsky and Herbert Newman. *Old Ways* derives from the country-influenced project rejected by David Geffen after *Trans*. Young then went back to the drawing board and created an out-and-out country album, recruiting Waylon Jennings and Willie Nelson for added authenticity. "The Wayward Wind" is a cover of the 1956 Gogi Grant hit that Young claimed was a favorite from his childhood. "California Sunset" was taken from a live performance at the Opry in Austin for *Austin City Limits*.

Landing on Water 1986

Recorded at Broken Arrow Ranch, Woodside, CA and Record One, Los Angeles

Produced by Neil Young and Danny Kortchmar

Personnel
– Neil Young: guitar, synthesizer, vocals
– Steve Jordan: drums
– Danny Kortchmar: guitar, synthesizer, vocals

Additional credit
San Francisco Boys Choir

Cover art
– Art direction: Neil Young (as Bernard Shakey)
– Photography: Laura LiPuma

Tracks
"Weight of the World"
"Violent Side"
"Hippie Dream"
"Bad News Beat"
"Touch the Night"
"People on the Street"
"Hard Luck Stories"
"I Got a Problem"
"Pressure"
"Drifter"

Release date
July 21, 1986

Label and catalogue numbers
US/Canada: Geffen 24109
UK: Geffen 924 109-1

Highest chart position on release
US 58

Notes
All songs by Neil Young. An attempt at a contemporary 1980s synthesizer-influenced sound that, again, frustrated fans. Several songs were salvaged from aborted Neil Young & Crazy Horse sessions and revamped using synthesizers.

Life 1987

Recorded November 18–19, 1986 at the Universal Amphitheatre, Hollywood and Record One, Los Angeles

Produced by Neil Young, David Briggs, and Jack Nitzsche

Credited to Neil Young & Crazy Horse

Personnel
– Neil Young: guitar, keyboards, harmonica, vocals
Crazy Horse
– Ralph Molina: drums, vocals
– Frank Sampedro: guitar, keyboards, vocals
– Billy Talbot: bass, vocals

Cover art
– Design and direction: Norman Moore
– Photography: Phillip Dixon, Al Seib/ *Los Angeles Times*

Tracks
"Mideast Vacation"
"Long Walk Home"
"Around the World"

"Inca Queen"
"Too Lonely"
"Prisoners of Rock 'n' Roll"
"Cryin' Eyes"
"When Your Lonely Heart Breaks"
"We Never Danced"

Release date
June 30, 1987

Label and catalogue numbers
US/Canada: Geffen 24154
UK: Geffen WX 108

Highest chart position on release
US 75

Notes
All songs by Neil Young. The commercial nadir of the Geffen years, *Life* was Young's final album for the label before he rejoined Reprise.

This Note's for You 1988

Recorded at Studio Instrument Rentals (SIR) Stage 6, Los Angeles using the Record Plant remote truck; the Omni, Oakland, CA; and Redwood Digital, San Francisco

Produced by Neil Young and Niko Bolas (The Volume Dealers)

Credited to Neil Young & the Bluenotes

Personnel
– Neil Young: guitar, vocals
– Tom Bray: trumpet
– Claude Cailliet: trombone
– Larry Cragg: baritone saxophone
– Chad Cromwell: drums
– John Fumo: trumpet
– Ben Keith: alto saxophone
– Steve Lawrence: tenor saxophone
– Rick Rosas: bass

Additional credits
Ralph Molina, drums; Steve Onuska, tambourine; George Whitsell, bass

Cover art
– Design: Glenn Parsons
– Photography: Bob Scott, Christine Cragg

Tracks
"Ten Men Workin'"
"This Note's for You"
"Coupe de Ville"
"Life in the City"
"Twilight"
"Married Man"
"Sunny Inside"
"Can't Believe Your Lyin'"
"Hey Hey"
"One Thing"

Release date
April 11, 1988

Label and catalogue numbers
US/Canada: Reprise 25719
UK: Reprise 925 719-1

Highest chart position on release
US 61

Notes
All songs by Neil Young. With renewed vigor, Young presented Reprise with a lively album of original R&B-flavored songs backed by an entirely new band featuring a six-piece horn section. Inspired by a bluesy jam with the reunited Squires at Winnipeg's funky Blue Note Café in June 1987, Young set about assembling a big band. The title track became a surprise hit single, reaching number nineteen. In addition, although initially banned by MTV, the promo for the song, which lampooned the commercialization of rock music, ended up winning the station's Video of the Year. A live double album by the band was recorded but not released. Two of the tracks, "Ain't It the Truth" (an old Squires song) and "This Note's for You," were included on Geffen's 1993 compilation *Lucky Thirteen*.

Eldorado 1989

Recorded at the Hit Factory, New York

Produced by Neil Young and Niko Bolas (The Volume Dealers)

Credited to Neil Young & the Restless

Personnel
– Neil Young: guitar, vocals
– Chad Cromwell: drums
– Rick Rosas: bass

Cover art
– Art direction: Neil Young
– Design: Diane Painter
– Cover assemblage: George Herms
– Photography: Glenn Viguers
– Creative consultant: James Mazzeo

Tracks
"Cocaine Eyes"
"Don't Cry"
"Heavy Love"
"On Broadway"
"Eldorado"

Release date
April 17, 1989 (Japan and Australia)

Label and catalogue number
Japan: Reprise 20P2 2651
Australia: Reprise 25919-1

Highest chart position on release
Released only in Japan and Australia

Notes
All songs written by Neil Young except "On Broadway" by Barry Mann, Cynthia Weil, Jerry Leiber, and Mike Stoller. A five-track EP CD taken from sessions for the aborted *Times Square* album, *Eldorado* takes Young almost into heavy metal territory with loud, crunchy guitars and manic vocals.

Freedom 1989

Recorded at the Barn-Redwood Digital, Broken Arrow Ranch, Woodside, CA; the Hit Factory, New York; and live at Jones Beach, New York

Produced by Neil Young and Niko Bolas (The Volume Dealers)

Personnel
– Neil Young: guitar, vocals
– Chad Cromwell: drums
– Ben Keith: pedal steel guitar, keyboards, alto saxophone, vocals
– Linda Ronstadt: vocals
– Rick Rosas: bass
– Frank Sampedro: guitar

Additional credits
Tommy Bray, trumpet; Claude Cailliet, trombone; Larry Cragg, baritone saxophone; John Fumo, trumpet; Steve Lawrence, tenor saxophone

Cover art
– Design and direction: Gary Burden for R. Twerk
– Package development: Don Brown
– Photography: Ebet Roberts

Tracks
"Rockin' in the Free World" (live)
"Crime in the City (Sixty to Zero Pt. I)"
"Don't Cry"
"Hangin' on a Limb"
"Eldorado"
"The Ways of Love"
"Someday"
"On Broadway"
"Wrecking Ball"
"No More"
"Too Far Gone"
"Rockin' in the Free World"

Release date
October 2, 1989

Label and catalogue numbers
US/Canada: Reprise 25899
UK: Reprise 925 889-1

Highest chart position on release
US 35

Notes

All songs written by Neil Young except "On Broadway" by Barry Mann, Cynthia Weil, Jerry Leiber, and Mike Stoller. *Freedom* captures the zeitgeist as exemplified by the collapse of the Berlin Wall and the Iron Curtain. "Rockin' in the Free World" became a metal-influenced anthem. Like *Rust Never Sleeps* a decade before, the album is bookended by an acoustic and a raucous electric version of the same song. Several tracks were from the aborted *Times Square* sessions in New York, while others date back to the Bluenotes. Young ended what was a very confusing decade on a high note.

Ragged Glory 1990

Recorded at Plywood Digital, Woodside, CA and at the Hoosier Dome, Indianapolis, IN

Produced by Neil Young and David Briggs

Credited to Neil Young & Crazy Horse

Personnel
- Neil Young: guitar, harmonica, vocals
Crazy Horse
- Ralph Molina: drums, vocals
- Frank Sampedro: guitar, vocals
- Billy Talbot: bass, vocals

Cover art
- Design and direction: Janet Levinson
- Photography: Larry Cragg

Tracks
"Country Home"
"White Line"
"F*!#in' Up"
"Over and Over"
"Love to Burn"
"Farmer John"
"Mansion on the Hill"
"Days That Used to Be"
"Love and Only Love"
"Mother Earth (Natural Anthem)"

Release date
September 9, 1990

Label and catalogue numbers
US/Canada: Reprise 26315
UK: Reprise 7599-26315-1

Highest chart position on release
US 31

Notes

All songs written by Neil Young except "Farmer John" by Don Harris and Dewey Terry (Don & Dewey). A fine return to form for Young and Crazy Horse with a sound that harkened back to the glory days of *Everybody Knows This Is Nowhere* and *Zuma*. Recorded over a couple of days without overdubs, just raw and ragged. Young stated that he was inspired to get back to basics after working on his Archives box set. This would be the album that anointed Young as the "Godfather of Grunge" in the eyes of a whole new generation of rockers weaned on Nirvana et al. "F*!#in' Up" is a personal statement by Young while "Mother Earth (Natural Anthem)," recorded live and solo, became a show-closing anthem.

Harvest Moon 1992

Recorded at Redwood Digital, Woodside, CA and live at the Portland Auditorium, Portland, Oregon; strings overdubbed at Sunset Sound, Hollywood

Produced by Neil Young and Ben Keith (production assistant: Joel Bernstein)

Personnel
- Neil Young: vocals, guitar, banjo-guitar, piano, pump organ, vibraphone
The Stray Gators
- Kenny Buttrey: drums
- Larry Cragg: vocals
- Tim Drummond: bass, marimba, broom
- Ben Keith: vocals, pedal steel guitar, dobro, bass marimba
- Nicolette Larson: vocals
- Spooner Oldham: piano, pump organ, keyboards
- Linda Ronstadt: vocals
- James Taylor: vocals
- Astrid Young: vocals

Additional credit
Jack Nitzsche: string arrangement ("Such a Woman")

Cover art
- Direction: Janet Levinson and Joel Bernstein
- Design: Janet Levinson
- Painting: Rebecca Holland
- Photography: Joel Bernstein and Larry Cragg

Tracks
"Unknown Legend"
"From Hank to Hendrix"
"You and Me"
"Harvest Moon"
"War of Man"
"One of These Days"
"Such a Woman"
"Old King"
"Dreamin' Man"
"Natural Beauty"

Release date
November 2, 1992

Label and catalogue numbers
US/Canada: Reprise 45057
UK: Reprise 9362 – 45057-2

Highest chart position on release
US 16

Notes

All songs written by Neil Young. The album bears the dedication "For Pegi" and many of the songs are paeans to his wife, including "Unknown Legend," "You and Me," "Harvest Moon," and "Such a Woman." "Natural Beauty" was recorded live at Portland Auditorium with overdubs at Redwood Digital. The album marked the return to Young's inner circle of several stalwarts from the *Harvest* period such as Ben Keith, Kenny Buttrey, Tim Drummond, and Jack Nitzsche, hence the naming of the band after the original *Harvest* group. The album was certified platinum in February 1993 (double platinum in 1997). Critics hailed the return of Young's mellow country-folk sound. *Harvest Moon* earned the 1993 Juno Award for Album of the Year from the Canadian Academy of Recording Arts and Sciences (CARAS).

Sleeps with Angels 1994

Recorded at the Complex Studios, Los Angeles

Produced by Neil Young and David Briggs

Credited to Neil Young & Crazy Horse

Personnel
- Neil Young: guitar, piano, accordion, flute, harmonica, vocals
Crazy Horse
- Ralph Molina: drums, vocals
- Frank Sampedro: guitar, keyboards, vocals
- Billy Talbot: bass, vibes, vocals

Cover art
- Design and direction: Elan Soltes and Jessica Narkunski/FX design

Tracks
"My Heart"
"Prime of Life"
"Driveby"
"Sleeps with Angels"
"Western Hero"
"Change Your Mind"
"Blue Eden"
"Safeway Cart"
"Train of Love"
"Trans Am"
"Piece of Crap"
"A Dream That Can Last"

Release date
August 6, 1994

Label and catalogue numbers
US/Canada: Reprise 45749
UK: Reprise 9362-45749-1

Highest chart position on release
US 9

Notes
All songs written by Neil Young except "Blue Eden" co-written with Molina, Sampedro and Talbot. Much of this album was recorded before Nirvana's Kurt Cobain committed suicide; however, when Cobain cited Young's lyrics from "My My, Hey Hey (Out of the Blue)" in his suicide note, Young was devastated. The title song was written as a tribute soon after, which further endeared Young to the grunge crowd. A dark and brooding album and Young's last with producer David Briggs.

Mirror Ball 1995

Recorded at Bad Animals, Seattle
Produced by Brendan O'Brien

Personnel
– Neil Young: guitar, pump organ, vocals
– Jeff Ament: bass
– Stone Gossard: guitar
– Jack Irons: drums
– Mike McCready: guitar
– Brendan O'Brien: guitar, piano, vocals
– Eddie Vedder: vocals

Cover art
– Design and direction: Gary Burden for R. Twerk
– Photography: Henry Diltz
– Mosaic portrait: Joel Bernstein

Tracks
"Song X"
"Act of Love"
"I'm the Ocean"
"Big Green Country"
"Truth Be Known"
"Downtown"
"What Happened Yesterday"
"Peace and Love"
"Throw Your Hatred Down"
"Scenery"
"Fallen Angel"

Release date
June 27, 1995

Label and catalogue numbers
US/Canada: Reprise 45934
UK: Reprise 9362-45934-1

Highest chart position on release
US 5

Notes
All songs written by Neil Young. Recorded in two marathon sessions at Heart's Bad Animals studio with backing by leading grunge rockers Pearl Jam who had to be credited individually for contract reasons. Young regarded it as "a challenge" to attempt recording with younger players. The band offered him a different sound and solid backing although Young's sound remains dominant. Some of the song themes explore the differences between 1960s and 1990s ideals. Pearl Jam (minus lead singer Eddie Vedder) later backed Young on tour in support of the album. Both earned credibility by associating with the other although this would be a one-off experiment. The album was nominated for a Grammy award.

Broken Arrow 1996

Recorded at Plywood Digital, Woodside, CA and live at Old Princeton Landing, Princeton-by-the-Sea, CA

Produced by Neil Young

Credited to Neil Young with Crazy Horse

Personnel
– Neil Young: guitar, piano, harmonica, vocals
Crazy Horse
– Ralph Molina: drums, percussion, vocals
– Frank Sampedro: guitar, vocals
– Billy Talbot: bass, tambourine, vocals

Cover art
– Design and direction: Gary Burden
– Front cover: George Catlin
– Back cover: K.P.O.B.
– Band photo: Larry Cragg

Tracks
"Big Time"
"Loose Change"
"Slip Away"
"Changing Highways"
"Scattered (Let's Think About Livin')"
"This Town"
"Music Arcade"
"Baby What You Want Me to Do"
"Interstate"

Release date
July 2, 1996

Label and catalogue numbers
US/Canada: Reprise 46291
UK: Reprise 9362-46291-2

Highest chart position on release
US 31

Notes
All songs written by Neil Young except "Baby What You Want Me to Do" by Jimmy Reed, recorded live on an audience tape recorder during a gig at Old Princeton Landing on March 21, 1996. "Interstate" was available only on the vinyl version of the album. One reviewer termed the album "directionless" and wondered why it was even recorded.

Silver & Gold 2000

Recorded at Redwood Digital, Woodside, CA with additional recording at Arlyn Studios, Austin, TX

Produced by Neil Young and Ben Keith

Personnel
– Neil Young: guitar, piano, harmonica, vocals
– Donald "Duck" Dunn: bass
– Ben Keith: pedal steel guitar, vocals
– Jim Keltner: drums
– Spooner Oldham: piano, organ

Additional credits
Oscar Butterworth, drums; Emmylou Harris, vocals; Linda Ronstadt, vocals

Cover art
– Design and direction: Gary Burden and Jenice Heo for R. Twerk
– Photography: Amber Young, Pegi Young

Tracks
"Good to See You"
"Silver & Gold"
"Daddy Went Walkin'"
"Buffalo Springfield Again"
"The Great Divide"
"Horseshoe Man"
"Red Sun"
"Distant Camera"
"Razor Love"
"Without Rings"

Release date
April 25, 2000

Label and catalogue numbers
US/Canada: Reprise 47305
UK: Reprise 9362-47305-2
Highest chart position on release
US 22

Notes
All songs by Neil Young. A mellower album than recent Young releases, eschewing the grungy guitar excursions for a laidback funk. "Silver & Gold" and "Razor Love" date back to the 1980s, while the other songs are more recent.

Are You Passionate? 2002

Recorded at the Site, Marin County, CA and Toast, San Francisco

Produced by Neil Young and Booker T. Jones with Donald "Duck" Dunn and Frank Sampedro

Personnel
- Neil Young: guitar, piano, vocals
- Tom Bray: trumpet
- Donald "Duck" Dunn: bass
- Booker T. Jones: organ, vibes, vocals
- Ralph Molina: drums, vocals
- Steve Potts: drums, bongos, tambourine
- Frank Sampedro: guitar, vocals
- Billy Talbot: bass, vocals
- Astrid Young: vocals
- Pegi Young: vocals

Cover art
- Design and direction: Gary Burden, Jenice Heo
- Photography: Neil Young (as Joe Yankee), Gary Burden

Tracks
"You're My Girl"
"Mr. Disappointment"
"Differently"
"Quit (Don't Say You Love Me)"
"Let's Roll"
"Are You Passionate?"
"Goin' Home"
"When I Hold You in My Arms"
"She's a Healer"
"Be with You"
"Two Old Friends"

Release date
April 9, 2002

Label and catalogue numbers
US/Canada: Reprise 48111
UK: Reprise 9 48111-2

Highest chart position on release
US 10

Notes
All songs by Neil Young. "Goin' Home" was recorded February 8, 2000 with Crazy Horse at Toast, San Francisco. The rest of the tracks were recorded with the nucleus of Booker T. & the M.G.s, who also toured with Young to promote the album. They gave the tracks the light soul feel that Young sought. "Let's Roll" was inspired by events on September 11, 2001 and, in particular, the heroism of passengers on United Airlines Flight 93 who were able to overcome their hijackers and crash the plane before it could strike any strategic targets.

Greendale 2003

Recorded at Plywood Analog studios, Woodside, CA

Produced by Neil Young and L. A. Johnson

Credited to Neil Young & Crazy Horse

Personnel
- Neil Young: guitar, organ, harmonica, vocals
Crazy Horse
- Ralph Molina: drums, vocals
- Billy Talbot: bass, vocals
The Mountainettes
- Twink Brewer: vocals
- Nancy Hall: vocals
- Sue Hall: vocals
- Pegi Young: vocals

Tracks
"Falling From Above"
"Double E"
"Devil's Sidewalk"
"Leave the Driving"
"Carmichael"
"Bandit"
"Grandpa's Interview"
"Bringin' Down Dinner"
"Sun Green"
"Be the Rain"

Release date
August 19, 2003

Label and catalogue numbers
US/Canada: Reprise 48533
UK: Reprise 9 48533-2

Highest chart position on release
US 22

Notes
All songs by Neil Young. *Greendale* was Young's first "rock opera." It was staged as complete piece including sets and props. The album/CD included a live bonus DVD of a solo concert in Dublin called *Live at Vicar St.* A *Greendale* film was later directed by Young and released on DVD. Crazy Horse guitarist Frank Sampedro was asked to sit out the sessions because Young felt the music required only one guitar.

Prairie Wind 2005

Recorded at Masterlink Studios, Nashville

Produced by Ben Keith and Neil Young

Personnel
- Neil Young: guitar, piano, harmonica, vocals
- Chad Cromwell: drums, percussion
- Karl Himmel: drums, percussion
- Ben Keith: dobro, pedal steel, slide guitar
- Spooner Oldham: piano, Hammond B3 organ, Wurlitzer electric piano
- Rick Rosas: bass

Additional credits
Grant Boatwright, acoustic guitar & backing vocals; Chuck Cochran, string arranger; Anthony Crawford, backing vocals; Diana DeWitt, backing vocals; Fisk University Jubilee Choir directed by Paul Kwami; Clinton Gregory, fiddle; Emmylou Harris, backing vocals; Wayne Jackson, horns; Thomas McGinley, horns; Gary Pigg, backing vocals; Curtis Wright, backing vocals; Pegi Young, backing vocals

Cover art
- Design and direction: Gary Burden and Jenice Heo for R. Twerk
- Photography: L. A. Johnson, Larry Cragg

Tracks
"The Painter"
"No Wonder"
"Falling Off the Face of the Earth"
"Far from Home"
"It's a Dream"
"Prairie Wind"
"Here for You"
"This Old Guitar"
"He Was the King"
"When God Made Me"

Release date
September 27, 2005

Label and catalogue numbers
US/Canada: Reprise 49494
UK: Reprise 9 49494-2

Highest chart position on release
US 11

Notes
All songs by Neil Young. The album bears a dedication to Young's father, Scott, who passed away in June 2005 after suffering from Alzheimer's disease. Young debuted the entire album live at the Ryman Auditorium in Nashville over two concerts on August 18 and 19, 2005. The shows were filmed by Oscar-winning director Jonathan Demme (and produced by Tom Hanks's Playtone Productions) for the feature-length documentary *Neil Young: Heart of Gold*, which was released in February 2006. Many of the songs reflect on the theme of mortality—not only had he recently lost his father but Young also suffered a mild brain aneurysm and had surgery in March 2005, just weeks before the sessions began.

Living with War 2006

Recorded at Redwood Digital Studios, Woodside, CA and Capitol Recording Studios, Hollywood

Produced by Neil Young and Niko Bolas (The Volume Dealers) with assistance from L. A. Johnson

Personnel
- Neil Young: guitar, piano, harmonica, vocals
- Tom Bray: trumpet
- Chad Cromwell: drums, percussion
- Rick Rosas: bass

Additional credit
100-voice choir under the direction of Darrell Brown

Cover art
- Design and direction: Gary Burden and Jenice Heo for R. Twerk
- Photography: L. A. Johnson, Larry Cragg

Tracks
"After the Garden"
"Living with War"
"The Restless Consumer"
"Shock and Awe"
"Families"
"Flags of Freedom"
"Let's Impeach the President"
"Lookin' for a Leader"
"Roger and Out"
"America the Beautiful"

Release date
May 2, 2006

Label and catalogue numbers
US/Canada: Reprise 44335
UK: Reprise 9362 44335-2

Highest chart position on release
US 15

Notes
All songs by Neil Young except "America the Beautiful" written by Katherine Lee Bates and Samuel A. Ward. The album conveyed Young's fury at President George W. Bush and the ongoing conflicts in Iraq and Afghanistan after seeing photos of wounded American soldiers on the front page of a newspaper. Being a Canadian citizen, he was attacked for having no right to criticize American foreign policy (no one bothered to note that, as a US resident since 1966, Young had paid millions in taxes). During the CSNY tour that summer, some people showed their feelings about Young's overtly political stance by walking out when songs from the album were played.

Released in December 2006, *Living with War: "In the Beginning"* (Reprise 43265) contained stripped-down takes of all the songs on the original, minus "America the Beautiful." The CD came with a limited-edition DVD showing studio footage of Young and the band.

Chrome Dreams II 2007

Recorded at Feelgood's Garage, near Redwood City, CA

Produced by Neil Young and Niko Bolas (The Volume Dealers)

Personnel
- Neil Young: guitar, banjo, harmonica, piano, pump organ, vibes, percussion, vocals
- Ben Keith: pedal steel guitar, lap steel guitar, dobro, guitar, organ, vocals
- Ralph Molina: drums, percussion, vocals
- Rick Rosas: bass, vocals

Additional credits
On "Ordinary People"
Tom Bray, trumpet; Claude Cailliet, trumpet; Joe Canuck, vocals; Larry Cragg, baritone saxophone; Chad Cromwell, drums; John Fumo, trumpet; Steve Lawrence, tenor saxophone & keyboards; Frank Sampedro, guitar

Background singers
- *The Wyatt Earps*: Ben Keith, Ralph Molina, Neil Young
- *The Jane Wyatts*: Nancy Hall, Annie Stocking, Pegi Young
- *The Dirty Old Men*: Larry Cragg, Ben Keith, Ralph Molina, Rick Rosas, Neil Young
- *The Way Choir*: The Young People's Chorus of New York (Francisco J. Núñez, Artistic Director/Founder, Elizabeth Núñez, Conductor)

Cover art
- Design and direction: Gary Burden and Jenice Heo for R. Twerk
- Photography: Anthony Crawford, Larry Cragg

Tracks
"Beautiful Bluebird"
"Boxcar"
"Ordinary People"
"Shining Light"
"The Believer"
"Spirit Road"
"Dirty Old Man"
"Ever After"
"No Hidden Path"
"The Way"

Release date
October 23, 2007

Label and catalogue numbers
US/Canada: Reprise 311932
UK: Reprise 9362-49917-1

Highest chart position on release
US 11

Notes
All songs by Neil Young. The "II" in the album's title refers to a *Chrome Dreams* album Young conceived and recorded tracks for in 1977 before scrapping it in favor of *American Stars 'n Bars*. "Beautiful Bluebird" was first recorded in 1985 for *Old Ways*. "Boxcar" dates from the aborted *Times Square* album sessions in 1988, while the eighteen-minute epic "Ordinary People" also dates from this period and was a major crowd-pleaser whenever Young played it live. Much of the album was recorded live in the studio. The album was also released as a double vinyl album.

Fork in the Road 2009

Recorded at Legacy Studios, New York City and Rak Studios, London

Produced by Neil Young and Niko Bolas (The Volume Dealers)

Personnel
- Neil Young: guitar, vocals
- Anthony Crawford: guitar, piano, organ, vocals
- Chad Cromwell: drums
- Ben Keith: lap steel guitar, guitar, organ, vocals
- Rick Rosas: bass
- Pegi Young: vibes, guitar, vocals

Cover art
- Design and direction: Gary Burden and Jenice Heo for R. Twerk
- Cover photos: courtesy of Shakey Pictures
- Inside photo: L. A. Johnson

Tracks
"When Worlds Collide"
"Fuel Line"
"Just Singing a Song"
"Johnny Magic"
"Cough Up the Bucks"
"Get Behind the Wheel"
"Off the Road"
"Hit the Road"
"Light a Candle"
"Fork in the Road"

Release date
April 7, 2009

Label and catalogue numbers
US/Canada: Reprise 518040
UK: Reprise 9362-49787-2

Highest chart position on release
US 19

Notes
All songs by Neil Young. The album's theme draws from Young's recent experiments with an electric automobile, LincVolt, and America's doomed dependence on oil and gas.

Le Noise 2010

Recorded at Daniel Lanois's home studio in Silver Lake, Los Angeles

Produced by Daniel Lanois

Personnel
- Neil Young: guitar, vocals

Cover art
- Design and direction: Gary Burden and Jenice Heo for R. Twerk
- Photography: Adam C. K. Vollick

Tracks
"Walk with Me"
"Sign of Love"
"Someone's Gonna Rescue You"
"Love and War"
"Angry World"
"Hitchhiker"
"Peaceful Valley Boulevard"
"Rumblin'"

Release date
September 28, 2010

Label and catalogue numbers
US/Canada: Reprise 525956-2
UK: Reprise 9362-49618-6

Highest chart position on release
US 14

Notes
All songs by Neil Young. What began as an acoustic album transformed into a solo electric tour de force with Lanois applying his characteristic dark sonic ambience to Young's personal songs. Sessions were interrupted for several weeks after Lanois was hospitalized following a motorcycle accident. "Hitchhiker" is the first song to address Young's drug use over the decades.

Americana 2012

Recorded at Audio Casa Blanca, Broken Arrow Ranch, Redwood City, CA

Produced by Neil Young, John Hanlon, and Mark Humphreys

Credited to Neil Young with Crazy Horse

Personnel
- Neil Young: guitar, vocals
Crazy Horse
- Ralph Molina: drums, vocals
- Frank Sampedro: guitar, vocals
- Billy Talbot: bass, vocals

Additional credits
Americana Choir directed by Darrell Brown; Dan Greco, orchestral cymbals & tambourine; Stephen Stills, vocals; Pegi Young, vocals

Cover art
- Design and direction: Gary Burden and Jenice Heo for R. Twerk
- Original cover art: Tom Wilkes (photographed by Hannah Johnson)
- Back cover: Frontier wagons image courtesy of Washington State Historical Society
- Crazy Horse logo: Rebecca Holland
- Inside jacket: Montage of F. F. Palmer painting "Across the Continent: Westward the Course of Empire Takes Its Way"
- "Freedom of Speech" flag painting: Jenice Heo
- Liner notes: Neil Young

Tracks
"Oh Susannah" (Stephen Collins Foster; Arrangement: Tim Rose)
"Clementine" (Traditional; Arrangement: Young)
"Tom Dula" (Traditional; Arrangement: Young)
"Gallows Pole" (Traditional; Arrangement: Odetta Felious Gordon)
"Get a Job" (Richard Lows/Earl Beal/Raymond Edwards/William Horton)
"Travel On" (Traditional; Arrangement: Paul Clayton/Larry Ehrlich/David Lazar/Tom Six)
"High Flyin' Bird" (Billy Edd Wheeler)
"Jesus' Chariot (She'll Be Coming Round the Mountain)" (Traditional; Arrangement: Young)
"This Land Is Your Land" (Woody Guthrie)
"Wayfarin' Stranger" (Traditional; Arrangement: Burl Ives)
"God Save the Queen" (Thomas Augustine Arne; Medley arrangement: Young)

Release date
June 5, 2012

Label and catalogue numbers
US/Canada: Reprise 531195-2
UK: Reprise 9362-49508-5

Highest chart position on release
US 4

Notes
While writing the first volume of his autobiography, *Waging Heavy Peace*,

Young realized that his brief experiment with rocking up traditional folk songs back in 1965 in Canada had never been recorded. Suitably inspired, and after delving into the history of each of the songs, he convened Crazy Horse and banged out the tracks for the album pretty much live off the studio floor in a couple of days. The album received mixed reviews.

Psychedelic Pill 2012

Recorded at Audio Casa Blanca, Broken Arrow Ranch, Redwood City, CA and Lava Tracks, Kamuela, HI

Produced by Neil Young, John Hanlon, and Mark Humphreys

Credited to Neil Young & Crazy Horse

Personnel
- Neil Young: guitar, pump organ, stringman, whistling, vocals
Crazy Horse
- Ralph Molina: drums, vocals
- Frank Sampedro: guitar, vocals
- Billy Talbot: bass, vocals

Additional credit
Dan Greco: tambourine, bell

Cover art
- Design and direction: Gary Burden and Jenice Heo for R. Twerk
- Pill illustration: Lori Anzalone
- Photography: Russ Avarella

Tracks
"Driftin' Back"
"Psychedelic Pill"
"Ramada Inn"
"Born in Ontario"
"Twisted Road"
"She's Always Dancing"
"For the Love of Man"
"Walk Like a Giant"
"Psychedelic Pill" (alt mix)

Release date
October 30, 2012

Label and catalogue numbers
US/Canada: Reprise 531980-2
UK: Reprise 9362-49485-9

Highest chart position on release
US 8

Notes
All songs written by Neil Young. The double album marks a return to Young's longer jam songs with Crazy Horse. "Driftin' Back" clocks in at over twenty-seven minutes while "Ramada Inn" and "Walk Like a Giant" both run for over

sixteen minutes each. The album emerged from jam sessions immediately following the *Americana* sessions.

A Letter Home 2014

Recorded at Third Man Records, Nashville

Produced by Jack White and Neil Young

Personnel
- Neil Young: guitar, harmonica, piano, vocals
- Jack White: guitar, piano, vocals

Cover art
- Design and direction: Gary Burden and Jenice Heo for R. Twerk
- Hand lettering: Julian Baker
- Photography: Will Mitchell, Jo McGaughey

Tracks
"A Letter Home Intro"
"Changes" (Phil Ochs)
"Girl from the North Country" (Bob Dylan)
"Needle of Death" (Bert Jansch)
"Early Morning Rain" (Gordon Lightfoot)
"Reason to Believe" (Tim Hardin)
"On the Road Again" (Willie Nelson)
"If You Could Read My Mind" (Gordon Lightfoot)
"Since I Met You Baby" (Ivory Joe Hunter)
"My Hometown" (Bruce Springsteen)
"I Wonder If I Care as Much" (Don and Phil Everly)

Release date
April 22, 2014

Label and catalogue numbers
US/Canada: Third Man Records TMR 245/Reprise 2-541532
UK: Reprise 9362-49399-9

Highest chart position on release
US 13

Notes
A bizarre experiment even for Young, the album was recorded in Jack White's refurbished 1947 Voice-O-Graph direct-to-vinyl recording booth. This gave the tracks an old-timey, scratchy quality. Two spoken intros find Young sending a message to his long dead mother, Rassy.

Storytone 2014

Recorded at Capitol Studios, Hollywood, CA; Sony Scoring Stage, Hollywood; and East West Studios, Hollywood

Produced by Neil Young and Niko Bolas (The Volume Dealers)

Personnel
- Neil Young: guitar, vocals
- Chris Walden: arrangements, orchestration, conducting, and co-producing
- Michael Bearden: arrangements, conducting and co-producing
- Patrick Russ: orchestrations

Cover art
- Design and direction: Gary Burden and Jenice Heo for R. Twerk
- Cover Painting: Neil Young
- Photography: Garth Lenz

Tracks
"Plastic Flowers"
"Who's Gonna Stand Up?"
"I Want to Drive My Car"
"Glimmer"
"Say Hello to Chicago"
"Tumbleweed"
"Like You Used to Do"
"I'm Glad I Found You"
"When I Watch You Sleeping"
"All Those Dreams"

Release date
November 4, 2014

Label and catalogue numbers
US/Canada: Reprise 546105-2
UK: Reprise 9362-49324-0

Highest chart position on release
US 33

Notes
Young recorded the tracks both solo and orchestrated, offering both versions on one double album. *Storytone* is his thirty-ninth Top Forty album, which puts him in seventh place on the all-time list, just ahead of Elton John (who has thirty-eight).

The Monsanto Years 2015

Recorded at the Teatro Theatre, Oxnard, CA

Produced by Neil Young and John Hanlon

Credited to Neil Young and Promise of the Real

Personnel
- Neil Young: guitar, vocals
Promise of the Real
- Anthony Logerfo: drums
- Corey McCormick: bass
- Tato Melgar: percussion
- Lukas Nelson: guitar, vocals

Additional credit
Micah Nelson: guitar

Cover art
- Design and direction: Gary Burden and Jenice Heo for R. Twerk

Tracks
"A New Day for Love"
"Wolf Moon"
"People Want to Hear about Love"
"Big Box"
"A Rock Star Bucks a Coffee Shop"
"Workin' Man"
"Rules of Change"
"Monsanto Years"
"If I Don't Know"

Release date
June 30, 2015

Notes
Young invited Willie Nelson's sons Lukas and Micah to join him for a set-closing "Rockin' in the Free World" at Farm Aid in September 2014 and four months later they, and Lukas's band Promise of the Real (named after a lyric in the *On the Beach* track "Walk On"), were recording with him. *The Monsanto Years* expresses Young's concern at the influence of the agribusiness giant.

The package also included a DVD containing footage of the album being recorded at the historic Teatro Theatre.

LIVE ALBUMS

Time Fades Away 1973

Recorded at UCLA's Royce Hall, Los Angeles; Public Hall, Cleveland; Myriad, Oklahoma City; Seattle Coliseum, Seattle; San Diego Sports Arena, San Diego; Phoenix Coliseum, Phoenix; and Memorial Auditorium, Sacramento

Produced by Elliot Mazer and Neil Young

Personnel
- Neil Young: vocals, guitar, piano, harmonica, bass (as Joe Yankee)
The Stray Gators
- Johnny Barbata: drums
- Ken Buttrey: drums
- Tim Drummond: bass
- Ben Keith: pedal steel guitar
- Jack Nitzsche: piano, slide guitar

Additional credits
David Crosby, guitar & vocals; Graham Nash, guitar & vocals

Cover art
- Design: Tom Wilkes

Tracks
"Time Fades Away"
"Journey through the Past"
"Yonder Stands the Sinner"
"L.A."
"Love in Mind"
"Don't Be Denied"
"The Bridge"
"Last Dance"

Release date
October 15, 1973

Label and catalogue numbers
US/Canada: Reprise MS 22151
UK: Reprise K 54010

Highest chart position on release
US 22

Notes
All songs by Neil Young. Recorded during Young's first major arena tour, which was plagued by excessive volume, extortionate money demands from his band, and the loss of his voice part way through. David Crosby and Graham Nash were enlisted to help shore up his vocals. All songs on the album were brand new and received mixed reaction from audiences. The B-side of the "Times Fades Away" single is a rare live version of "Last Trip to Tulsa" recorded with Crazy Horse. One of only two Neil Young albums not released on CD (the other is *Journey through the Past*). Young has stated he does not wish to relive the nightmarish

experience of that tour by releasing the album on CD.

Live Rust 1979

Recorded between October 4 and 22, 1978 at the Boston Gardens, Chicago Stadium, the Civic Center, St. Paul, McNichols Arena, Denver, and San Francisco's Cow Palace.

Produced by Neil Young (as Bernard Shakey), David Briggs, and Tim Mulligan

Credited to Neil Young & Crazy Horse

Personnel
- Neil Young: guitar, keyboards, harmonica, vocals
Crazy Horse
- Ralph Molina: drums, vocals
- Frank Sampedro: guitar, keyboards, vocals
- Billy Talbot: bass, vocals

Cover art
Uncredited

Tracks
"Sugar Mountain"
"I Am a Child"
"Comes a Time"
"After the Gold Rush"
"My My, Hey Hey (Out of the Blue)"
"When You Dance I Can Really Love"
"The Loner"
"The Needle and the Damage Done"
"Lotta Love"
"Sedan Delivery"
"Powderfinger"
"Cortez the Killer"
"Cinnamon Girl"
"Like a Hurricane"
"Hey Hey, My My (Into the Black)"
"Tonight's the Night"

Release date
November 14, 1979

Label and catalogue numbers
US/Canada: Reprise 2-2296
UK: Reprise K 64041

Highest chart position on release
US 15

Notes
All songs by Neil Young except "My My, Hey Hey (Out of the Blue)" co-written with Jeff Blackburn. Soundtrack to Young's feature film *Rust Never Sleeps*. Double live album recorded during Young's 1978 Rust Never Sleeps tour, which employed giant amplifier and microphone props as well as roadies dressed as *Star Wars* Ewok characters scurrying about the stage.

Weld 1991

Recorded live at various venues between February and April 1991

Produced by Neil Young and David Briggs

Credited to Neil Young & Crazy Horse

Personnel
- Neil Young: guitar, harmonica, vocals
Crazy Horse
- Ralph Molina: drums, vocals
- Frank Sampedro: guitar, keyboards, vocals
- Billy Talbot: bass, vocals

Cover art
- Design and direction: Rebecca Holland
- Photography: Joel Bernstein, Larry Cragg

Tracks
"Hey Hey, My My (Into the Black)"
"Crime in the City"
"Blowin' in the Wind"
"Welfare Mothers"
"Love to Burn"
"Cinnamon Girl"
"Mansion on the Hill"
"F*!#in' Up"
"Cortez the Killer"
"Powderfinger"
"Love and Only Love"
"Rockin' in the Free World"
"Like a Hurricane"
"Farmer John"
"Tonight's the Night"
"Roll Another Number"

Release date
October 23, 1991

Label and catalogue numbers
US/Canada: Reprise 26671
UK: Reprise 7599-26671-2

Highest chart position on release
US 154

Notes
All songs written by Neil Young except "Blowin' in the Wind" by Bob Dylan and "Farmer John" by Don Harris and Dewey Terry (Don & Dewey). Coming off the critical and commercial success of *Ragged Glory*, the Smell the Horse tour was a major triumph for Young and the album captures the shows in all their glory. One critic termed the double album "the soundtrack to the Gulf War" which was going on at the time. *Weld* was available as a double-disc set or as a limited edition three-disc set with the inclusion of *Arc*, an album of feedback noises recorded on the tour.

Unplugged 1993

Recorded February 7, 1993 at Universal Studios, Universal City, CA

Produced by David Briggs

Personnel
- Neil Young: guitar, harmonica, piano, pump organ, vocals
- Oscar Butterworth: drums
- Larry Cragg: broom
- Tim Drummond: bass
- Ben Keith: dobro
- Nicolette Larson: vocals
- Nils Lofgren: guitar, autoharp, accordion, vocals
- Spooner Oldham: piano, organ
- Astrid Young: vocals

Cover art
- Design and direction: Janet Levinson
- Photography: Joel Bernstein

Tracks
"The Old Laughing Lady"
"Mr. Soul"
"World on a String"
"Pocahontas"
"Stringman"
"Like a Hurricane"
"The Needle and the Damage Done"
"Helpless"
"Harvest Moon"
"Transformer Man"
"Unknown Legend"
"Look Out for My Love"
"Long May You Run"
"From Hank to Hendrix"

Release date
June 8, 1993

Label and catalogue numbers
US/Canada: Reprise 45310
UK: Reprise 9362-45310-2

Highest chart position on release
US 23

Notes
All songs written by Neil Young. The album was recorded for a March 10, 1993 broadcast of MTV's popular *Unplugged* series. "Stringman" was an unreleased song dating back to the mid-1970s. The unplugged format allowed Young to reimagine many of his best-known songs in stripped-down arrangements. The show was later released on DVD.

Year of the Horse 1997

Recorded live at various venues between May 9 and November 8, 1996.

Produced by "Horse"

Credited to Neil Young & Crazy Horse

Personnel
- Neil Young: guitar, piano, harmonica, vocals
Crazy Horse
- Ralph Molina: drums, percussion, vocals
- Frank Sampedro: guitar, keyboards, vocals
- Billy Talbot: bass, vocals

Cover art
- Design and direction: Gary Burden and Jenice Heo for R. Twerk
- Photography: Lars Larson, L. A. Johnson, Jim Jarmusch

Tracks
"When You Dance, I Can Really Love" (The Meadows, Hartford, Nov. 8)
"Barstool Blues" (The Catalyst, Santa Cruz, May 9)
"When Your Lonely Heart Breaks" (The Catalyst, Santa Cruz, May 9)
"Mr. Soul" (Shoreline Amphitheatre, Mountain View, Oct. 19)
"Big Time" (Jones Beach, Wantagh, NY, Aug. 25)
"Pocahontas" (Agridome, Regina, Oct. 26)
"Human Highway" (Shoreline Amphitheatre, Mountain View, Oct. 20)
"Slip Away" (The Forum, Los Angeles, Sept. 11)
"Scattered" (The Meadows, Hartford, Nov. 8)
"Danger Bird" (Cal Expo, Sacramento, Sept. 16)
"Prisoners" (Waldbühne, Berlin, July 9)
"Sedan Delivery" (Molson Park, Ontario, Aug. 31)

Release date
June 17, 1997

Label and catalogue numbers
US/Canada: Reprise 46652
UK: Reprise 9362-46652-2

Highest chart position on release
US 57

Notes
All songs written by Neil Young. There was also a Jim Jarmusch documentary film of the same name that followed Young and Crazy Horse on tour. This album, however, is not directly connected to the film and is not a soundtrack of the film. "Sedan Delivery" was not included on the original vinyl album release.

Road Rock Vol. I 2000

Recorded live at various venues between August 29 and October 1, 2000

Produced by Neil Young and Ben Keith

Credited to Neil Young Friends & Relatives

Personnel
- Neil Young: guitar, piano, vocals
- Donald "Duck" Dunn: bass
- Ben Keith: pedal steel guitar, vocals
- Jim Keltner: drums
- Spooner Oldham: piano, organ
- Astrid Young: vocals
- Pegi Young: vocals

Additional credit
Chrissie Hynde: guitar, vocals

Cover art
- Design and direction: Gary Burden and Jenice Heo for R. Twerk
- Photography: Danny Clinch

Tracks
"Cowgirl in the Sand" (Coors Amphitheatre, San Diego, Sept. 25)
"Walk On" (GM Place, Vancouver, Oct. 1)
"Fool for Your Love" (Santa Barbara Bowl, CA, Sept. 28)
"Peace of Mind" (GM Place, Vancouver, Oct. 1)
"Words" (GM Place, Vancouver, Oct. 1)
"Motorcycle Mama" (Coors Amphitheatre, San Diego, Sept. 25)
"Tonight's the Night" (Coors Amphitheatre, San Diego, Sept. 25)
"All Along the Watchtower" (Blossom Music Center, Cuyahoga Falls, OH, Aug. 29)

Release date
December 5, 2000

Label and catalogue numbers
US/Canada: Reprise 48306
UK: Reprise 9 48036-2

Highest chart position on release
US 22

Notes
All songs by Neil Young except "All Along the Watchtower" by Bob Dylan. This track features the Pretenders' Chrissie Hynde. "Fool for Your Love" is an unreleased song dating back to the late 1980s. A companion DVD was also released.

SOUNDTRACKS

Journey through the Past 1972

Soundtrack double album to Young's quirky, dreamlike film of the same name, featuring tracks recorded between 1967 and 1972 in various contexts, including television broadcasts with Buffalo Springfield, live recordings with Crosby, Stills, Nash & Young, and outtakes from the *Harvest* sessions

Produced by Neil Young and L. A. Johnson

Personnel
- Neil Young: vocals, guitar, piano, harmonica
- Johnny Barbata: drums
- The Beach Boys
- Ken Buttrey: drums
- David Crosby: guitar, vocals
- Tim Drummond: bass
- Richie Furay: guitar, vocals
- Ben Keith: pedal steel guitar
- Dewey Martin: drums, vocals
- Ralph Molina: drums, vocals
- Graham Nash: guitar, keyboards, vocals
- Jack Nitzsche: piano, slide guitar
- Bruce Palmer: bass
- Calvin "Fuzzy" Samuels: bass
- Stephen Stills: guitar, keyboards, vocals
- Billy Talbot: bass, vocals
- Danny Whitten: guitar, vocals

Cover art
- Design: Gamache and Gundelfinger
- Photography: Frederic Underhill

Tracks
"For What It's Worth" (Stephen Stills)
"Mr. Soul"
"Rock & Roll Woman" (Stephen Stills)
"Find the Cost of Freedom" (Stephen Stills)
"Ohio"
"Southern Man"
"Are You Ready for the Country?"
"Let Me Call You Sweetheart" (Leo Friedman and Beth Slater Whitson)
"Alabama"
"Words"
"Relativity Invitation"
"Handel's Messiah" (George Frideric Handel)
"King of Kings" (Miklós Rózsa)
"Soldier"
"Let's Go Away for Awhile" (Brian Wilson)

Release date
November 1, 1972

Label and catalogue numbers
US/Canada: Reprise 2XS 6480
UK: Reprise K 64015

Highest chart position on release
US 45

Notes
All songs by Neil Young except where noted. Critics labeled the film and soundtrack self-indulgent, a criticism Young copped to in 1975 when he claimed he made the movie for himself without a script or plan.

Dead Man 1996

Recorded at Mason St. Studios, San Francisco

Produced by Neil Young and John Hanlon

Personnel
- Neil Young: guitar, piano, organ

Cover art
- Design and direction: Gary Burden
- Photography: Jim Jarmusch, Christine Parry

Tracks
Seven instrumental tracks recorded by Young solo interspersed with movie dialogue

Release date
February 27, 1996

Label and catalogue numbers
US/Canada: Vapor 9 46171-2

Highest chart position on release
DNC

Notes
All tracks composed spontaneously by Neil Young as he sat alone in the studio with his guitar watching a rough cut of Jim Jarmusch's movie of the same name starring Johnny Depp.

COMPILATIONS

Decade

Released October 28, 1977
US/Canada: Reprise 3RS 2257
UK: Reprise K 64037
Chart: US 43

Tracks
"Down to the Wire"
"Burned"
"Mr. Soul"
"Broken Arrow"
"Expecting to Fly"
"Sugar Mountain"
"I Am a Child"
"The Loner"
"The Old Laughing Lady"
"Cinnamon Girl"
"Down by the River"
"Cowgirl in the Sand"
"I Believe in You"
"After the Gold Rush"
"Southern Man"
"Helpless"
"Ohio"
"Soldier"
"Old Man"
"A Man Needs a Maid"
"Harvest"
"Heart of Gold"
"Star of Bethlehem"
"The Needle and the Damage Done"
"Tonight's the Night"
"Tired Eyes"
"Walk On"
"For the Turnstiles"
"Winterlong"
"Deep Forbidden Lake"
"Like a Hurricane"
"Love Is a Rose"
"Cortez the Killer"
"Campaigner"
"Long May You Run"

Notes
Triple album featuring tracks from 1966 to 1977, including Buffalo Springfield, solo, Crazy Horse, and CSNY songs, individually annotated by Young on the inner sleeve. All songs written by Neil Young. Some songs were previously unreleased; "Sugar Mountain" made its first album appearance. A three-disc package may have seemed ambitious, but the album was a well-received compilation of Young's recording oeuvre and a measure of his incredible talent.

Lucky Thirteen

Released January 13, 1993
US/Canada: Geffen 24452
UK: Geffen GED 24452
Chart: DNC

Tracks
"Sample and Hold"
"Transformer Man"
"Depression Blues"
"Get Gone"
"Don't Take Your Love Away from Me"
"Once an Angel"
"Where Is the Highway Tonight?"
"Hippie Dream"
"Pressure"
"Around the World"
"Mideast Vacation"
"Ain't It the Truth"
"This Note's for You"

Notes
A compilation of tracks chosen by Young from his various Geffen albums between 1982 and 1988. All songs written by Neil Young. "Depression

Blues" is an outtake from the *Old Ways* sessions. "Get Gone" and "Don't Take Your Love Away from Me" were recorded in Dayton, OH in 1983 by the Shocking Pinks for a television special, and "Ain't It the Truth" and "This Note's for You" date from the aborted 1988 Neil Young & the Bluenotes live album.

Greatest Hits

Released November 16, 2004
US/Canada: Reprise 49494
UK: Reprise 9 49494-2
Chart: US 27

Tracks
"Down by the River"
"Cowgirl in the Sand"
"Cinnamon Girl"
"Helpless"
"After the Gold Rush"
"Only Love Can Break Your Heart"
"Southern Man"
"Ohio"
"The Needle and the Damage Done"
"Old Man"
"Heart of Gold"
"Like a Hurricane"
"Comes a Time"
"Hey Hey, My My (Into the Black)"
"Rockin' in the Free World"
"Harvest Moon"

Notes
All songs by Neil Young. With the exception of "Harvest Moon," all the tracks date from 1969 to 1979, Young's most successful years creatively and commercially. Furthermore, with the exception of the final four tracks, all had already been included on the 1977 *Decade* compilation.

ARCHIVES SERIES

Live at the Fillmore East 2006

Recorded live at the Fillmore East, New York, March 6 and 7, 1970

Produced by Paul Rothchild

Credited to Neil Young & Crazy Horse

Personnel
– Neil Young: guitar, vocals
Crazy Horse
– Ralph Molina: drums, vocals
– Jack Nitzsche: electric piano
– Billy Talbot: bass
– Danny Whitten: guitar, vocals

Cover art
– Design and direction: Gary Burden and Jenice Heo for R. Twerk
– Photography: Joel Bernstein, Joe Sia

Tracks
"Everybody Knows This Is Nowhere"
"Winterlong"
"Down by the River"
"Wonderin'"
"Come On Baby Let's Go Downtown"
"Cowgirl in the Sand"

Release date
November 14, 2006

Label and catalogue numbers
US/Canada: Reprise 44429
UK: Reprise 444992-2

Highest chart position on release
US 55

Notes
All songs by Neil Young except "Come On Baby Let's Go Downtown" by Danny Whitten. Recorded during Young's first tour with Crazy Horse. The only live recordings of Young with Whitten. The album features only the electric songs from their shows (Young played an acoustic opening set). The album is the first release in Young's Archives Performance Series.

Live at Massey Hall 1971 2007

Recorded live at Toronto's Massey Hall, January 19, 1971

Produced by David Briggs and Neil Young

Personnel
– Neil Young: guitar, harmonica, piano, vocals

Cover art
– Design and direction: Gary Burden and Jenice Heo for R. Twerk
– Photography: Wim van der Linden, David Toms, Joel Bernstein

Tracks
"On the Way Home"
"Tell Me Why"
"Old Man"
"Journey through the Past"
"Helpless"
"Love in Mind"
"A Man Needs a Maid/ Heart of Gold Suite"
"Cowgirl in the Sand"
"Don't Let It Bring You Down"
"There's a World"
"Bad Fog of Loneliness"
"The Needle and the Damage Done"
"Ohio"
"See the Sky About to Rain"
"Down by the River"
"Dance Dance Dance"
"I Am a Child"

Release date
March 13, 2007

Label and catalogue numbers
US/Canada: Reprise 43328
UK: Reprise 9362 43328-2

Highest chart position on release
US 6

Notes
All songs by Neil Young. Recorded on Young's 1970–1971 Journey through the Past solo tour, which brought him back to Canada for several shows. A number of songs are now familiar as tracks on *Harvest*, but at the time they had yet to be released, or even recorded. The release included a DVD of images and concert footage from a Dutch documentary (but no footage of the Massey Hall performance).

Sugar Mountain: Live at Canterbury House 1968 2008

Recorded live on November 9, 1968 at Canterbury House, Ann Arbor, MI

Produced by Neil Young

Personnel
– Neil Young: guitar, harmonica, vocals

Cover art
– Design and direction: Gary Burden and Jenice Heo for R. Twerk
– Archivist: Joel Bernstein
– Photography: Linda McCartney

Tracks
(Emcee intro)
"On the Way Home"
(Songwriting rap)
"Mr. Soul"
(Recording rap)
"Expecting to Fly"
"The Last Trip to Tulsa"
(Bookstore rap)
"The Loner"
("I Used to" rap)
"Birds"
"Winterlong" (excerpt) and "Out of My Mind" (intro)
"Out of My Mind"
"If I Could Have Her Tonight"
(Classical Gas rap)
"Sugar Mountain" (intro)
"Sugar Mountain"
"I've Been Waiting for You"
(Songs rap)
"Nowadays Clancy Can't Even Sing"
(Tuning rap) and "The Old Laughing Lady" (intro)
"The Old Laughing Lady"
"Broken Arrow"

Release date
December 2, 2008

Label and catalogue numbers
US/Canada: Reprise 516758
UK: Reprise 9362-49839-8

Highest chart position on release
US 40

Notes
All songs by Neil Young. Recorded on Young's first ever solo tour in the fall of 1968. Only "Sugar Mountain" had previously been released from this recording. Young brought his Sony reel-to-reel tape recorder with him to record the show and archived the tapes for some forty years.

Archives Vol. 1 1963–1972 2009

Box set produced by Neil Young and Joel Bernstein

Cover art
– Design and direction: Gary Burden for R. Twerk

Tracks
Disc 00: Early Years (1963-1968)
"Aurora" (The Squires)
"The Sultan" (The Squires)
"I Wonder" (The Squires)
"Mustang" (The Squires)
"I'll Love You Forever" (The Squires)
"(I'm a Man and) I Can't Cry" (The Squires)
"Hello Lonely Woman" (with Comrie Smith)
"Casting Me Away from You" (with Comrie Smith)
"There Goes My Babe" (with Comrie Smith)
"Sugar Mountain"
"Nowadays Clancy Can't Even Sing"
"Runaround Babe"
"The Ballad of Peggy Grover"
"The Rent Is Always Due"
"Extra, Extra"
"I Wonder" (The Squires) – (hidden track)
"Nowadays Clancy Can't Even Sing" (Buffalo Springfield) – (hidden track)

Disc 01: Early Years (1963-1968)
"Flying on the Ground Is Wrong"
"Burned" (Buffalo Springfield)
"Out of My Mind" (Buffalo Springfield)
"Down Down Down"
"Kahuna Sunset" (Buffalo Springfield) (Young, Stills)
"Mr. Soul" (Buffalo Springfield)
"Sell Out" (Buffalo Springfield)
"Down to the Wire"
"Expecting to Fly" (Buffalo Springfield)
"Slowly Burning"

"One More Sign"
"Broken Arrow" (Buffalo Springfield)
"I Am a Child" (Buffalo Springfield)
"Do I Have to Come Right Out and Say It" (Buffalo Springfield) – (hidden track)
"Flying on the Ground Is Wrong" (Buffalo Springfield) – (hidden track)
"For What It's Worth" (Buffalo Springfield) (Stills) – (hidden track)
"This Is It!" (Buffalo Springfield) – (hidden track)

Disc 02: Topanga 1 (1968–1969)
"Everybody Knows This Is Nowhere"
"The Loner"
"Birds"
"What Did You Do to My Life?"
"The Last Trip to Tulsa"
"Here We Are in the Years"
"I've Been Waiting for You"
"The Old Laughing Lady"
"I've Loved Her So Long"
"Sugar Mountain"
"Nowadays Clancy Can't Even Sing"
"Down by the River" (with Crazy Horse)
"Cowgirl in the Sand" (with Crazy Horse)
"Everybody Knows This Is Nowhere" (with Crazy Horse)
"The Emperor of Wyoming" (hidden Track)

Disc 03: Live at the Riverboat (1969)
"Sugar Mountain"
"The Old Laughing Lady"
"Flying on the Ground Is Wrong"
"On the Way Home"
"I've Loved Her So Long"
"I Am a Child"
"1956 Bubblegum Disaster"
"The Last Trip to Tulsa"
"Broken Arrow"
"Whiskey Boot Hill"
"Expecting to Fly"

Disc 04: Topanga 2 (1969–1970)
"Cinnamon Girl" (with Crazy Horse)
"Running Dry (Requiem for the Rockets)" (with Crazy Horse)
"Round and Round (It Won't Be Long)" (with Crazy Horse)
"Oh Lonesome Me" (with Crazy Horse)
"Birds" (with Crazy Horse)
"Everybody's Alone" (with Crazy Horse)
"I Believe in You" (with Crazy Horse)
"Sea of Madness" (CSNY)
"Dance Dance Dance" (with Crazy Horse)
"Country Girl" (CSNY)
"Helpless" (CSNY)
"It Might Have Been" (with Crazy Horse) (Ronnie Green, Harriet Kane)
"I Believe in You" (with Crazy Horse) – (hidden track)
"I've Loved Her So Long" (CSNY) – (hidden track)

Disc 05: Neil Young & Crazy Horse – Live at the Fillmore East (1970)
"Everybody Knows This Is Nowhere"
"Winterlong"
"Down by the River"
"Wonderin'"
"Come On Baby, Let's Go Downtown" (Whitten)
"Cowgirl in the Sand"

Disc 06: Topanga 3 (1970)
"Tell Me Why"
"After the Gold Rush"
"Only Love Can Break Your Heart"
"Wonderin'"
"Don't Let It Bring You Down"
"Cripple Creek Ferry"
"Southern Man"
"Till the Morning Comes"
"When You Dance I Can Really Love" (with Crazy Horse)
"Ohio" (CSNY)
"Only Love Can Break Your Heart" (CSNY)
"Tell Me Why" (CSNY)
"Music Is Love" (with David Crosby and Graham Nash)
"See the Sky About to Rain"
"When You Dance I Can Really Love" (with Crazy Horse) – (hidden track)
"Birds" (hidden track)

Disc 07: Live at Massey Hall (1971)
"On the Way Home"
"Tell Me Why"
"Old Man"
"Journey through the Past"
"Helpless"
"Love in Mind"
"A Man Needs a Maid/ Heart of Gold Suite"
"Cowgirl in the Sand"
"Don't Let It Bring You Down"
"There's a World"
"Bad Fog of Loneliness"
"The Needle and the Damage Done"
"Ohio"
"See the Sky About to Rain"
"Down by the River"
"Dance Dance Dance"
"I Am a Child"

Disc 08: North Country (1971–1972)
"Heart of Gold"
"The Needle and the Damage Done"
"Bad Fog of Loneliness" (with the Stray Gators)
"Old Man" (with the Stray Gators)
"Heart of Gold" (with the Stray Gators)
"Dance Dance Dance"
"A Man Needs a Maid" (with the London Symphony Orchestra)
"Harvest" (with the Stray Gators)
"Journey through the Past" (with the Stray Gators)
"Are You Ready for the Country?" (with the Stray Gators)
"Alabama" (with the Stray Gators)

"Words (Between the Lines of Age)"
 (with the Stray Gators)
"Soldier"
"War Song" (with Graham Nash and
 the Stray Gators)

Disc 09: A Journey through the Past DVD

Release date
June 2, 2009

Label and catalogue numbers
US/Canada: Reprise 175292
UK: Reprise 476732-2

Highest chart position on release
US 102

Notes
All songs by Neil Young unless otherwise noted. Some fifteen years in the making, *Archives Vol. 1* was a massive undertaking and set the bar high for any other career retrospective box sets.

Dreamin' Man Live '92 2009

Recorded at various venues during the 1992 solo tour

Produced by Neil Young and John Hanlon

Personnel
– Neil Young: guitar, banjo, harmonica, piano, vocals

Cover art
– Design and direction: Gary Burden and Jenice Heo for R. Twerk
– Photography: Neil Young, Steve Babineau
– Artwork: Rebecca Holland

Tracks
"Dreamin' Man"
"Such a Woman"
"One of These Days"
"Harvest Moon"
"You and Me"
"From Hank to Hendrix"
"Unknown Legend"
"Old King"
"Natural Beauty"
"War of Man"

Release date
December 8, 2009

Label and catalogue numbers
US/Canada: Reprise 511277-2
UK: Reprise 9362-49855-3 2

Highest chart position on release
DNC

Notes
All songs written by Neil Young.

A Treasure 2011

Recording live at various venues during the 1984–1985 Old Ways tour

Produced by Neil Young and Ben Keith

Credited to Neil Young with the International Harvesters

Personnel
– Neil Young: guitar, vocals
International Harvesters
– Anthony Crawford: guitar, banjo, vocals
– Tim Drummond: bass
– Karl Himmel: drums
– Ben "Long Grain" Keith: pedal steel guitar, lap slide guitar, stringman, vocals
– Spooner Oldham: piano
– Rufus Thibodeaux: fiddle

Additional credits
Joe Allen, bass; Matraca Berg, vocals; Tracy Nelson, vocals; Hargus "Pig" Robbins, piano

Cover art
– Design and direction: Gary Burden and Jenice Heo for R. Twerk
– Photography: Joel Bernstein, Hannah Johnson
– Artwork: Ron Farnsworth

Tracks
"Amber Jean"
"Are You Ready for the Country?"
"It Might Have Been" (Ronnie Green, Harriet Kane)
"Bound for Glory"
"Let Your Fingers Do the Walking"
"Flying on the Ground Is Wrong"
"Motor City"
"Soul of a Woman"
"Get Back to the Country"
"Southern Pacific"
"Nothing Is Perfect"
"Grey Riders"

Release date
June 14, 2011

Label and catalogue numbers
US/Canada: Reprise 527650-2
UK: Reprise 9362-49579-3

Highest chart position on release
US 7

Notes
All songs written by Neil Young except where noted. "Amber Jean," "Let Your Fingers Do the Walking," "Soul of a Woman," "Nothing Is Perfect," and "Grey Riders" were previously unreleased songs.

Live at the Cellar Door 2013

Recorded live by Henry Lewy at the Cellar Door, Washington, DC between November 30 and December 2, 1970

Produced by Neil Young

Personnel
– Neil Young: guitar, piano, vocals

Cover art
– Design and direction: Gary Burden and Jenice Heo for R. Twerk
– Photography: Gary Burden
– Photograph: Courtesy of George Mason University

Tracks
"Tell Me Why"
"Only Love Can Break Your Heart"
"After the Gold Rush"
"Expecting to Fly"
"Bad Fog of Loneliness"
"Old Man"
"Birds"
"Don't Let It Bring You Down"
"See the Sky About to Rain"
"Cinnamon Girl"
"I Am a Child"
"Down by the River"
"Flying on the Ground Is Wrong"

Release date
December 10, 2013

Label and catalogue numbers
US/Canada: Reprise 535854-2
UK: Reprise 9362-49434-5

Highest chart position on release
US 27

Notes
All songs written by Neil Young.

SINGLES

This selection is not exhaustive and does not include every promo, reissue, and alternative B-side. US releases unless otherwise stated.

– *November 1968*: "The Loner"/ "Sugar Mountain"
– *March 1969*: "Everybody Knows This Is Nowhere"/"The Emperor of Wyoming"
– *July 1969*: "Down by the River"/ "The Losing End"
– *October 1969 (UK)*: "Pretty Girl Why"/"Questions"
– *June 1970*: "Cinnamon Girl"/"Sugar Mountain"
– *August 1970 (UK)*: "Down by the River"/"Cinnamon Girl"
– *October 1970*: "Only Love Can Break Your Heart"/"Birds"

- *March 1971*: "When You Dance I Can Really Love"/"Sugar Mountain"
- *February 1971 (UK)*: "When You Dance I Can Really Love"/"After the Gold Rush"
- *January 1972*: "Heart of Gold"/ "Sugar Mountain"
- *April 1972*: "Old Man"/"The Needle and the Damage Done"
- *June 1972*: "War Song" (with Graham Nash)/"The Needle and the Damage Done"
- *November 1973*: "Times Fades Away"/ "The Last Trip to Tulsa"
- *June 1974*: "Walk On"/"For the Turnstiles"
- *September 1975*: "Lookin' for a Love"/ "Sugar Mountain"
- *January 1976*: "Drive Back"/ "Stupid Girl"
- *May 1976 (UK)*: "Don't Cry No Tears"/ "Stupid Girl"
- *August 1977*: "Hey Babe"/ "Homegrown"
- *September 1977*: "Like a Hurricane"/ "Hold Back the Tears"
- *December 1977*: "Sugar Mountain"/ "The Needle and the Damage Done"
- *October 1978*: "Comes a Time"/ "Motorcycle Mama"
- *October 1978 (UK)*: "Comes a Time"/ "Lotta Love"
- *December 1978*: "Four Strong Winds"/ "Human Highway"
- *December 1978 (UK)*: "Four Strong Winds"/"Motorcycle Mama"
- *September 1979*: "Hey Hey, My My (Into the Black)"/"My My, Hey Hey (Out of the Blue)"
- *December 1979*: "The Loner" (live)/ "Cinnamon Girl" (live)
- *November 1980*: "Hawks & Doves"/ "Union Man"
- *February 1981*: "Stayin' Power"/ "Captain Kennedy"
- *November 1981*: "Southern Pacific"/ "Motor City"
- *January 1982*: "Opera Star"/ "Surfer Joe and Moe the Sleaze"
- *December 1982*: "Little Thing Called Love"/"We R in Control"
- *January 1983*: "Sample and Hold"/ "Mr. Soul" (12" single)
- *February 1983*: "Mr. Soul Pt. 1"/ "Mr. Soul Pt. 2"
- *August 1983*: "Wonderin'"/ "Payola Blues"
- *October 1983*: "Cry, Cry, Cry"/ "Payola Blues"
- *September 1985*: "Get Back to the Country"/"Misfits"
- *November 1985*: "Old Ways"/ "Once an Angel"
- *July 1986*: "Weight of the World"/"Pressure"
- *June 1987*: "Mideast Vacation"/ "Long Walk Home"
- *June 1987 (UK)*: "Long Walk Home"/"Cryin' Eyes"

- *April 1988*: "Ten Men Workin'"/ "I'm Goin'"
- *May 1988*: "This Note's for You" (live)/"This Note's for You"
- *August 1989*: "Rockin' in the Free World"/"Rockin' in the Free World" (live)
- *September 1990*: "Mansion on the Hill"/"Don't Spook the Horse"
- *February 1991*: "Over and Over"/ "Don't Spook the Horse"
- *December 1992*: "Harvest Moon"/ "Old King"
- *December 1992*: "War of Man"
- *February 1993 (UK)*: "Harvest Moon"/"Winterlong"
- *February 1993 (UK)*: "Harvest Moon"/"Old King"/"The Needle and the Damage Done"/"Goin' Back"
- *July 1993 (UK)*: "The Needle and the Damage Done"/"You and Me"
- *October 1993 (UK)*: "Long May You Run"/"Sugar Mountain"
- *March 1994 (UK)*: "Philadelphia"/ "Such a Woman"/"Stringman"
- *June 1995*: "Peace and Love"
- *June 1995 (UK)*: "Downtown"/ "Big Green Country"
- *July 1996*: "Big Time"/"Interstate"
- *April 2002*: "Let's Roll"
- *October 2007*: "Ordinary People"
- *October 2014*: "Who's Gonna Stand Up?"

CROSBY, STIILS, NASH & YOUNG

STUDIO ALBUMS

Déjà Vu 1970

Recorded at Wally Heider's Studio C, San Francisco and Wally Heider's Studio III, Los Angeles

Produced by David Crosby, Stephen Stills, Graham Nash, and Neil Young

Personnel
- David Crosby: guitar, vocals
- Stephen Stills: guitar, keyboards, vocals
- Graham Nash: guitar, keyboards, vocals
- Neil Young: vocals, guitar

Additional credits
Jerry Garcia, pedal steel guitar; Greg Reeves, bass; John Sebastian, harmonica; Dallas Taylor, drums

Cover art
- Direction: Gary Burden
- Cover photo: Tom Gundelfinger
- Inside photos: Henry Diltz, Sally Sachs

Tracks
"Carry On" (Stills)
"Teach Your Children" (Nash)
"Almost Cut My Hair" (Crosby)
"Helpless" (Young)
"Woodstock" (Mitchell)
"Déjà Vu" (Crosby)
"Our House" (Nash)
"4+20" (Stills)
"Country Girl" – "Whiskey Boot Hill"/"Down, Down, Down"/"Country Girl (I Think You're Pretty)" (Young)
"Everybody I Love You" (Stills, Young)

Release date
March 11, 1970

Label and catalogue numbers
US/Canada: Atlantic SD 7200
UK: Atlantic 2401 001

Highest chart position on release
US 1

Notes
Sessions were fraught with frustration and delays due to Crosby's escalating drug use. Young's addition to the trio was intended to beef up their live sound but his songwriting added a further strength to the group. "Whiskey Boot Hill" and "Down, Down, Down" dated back to the Buffalo Springfield era. Young's "Ohio" and Stills's "Find the Cost of Freedom" were both recorded after the album sessions but released as a single as the album climbed the charts.

American Dream 1988

Recorded at Redwood Digital, Woodside, CA and Record One, Los Angeles

Produced by Neil Young and Niko Bolas (The Volume Dealers), David Crosby, Stephen Stills, Graham Nash, and Tim Mulligan

Personnel
- David Crosby: guitar, vocals
- Stephen Stills: guitar, keyboards, bass, percussion, vocals
- Graham Nash: guitar, piano, harmonica, vocals
- Neil Young: guitar, piano, harmonica, percussion, vocals

Additional credits
Chad Cromwell, drums; Tommy Bray, trumpet; Claude Cailliet, trombone; Larry Cragg, baritone saxophone; Mike Finnegan, organ & vocals; John Fumo, trumpet; Bob Glaub, bass; Joe Lala, percussion; Steve Lawrence, tenor saxophone; Joe Vitale, drums & vibes; The Volume Dealers Choir

Cover art
- Design: Gary Burden for R. Twerk
- Photography: Aaron Rapoport, Henry Diltz
- Border illustration: Delana Vettoli

Tracks
"American Dream" (Young)
"Got It Made" (Stills)
"Name of Love" (Young)
"Don't Say Goodbye" (Nash, Vitale)
"This Old House" (Young)
"Nighttime for the Generals" (Crosby)
"Shadowland" (Nash, Ryan, Vitale)
"Drivin' Thunder" (Stills, Young)
"Clear Blue Sky" (Nash)
"That Girl" (Stills, Vitale, Glaub)
"Compass" (Crosby)
"Soldiers of Peace" (Nash, Doerge, Vitale)
"Feel Your Love" (Young)
"Night Song" (Stills, Young)

Release date
November 22, 1988

Label and catalogue numbers
US/Canada: Atlantic 81888
UK: Atlantic WX 233

Highest chart position on release
US 16

Notes
Following Crosby's release from prison on drugs and firearms charges, Young made good on his promise that if Crosby cleaned up his act he would record a new CSNY album. Reviews were lukewarm with some

noting that even Young's tracks sounded tired. *Rolling Stone* magazine declared the album a "snoozefest."

Looking Forward 1999

Recorded at Ocean Studios, Burbank, CA; Redwood Digital, Woodside, CA; Ga Ga's Room, Los Angeles; Stray Gator Sound, Los Angeles; and Conway Studio A, Los Angeles

Produced by David Crosby, Stephen Stills, Graham Nash, Neil Young, Ben Keith, J. Stanley Johnston, and Joe Vitale

Personnel
- David Crosby: guitar, vocals
- Stephen Stills: guitar, bass, organ, cowbell, timbales, maracas, batá, percussion, vocals
- Graham Nash: guitar, vocals
- Neil Young: guitar, harmonica, celeste, vocals

Additional credits
Alex Acuña, timbales; Lenny Castro, percussion; Vince Charles, percussion; Luis Conte, congas, jombe, bass drum, batá & percussion; Craig Doerge, keyboards; Donald "Duck" Dunn, bass; Mike Finnegan, organ; Snuffy Garrett, guitar; Bob Glaub, bass; "Hutch" Hutchinson, bass; Gerald Johnson, bass; Ben Keith, pedal steel guitar & dobro; Jim Keltner, drums; Joe Lala, congas; Spooner Oldham, pump organ; James Raymond, piano; Danny Sarokin, guitar; Joe Vitale, drums, organ & batá

Cover art
- Design and direction: Gary Burden and Jenice Heo for R. Twerk
- Photography: Henry Diltz, R. Mac Holbert, Pegi Young

Tracks
"Faith in Me" (Stills, Vitale)
"Looking Forward" (Young)
"Stand and Be Counted" (Crosby, Raymond)
"Heartland" (Nash)
"Seen Enough" (Stills)
"Slowpoke" (Young)
"Dream for Him" (Crosby)
"No Tears Left" (Stills)
"Out of Control" (Young)
"Someday Soon" (Nash)
"Queen of Them All" (Young)
"Sanibel" (Sarokin)

Release date
October 26, 1999

Label and catalogue numbers
US/Canada: Reprise 47436
UK: Reprise 9-47436-2

Highest chart position on release
US 26

Notes
Looking Forward was initially to be a self-financed Crosby, Stills & Nash album, the trio having been dropped by Atlantic, but once Young became involved, his label, Reprise, signed the quartet to a one-off contract for the album.

LIVE ALBUMS

4 Way Street 1971

Recorded live in June and July 1970 at Fillmore East, New York; Auditorium Theatre, Chicago; and the Forum, Inglewood, CA

Produced by David Crosby, Stephen Stills, Graham Nash, and Neil Young

Personnel
- David Crosby: guitar, vocals
- Stephen Stills: guitar, keyboards, vocals
- Graham Nash: guitar, keyboards, vocals
- Neil Young: vocals, guitar

Additional credits
Johnny Barbata, drums; Calvin "Fuzzy" Samuels, bass

Cover art
- Direction: Gary Burden
- Photography: Henry Diltz, Joel Bernstein

Tracks
"Suite: Judy Blue Eyes" (Stills)
"On the Way Home" (Young)
"Teach Your Children" (Nash)
"Triad" (Crosby)
"The Lee Shore" (Crosby)
"Chicago" (Nash)
"Right Between the Eyes" (Nash)
"Cowgirl in the Sand" (Young)
"Don't Let It Bring You Down" (Young)
"49 Bye Byes"/"For What It's Worth"/"America's Children" (Stills)
"Love the One You're With" (Stills)
"Pre-Road Downs" (Nash)
"Long Time Gone" (Crosby)
"Southern Man" (Young)
"Ohio" (Young)
"Carry On" (Stills)
"Find the Cost of Freedom" (Stills)

Release date
April 7, 1971

Label and catalogue numbers
US/Canada: Atlantic SD 2-902
UK: Atlantic 2657 007

Highest chart position on release
US 1

Notes

The album represented both the acoustic or "wooden" music side of the group with individual solo spots as well as their electric side with extended workouts on several tracks. The group would break up before the album's release due to individual conflicts and clashing egos.

Déjà Vu Live 2008

Recorded on the 2006 Freedom of Speech Tour by Rob Clark and mixed live by Tim Mulligan and Dave Lohr, except "Living with War—Theme," which was recorded at Audio Resource, Honolulu

Produced by Neil Young and L. A. Johnson

Personnel
- David Crosby: guitar, vocals
- Stephen Stills: guitar, piano, vocals
- Graham Nash: guitar, piano, vocals
- Neil Young: guitar, piano, vocals

Additional credits
Tom Bray, trumpet; Chad Cromwell, drums; Ben Keith, pedal steel guitar; Spooner Oldham, keyboards; Rick Rosas, bass

Cover art
- Design and direction: Gary Burden and Jenice Heo for R. Twerk
- Photography: Larry Cragg

Tracks
"What Are Their Names" (Crosby)
"Living with War—Theme" (Young)
"After the Garden" (Young)
"Military Madness" (Nash)
"Let's Impeach the President" (Young)
"Déjà Vu" (Crosby)
"Shock and Awe" (Young)
"Families" (Young)
"Wooden Ships" (Crosby, Stills, Kantner)
"Looking for a Leader" (Young)
"For What It's Worth" (Stills)
"Living with War" (Young)
"Roger and Out" (Young)
"Find the Cost of Freedom" (Stills)
"Teach Your Children" (Nash)
"Living with War—Theme" (Young)

Release date
July 22, 2008

Label and catalogue numbers
US/Canada: Reprise 512606
UK: Reprise 9362-49839-1

Highest chart position on release
US 153

Notes

Soundtrack to a DVD of the same name. Crosby, Stills & Nash signed on for what was ostensibly a Neil Young tour in support of *Living with War*.

CSNY 1974 2014

Recorded live at various venues from August 19 to December 14, 1974

Produced by Graham Nash and Joel Bernstein with Crosby, Stills, Nash & Young

Personnel
- David Crosby: guitar, tambourine, vocals
- Stephen Stills: guitars, keyboards, bass, vocals
- Graham Nash: guitars, keyboards, harmonica, vocals
- Neil Young: guitar, keyboards, harmonica, banjo, vocals

Additional credits
Tim Drummond, bass; Russ Kunkel, drums; Joe Lala, percussion

Cover art
- Design and direction: Brian Porizek with Joel Bernstein and Graham Nash
- Photography: Joel Bernstein, Graham Nash

Tracks

Disc 1: First Set
"Love the One You're With" (Stills)
"Wooden Ships" (Crosby, Stills, Kantner)
"Immigration Man" (Nash)
"Helpless" (Young)
"Carry Me" (Crosby)
"Johnny's Garden" (Stills)
"Traces" (Young)
"Grave Concern" (Nash)
"On the Beach" (Young)
"Black Queen" (Stills)
"Almost Cut My Hair" (Crosby)

Disc 2: Second Set
"Change Partners" (Stills)
"The Lee Shore" (Crosby)
"Only Love Can Break Your Heart" (Young)
"Our House" (Nash)
"Fieldworker" (Nash)
"Guinnevere" (Crosby)
"Time after Time" (Crosby)
"Prison Song" (Nash)
"Long May You Run" (Young)
"Goodbye Dick" (Young)
"Mellow My Mind" (Young)
"Old Man" (Young)
"Word Game" (Stills)
"Myth of Sisyphus" (Stills, Passarelli)
"Blackbird" (Lennon, McCartney)

"Love Art Blues" (Young)
"Hawaiian Sunrise" (Young)
"Teach Your Children" (Nash)
"Suite: Judy Blue Eyes" (Stills)

Disc 3: Third Set
"Déjà Vu" (Crosby)
"My Angel" (Stills)
"Pre-Road Downs" (Nash)
"Don't Be Denied" (Young)
"Revolution Blues" (Young)
"Military Madness" (Nash)
"Long Time Gone" (Crosby)
"Pushed It Over the End" (Young)
"Chicago" (Nash)
"Ohio" (Young)

Bonus DVD
"Only Love Can Break Your Heart" (Young)
"Almost Cut My Hair" (Crosby)
"Grave Concern" (Nash)
"Old Man" (Young)
"Johnny's Garden" (Stills)
"Our House" (Nash)
"Déjà Vu" (Crosby)
"Pushed It Over the End" (Young)

Release date
July 7, 2014

Label and catalogue numbers
US/Canada: CSNY/Rhino R2-541729
UK: Reprise CSNY/Rhino 8122796035

Highest chart position on release
US 17

Notes
Long-awaited multi-disc set from the legendary 1974 tour. "Traces," "Goodbye Dick," "Love Art Blues," "Hawaiian Sunrise," and "Pushed It Over the End" are all previously unreleased Neil Young tracks.

COMPILATIONS

So Far 1974

Released July 1974 (US/Canada)/ August 1974 (UK)
US/Canada: Atlantic SD 18100
UK: Reprise K 50023
Chart: US 1

Tracks
"Déjà Vu" (Crosby)
"Helplessly Hoping" (Stills)
"Wooden Ships" (Crosby & Stills)
"Teach Your Children" (Nash)
"Ohio" (Young)
"Find the Cost of Freedom" (Stills)
"Woodstock" (Mitchell)
"Our House" (Nash)
"Helpless" (Young)
"Guinnevere" (Crosby)
"Suite: Judy Blue Eyes" (Stills)

SINGLES

- *March 1970*: "Woodstock"/"Helpless"
- *May 1970*: "Teach Your Children"/"Country Girl"
- *June 1970*: "Ohio"/"Find the Cost of Freedom"
- *September 1970*: "Our House"/ "Déjà Vu"
- *January 1989 (UK)*: "American Dream"/"Compass"
- *January 1989*: "This Old House"/ "Got It Made"
- *October 1999*: "No Tears Left"/ "Looking Forward"

THE STILLS-YOUNG BAND

STUDIO ALBUMS

Long May You Run 1976

Recorded at Criteria Studios, Miami

Produced by Stephen Stills, Neil Young, and Don Gehman

Personnel
- Stephen Stills: guitar, piano, vocals
- Neil Young: guitar, piano, harmonica, string synthesizer, vocals
- Jerry Aiello: organ, piano
- Joe Lala: percussion, vocals
- George "Chocolate" Perry: bass, vocals
- Joe Vitale: drums, flute, vocals

Cover art
- Design: Tom Wilkes

Tracks
"Long May You Run" (Young)
"Make Love to You" (Stills)
"Midnight on the Bay" (Young)
"Black Coral" (Stills)
"Ocean Girl" (Young)
"Let It Shine" (Young)
"12/8 Blues (All the Same)" (Stills)
"Fontainebleau" (Young)
"Guardian Angel" (Stills)

Release date
September 10, 1976

Label and catalogue numbers
US/Canada: Reprise MS 2253
UK: Reprise K 54081

Highest chart position on release
US 26

SINGLES

- *July 1976*: "Long May You Run"/ "12/8 Blues (All the Same)"
- *October 1976*: "Midnight on the Bay"/"Black Coral"

BOOKS

Young, Neil
Waging Heavy Peace: A Hippie Dream.
New York: Blue Rider Press, 2012 / London: Viking, 2012.

Young, Neil
Special Deluxe: A Memoir of Life & Cars.
New York: Blue Rider Press, 2014 / London: Viking, 2014.

Boyd, Glen
Neil Young FAQ: Everything Left to Know About the Iconic and Mercurial Rocker.
Milwaukee: Backbeat Books, 2012.

Chong, Kevin
Neil Young Nation: A Quest, an Obsession (and a True Story).
Vancouver: Greystone Books, 2005.

Einarson, John
Don't Be Denied: The Canadian Years.
Kingston, Ontario: Quarry Press, 1992 (revised 2012).

Einarson, John & Richie Furay
For What It's Worth:
The Story of Buffalo Springfield.
Kingston, Ontario: Quarry Music Books, 1997 (revised 2004, New York: Cooper Square Press).

Goodman, Fred
The Mansion on the Hill: Dylan, Young, Geffen, Springsteen, and the Head-On Collision of Rock and Commerce.
New York: Crown, 1997 / London: Times Books, 1997.

Inglis, Sam
Harvest (33 1/3 series).
London: Bloomsbury, 2003.

McDonough, Jimmy
Shakey: Neil Young's Biography.
New York: Random House, 2002 / London: Jonathan Cape, 2002.

Nash, Graham
Wild Tales: A Rock & Roll Life.
New York: Crown, 2013; London: Viking, 2013.

Rogan, Johnny
Neil Young Zero to Sixty:
A Critical Biography.
London: Rogan House, 2000.

Williams, Paul
Neil Young: Love to Burn, Thirty Years of Speaking Out 1966–1996.
London: Omnibus Press, 1997.

Wilson, Sharry
Young Neil: The Sugar Mountain Years.
Toronto: ECW Press, 2014.

Young, Scott
Neil and Me.
Toronto: McClelland & Stewart, 1984 (revised 1997).

SELECTED WEBSITES

Neil Young official website
www.neilyoung.com

Bad News Beat: All the Neil That's Fit to Print
www.bad-news-beat.org

CSNY official website
www.csny.com

4WaySite: The Crosby, Stills, Nash & Young Fansite
www.4waysite.com

Hyper Rust: The Unofficial Neil Young Pages
www.hyperrust.org

Neil Young Appreciation Society
www.nyas.org.uk

Sugar Mountain: Neil Young Set Lists
www.sugarmtn.org

Thrasher's Wheat:
A Neil Young Archives
www.thrasherswheat.org

Sources, Credits, and Acknowledgments

QUOTE SOURCES

All quotes come from previously unpublished interviews by Harvey Kubernik except where indicated.

7 "There really wasn't…" *Don't Be Denied: The Canadian Years* by John Einarson, Kingston, Ontario: Quarry Press, 1992 **8** "I never did…" NY interview with Cameron Crowe, *Rolling Stone*, August 14, 1975 **13** "I knew when…" *Don't Be Denied*, Einarson **16** "To me, Canada…" *Don't Be Denied*, Einarson **17** "Polio is the…" *Neil and Me* by Scott Young, Toronto: McClelland & Stewart, 1984 (revised 1997) **18** "I saw Neil…" *Don't Be Denied*, Einarson **19** "I wasn't into…" *Don't Be Denied*, Einarson **20** "Randy was definitely…" *Don't Be Denied*, Einarson **23** "I always believed…" *Don't Be Denied*, Einarson **23** "I always knew…" *Don't Be Denied*, Einarson **24** "His voice was…" *Don't Be Denied*, Einarson **24** "We got into…" *Don't Be Denied*, Einarson **25** "We didn't succeed…" *Waging Heavy Peace: A Hippie Dream* by Neil Young, New York: Blue Rider Press, 2012 **27** "I thought it…" *Don't Be Denied*, Einarson **28** "We were together…" *Don't Be Denied*, Einarson **29** "Canada just couldn't…" *Don't Be Denied*, Einarson **29** "Neil and I…" *Don't Be Denied*, Einarson **29** "Bruce and I…" *Don't Be Denied*, Einarson **30** "Something was happening…" *Waging Heavy Peace*, NY **34** "I was listening…" *Don't Be Denied*, Einarson **34** "Bruce and I…" *Don't Be Denied*, Einarson **34** "When the light…" *Don't Be Denied*, Einarson **37** "The real core…" *For What It's Worth: The Story of Buffalo Springfield* by John Einarson & Richie Furay, Kingston, Ontario: Quarry Music Books, 1997 (revised 2004, New York: Cooper Square Press) **38** "I always liked…" *For What It's Worth*, Einarson & Furay **41** "One day, I…" *Waging Heavy Peace*, NY **42** "Gold Star brought…" Stan Ross interview with Harvey Kubernik, *Goldmine* magazine, 2001 **46** "On Buffalo Springfield…" *Turn Up the Radio! Rock, Pop, & Roll in Los Angeles, 1956–1972* by Harvey Kubernik, Solana Beach, CA: Santa Monica Press, 2014 **46** "'Expecting to Fly'…" *For What It's Worth*, Einarson & Furay **46** "We were always…" Richie Furay interview with Harvey Kubernik, *Goldmine* magazine, 2001 **48** "We were fighting…" *For What It's Worth*, Einarson & Furay **48** "I just couldn't…" *For What It's Worth*, Einarson & Furay **49** "The band was…" Richie Furay interview with Harvey Kubernik, *Goldmine* magazine, 2001 **49** "Neil cut 'I…" Jim Messina interview with John Einarson, *DisCoveries* magazine, 2004 **49** "There have been…" NY in *Go* magazine, May 1968 **49** "Neil could not…" Richie Furay interview with John Einarson, *DisCoveries* magazine, 2004 **50** "First of all…" *Shakey: Neil Young's Biography* by Jimmy McDonough, New York: Random House, 2002 **51** "We just went…" *Shakey*, McDonough **54** "I plan to…" NY in *Go* magazine, May 1968 **54** "On my first…" NY radio interview with B. Mitchell Reed, KMET-FM (94.7), California, 1973 **55** "Sitting there last…" Ritchie Yorke, *Toronto Globe and Mail*, 1969 **57** "It will be…" NY interview with Mike Gormley, *Detroit Free Press*, February 28, 1969

60 "I don't know…" NY interview with Jon Stewart, *The Daily Show*, Comedy Central, November 28, 2012 **60** "Everybody Knows This…" NY radio interview with B. Mitchell Reed, KMET-FM (94.7), California, 1973 **62** "I think it…" NY radio interview with B. Mitchell Reed, KMET-FM (94.7), California, 1973 **63** "It was a…" Graham Nash interview with Harvey Kubernik, *Record Collector News*, 2014 **64** "Right from the…" / "I've known Neil…" / "Neil is just…" Ritchie Yorke, *A Rap with Crosby, Stills, Nash & Young*, copyright © Ritchie Yorke 1969 **64** "Woodstock was a…" *Shakey*, McDonough **67** "'When You Dance'…" *Shakey*, McDonough **67** "I think I'd…" Jack Nitzsche interview with Ritchie Yorke, 1970 **70** "I wrote 'Ohio'…" NY in *Songwriters on Songwriting* by Paul Zollo, Cambridge, MA: Da Capo Press, 1990 (revised 2003) **70** "At the first…" NY radio interview with B. Mitchell Reed, KMET-FM (94.7), California, 1973 **72** "I've been right…" NY interview with Ray Coleman, *Melody Maker*, August 25, 1973 **80** "I told them…" Johnny Cash interview with Sylvie Simmons, 1997 **81** "I wrote 'Heart…" *Songwriters on Songwriting*, Zollo **81** "I sang in…" Linda Ronstadt interview with Gary Strobl, 2015 **82** "More than anyone…" James Cushing in the *City on a Hill Press*, University of California Santa Cruz, April 13, 1972 **82** "Actually, 'Heart of…" NY interview with Ray Coleman, *Melody Maker*, 1972 **83** "I knew that…" *Waging Heavy Peace*, NY **84** "I thought *Time*…" NY interview with Cameron Crowe, *Rolling Stone*, 1975 **85** "Those huge concerts…" NY radio interview with B. Mitchell Reed, KMET-FM (94.7), California, 1973 **92** "My career is…" NY interview with Nick Kent, *MOJO*, December 1995 **96** "When we get…" Ralph Molina interview with Sylvie Simmons, 1997 **96** "Much like that…" *Neil Young FAQ: Everything Left to Know about the Iconic and Mercurial Rocker* by Glen Boyd, Milwaukee: Backbeat Books, 2012 **98** "You start to…" *Songwriters on Songwriting*, Zollo **100** "The stark tone…" Rob Mitchum in *Pitchfork*, 2003 **100** "So I'll write…" *Songwriters on Songwriting*, Zollo **101** "When I was…" Ian Tyson interview with Gary Strobl, 2015 **101** "The song 'Comes…" *Waging Heavy Peace*, NY **102** "When you look…" NY radio interview with Mary Turner, *Off the Record*, KMET-FM (94.7), California, 1979 **107** "The fact that…" NY interview on *Night Flight*, USA Network, June 5, 1984 **110** "Hawks & Doves…" Cynthia Rose in *New Musical Express*, November 1980 **110** "I was in…" *Waging Heavy Peace*, NY **113** "I could see…" NY interview with James Henke, *Rolling Stone*, June 2, 1988 **114** "I don't really…" *Songwriters on Songwriting*, Zollo **114** "The truth is…" David Geffen interviewed in *American Masters: Inventing David Geffen*, PBS-TV, 2014 **115** "I really believe…" NY interview with Jim Sullivan, *Boston Globe*, September 6, 1984 **116** "I see country…" NY interview with Adam Sweeting, *Melody Maker*, September 7, 1985 **118** "His great-grandpa worked…" "An Open Letter by Neil Young," read out at the first Farm Aid, September 22, 1985 **121** "I'm just me…" *Songwriters on Songwriting*, Zollo **125** "The Chili Peppers…" Flea, "100 Greatest Artists:

#36, Neil Young" in *Rolling Stone*, December 2, 2010 **128** "The spoofs—which…" Fred Goodman in *Rolling Stone*, August 11, 1988 **128** "I went along…" Tom Freston in *I Want My MTV: The Uncensored Story of the Music Video Revolution* by Rob Tannenbaum and Craig Marks, New York: Dutton Penguin, 2011 **132** "The song is…" NY interview with Mark Cooper, *Q* magazine, November 1989 **134** "Despite what some…" Steve Martin in *Pulse* magazine, 1991 **134** "We know each…" Billy Talbot interview with Sylvie Simmons, 2001 **134** "There's a rare…" Flea, "100 Greatest Artists: #36, Neil Young" in *Rolling Stone*, December 2, 2010 **135** "When I was…" Frank Sampedro interview with Sylvie Simmons, 2001 **135** "He's right up…" Jeff Tweedy, MusiCares Person of the Year speech, January 29, 2010 **136** "What's cool about…" Kirk Hammett in *MOJO*, February 2001 **137** "What this album…" NY interview with David Fricke, *Rolling Stone*, October 1992 **140** "He really, really…" NY interview with Nick Kent, *MOJO*, December 1994 **140** "And when I…" Eddie Vedder, Rock and Roll Hall of Fame induction speech for NY, January 12, 1995 **141** "David Briggs used…" *Waging Heavy Peace*, NY **146** "I asked myself…" NY interview for *Weltwoche* (Zürich), July 1996 **147** "Neil and the…" / "Crazy Horse have…" Jim Jarmusch interview with Harvey Kubernik, *Hits* magazine, 1996 **149** "There I was…" *Don't Be Denied*, Einarson **151** "I must have…" Ben Folds interview with Ed Condran, North Jersey.com, May 6, 2005 **152** "It is certainly…" *Neil Young FAQ*, Boyd **154** "It came song…" NY interview with David Sinclair, *Times* (London), May 23, 2003 **155** "The aneurysm gave…" NY interview with Charlie Rose, *Charlie Rose*, PBS-TV, July 17, 2008 **155** "What binds the…" John Metzger in *The Music Box*, September 2005, Volume 12, #9 **155** "You want the…" NY interview with George Varga, *San Diego Union-Tribune*, February 23, 2006 **155** "It looks like…" Jonathan Demme interview with George Varga, *San Diego Union-Tribune*, February 23, 2006 **162** "Neil Young's fierce…" Roy Trakin interview with Harvey Kubernik, *All Access*, February 2015 **163** "I was a…" NY interview with Andy Greene, *Rolling Stone*, January 29, 2008 **163** "Live seventies rock…" Barney Hoskyns in *Uncut*, January 2007 **163** "Chris Bellman's astonishingly…" Michael Fremer, MusicAngle.com, 2007 **164** "When I'm recording…" NY interview with Jaan Uhelszki, *Uncut*, December 2007 **166** "The car was…" NY interview with Sean Michaels, *Guardian*, November 18, 2010 **166** "Young's latest is…" Michael Metivier in *PopMatters*, April 6, 2009 **166** "I was writing…" *Special Deluxe: A Memoir of Life & Cars* by Neil Young, New York: Blue Rider Press, 2014 **170** "It's fantastic. It's…" David Gassman in *PopMatters*, September 26, 2010 **171** "I got the…" Rick Rosas in *Canyon of Dreams: The Magic and the Music of Laurel Canyon* by Harvey Kubernik, New York: Sterling, 2009 **171** "All during my…" *Turn Up the Radio!*, Kubernik **174** "We were supposed…" Stephen Stills interview with Andy Greene, *Rolling Stone*, November 5, 2012 **174** "*Americana* is, finally…" Stuart Henderson in *PopMatters*, June 5, 2012 **176** "*Psychedelic Pill* is…."

John Mulvey in *Uncut*, October 9, 2012 **176**
"*Waging Heavy Peace*..." David Carr in the *New York Times*, September 19, 2012 **177**
"I don't think..." NY interview with David Carr, *New York Times*, September 19, 2012 **178** "At this point..." NY interview with Andy Greene, *Rolling Stone*, January 8, 2015 **182** "My boss is..." NY interview with Jaan Uhelszki, *Uncut*, August 2012 **183** "It's gonna be..." NY interview with Garrett Kemps, *Spin.com*, May 2014 **187** "Often overlooked amidst..." Jim Beviglia in *American Songwriter*, November 4, 2014 **187** "We're going to..." NY in conversation with Nathan Brackett at the International Consumer Electronics Show, Las Vegas, January 2015 **187** "I went to..." Bruce Botnick interview with Michael Bonner, *Uncut*, January 2015 **188** "I don't know..." Graham Nash interview with Tom Pinnock, *Uncut*, January 2015 **189** "Neil is a..." Jonathan Demme interview with John Einarson, *Winnipeg Free Press*, November 13, 2005 **192** "I don't know..." NY interview with Andy Greene, *Rolling Stone*, January 8, 2015 **224** "I don't know..." NY interview with Jim Sullivan, *Boston Globe*, 1990

PICTURE CREDITS

Every effort has been made to trace and acknowledge the copyright holders. We apologize in advance for any unintentional omissions and would be pleased, if any such case should arise, to add appropriate acknowledgment in any future edition of the book. Please note below all sources for copyright associated where applicable with the images used.

T: top; B: bottom; R: right; L: left; C: center

Getty Images: endpapers (Redferns/Stefan M. Prager); 6 (FilmMagic/Paul R. Giunta); 9, 81 (Michael Putland); 17BC, 148TL, 180TL (*Toronto Star*); 18 inset (CBS Photo Archive); 20–21 (Simon Lees/*Guitarist* magazine); 21TR (Gamma-Keystone); 31, 36BR, 36TL, 43B, 44, 50L, 52–3, 55, 102TL, 147T (Michael Ochs Archives); 35TR, 58–9 (Hulton Archive); 35BR (The *Life* Images Collection/Julian Wasser); 40 (Moviepix); 41, 18, 115 (iStock); 50R, 97, 98 (Gijsbert Hanekroot); 59TL, 64B (Blank Archives); 64T (*New York Daily News* Archive); 65 (Archive Photos); 66 (Redferns); 71 (Howard Ruffner); 80 (ABC Photo Archives); 99L (Ed Perlstein); 102BL (*Evening Standard*/Graham Wood); 106, 224 (Rob Verhorst); 108TR (Peter Carrette Archive); 113BL (Harry Langdon); 114 (Paul Natkin); 118R, 120–21, 124, 135, 188 (Ebet Roberts); 123T, 150, 151T, 152R, 154 inset, 163L, 174, 174–5 (Tim Mosenfelder); 128R (Robin Platzer); 132L (Phil Dent); 133, 183B (NBC/NBCU Photobank); 134L (Martin Goodacre); 136 (Contour/Ken Regan/Camera 5); 144L (WireImage/George Pimentel); 146B (Mick Hutson); 158, 165 (*New York Post*/WireImage/Joe Kohen); 167B (Peter Still); 169 (*Washington Post*/Tracy A. Woodward); 171 (Darren Hauck); 172–3 (Douglas Mason); 175TR (Peter Bregg); 179 (Contour/Jeff Vespa); 181 (Angela Weiss); 186 (*New Yorker*/Thos Robinson); 191 (Tommaso Boddi); 192–3 (Frazer Harrison); **Corbis:** 1 (EPA/Klaus Hans Techt); 23, 25R, 42, 58C, 62, 73, 77, 88–9

(Henry Diltz); 29R, 35TL, 118C (Bettmann); 37 inset (Zuma Press/Brian Cahn); 45R (Hulton Deutsch Collection/H. Thompson); 91, 138–9, 149T (Neal Preston); 94CR (Lynn Goldsmith); 112T, 112B (Caterine Milinaire/Sygma); 120 (Roger Ressmeyer); 129, 130 (Aaron Rapaport); 166 (Zuma Press/Barry Sweet); 168 (Troy Wayrynen); 170 (Zuma Press/Martin Klimek); 190 (Denis Balibouse); **Henry Diltz:** 2–3, 10–11, 29L, 33BL, 48, 78–9, 83; **John Einarson:** 13, 14L, 14C, 14–15, 16T, 17TL, 17BL, 17BR, 19, 32B, 34, 36TR, 37, 148B; **Gary Pig Gold:** 14R, 58BR; **Toronto Public Library/Valentine and Sons United Publishing Company:** 17; **John Conrad/Randy Bachman:** 21BR; **Owen Clark:** 22L, 24; **Getstock/Reg Innell:** 25; **Manfred Buchheit:** 26–7; **Rick Mason:** 28; **Library and Archives Canada/Frank Prazak:** 29L; **Jeff Gold/Record Mecca:** 32TL; **John Van Hamersveld:** 33TR; **Press Association Images:** 35BL (AP/EW); 141R (Kevork Djansezian); 142 (Mark Humphrey); 180BL (Landov/Mike Theiler); 167 (Yui Mok); **Jini Dellacio Collection:** 38–9, 41; **Nurit Wilde:** 47, 51; **Tom Gundelfinger O'Neal:** 56, 63; **Amalie R. Rothschild:** 61, 68–9; **Topfoto:** 74R (Topham Picturepoint); 118L (AP); 103 (Ullstein Bilderdienst); **The Kobal Collection:** 76 (Universal); 104–5 (Shakey Pictures/Crest Productions); 127 (Columbia); **Dave Collis:** 84; **Frank White Photo Agency/Ed Finnell:** 86–7; **Vincent Miles:** 90R; **Sheri Lynn Behr:** 93; **Alamy:** 101T (Robert Landau); 144R (Pictorial Press); 140T (The Cover Version); 164 (Zuma Press); **Courtesy of the DEVO Archives:** 111T; **Scott Newton/***Austin City Limits***:** 115B, 116–17; **Associated Press:** 141L; **Francesco Lucarelli:** 148C, 177TR; **CP Images/Adrian Wyld:** 155; **Rex Shutterstock:** 156–7 (Paramount); 175B (Everett); **Penguin Randomhouse Publishing/Viking:** 177B; **Chris Schmitt:** 184–5

Album/Single Covers
Courtesy of Cyril Kieldsen: 22R (V Records); 32TC, 33TL, 49 (Atco/Warner Music Group); 43T, 45L, 46, 59C (Atlantic Records); 54T, 59TR, 82, 88 inset, 90L, 100, 102R, 111BL, 111BR, 128L, 131, 137, 140B, 146TL, 151B, 154, 160–61, 163R, 166 inset, 170 inset, 176–7 (Reprise Records/Warner Music Group); 113TL, 114 inset, 115T, 115C, 121 inset (Geffen Records); **Getty Images/GAB Archive:** 54B, 70R, 74L, 85, 96 (Reprise Records/Warner Music Group); **Courtesy of the Wooden Nickel Archives:** 74R, 132R (Reprise Records/Warner Music Group); **Alamy/Pictorial Press:** 134C (DGC Records)

Printed Ephemera
Courtesy of the Wooden Nickel Archives: 58L, 59TR, 74C, 75L, 75R, 94CL, 109L, 109R, 113TR, 123B, 135 inset, 141B, 144C, 146TR, 147B, 152, 153, 156, 180TR; **Courtesy of Cyril Kieldsen:** 94TR, 94L, 94B, 95, 101B, 126, 134R; **Private Collection:** 14R, 103 inset, 108TL, 120 inset

ACKNOWLEDGMENTS

I wish to thank Colin Webb at Palazzo Editions for commissioning this endeavor and for his ongoing project support, and Palazzo editor James Hodgson for his instructive notes.

I'm extremely grateful to my West Coast editorial direction team of word and voice hurlers, Kenneth Kubernik and Rob Hill, for their random kudos, barbed remarks, writing, and audible play execution around my game calling.

My deepest appreciation to the Henry Diltz Studio and particularly Gary Strobl, chief archivist and photo librarian.

Thanks to Joseph McCombs, who copy-edited the first chapter of my manuscript, and Yogananda devotee Chris Darrow for his administrative cataloging abilities.

The physical passing of David A. Barmack, Bobby Womack, Jack Nitzsche, Kim Fowley, Dave Diamond, Ray Manzarek, Bob Crewe, Rick Rosas, and Greg Strobl informed and guided these pages.

I cite several authors who provided access to their own Neil Young data and interviews: Larry LeBlanc, John Einarson, Paul Zollo, Jan Alan Henderson, Sharry Wilson, Sylvie Simmons, Dan Kessel, and Ritchie Yorke.

Numerous publicists, writers, record label employees, chroniclers, friends, and relatives aided my efforts: my mother, Hilda Kubernik, and cousin Shelia, Roger Steffens, Don Peake, Lanny Waggoner, Gene Aguilera, Rosemarie Renee Patronette in Hawaii, Gary Pig Gold, Wes Seely, Dr. James Cushing and Celeste Goyer in SLO, Burton Cummings, Elliott Lefko, Carol Shoenman and MsMusic, Nurit Wilde, Cary Baker, Sherry Hendrick and Alley Culture in Detroit, Travis Pike, Sue Michelson, Lonn Friend, Matt King, Neil Norman and GNP Crescendo Records, Richard Bosworth, Harold Sherrick, Colin Cowherd, Josh Mills, Mark Guerrero, Stuart Cornfeld, Mick Vranich, *The Dan Patrick Show*, Aime from Burbank and Sophie in Toronto, Rebekah, "Mary, Mary," Juliette Jagger, Jim Kaplan at *Record Collector News*, Jensen Communications, Chris Campion, Mark Weitz, Michelle Szeto, Jeffrey Goldman, Roger Staubach, Dr. David B. Wolfe, Guy Webster, Roy Trakin, David Kessel, Harry E. Northup, Daniel Weizmann, Kirk Silsbee, Rod Serling, Little Steven, Justin Pierce, David Leaf, Gary Schneider and Open Mynd Collectibles, Ciggy Sherman, Mike Johnson, Frank Orlando, Greg Franco, Dean Dean the Taping Machine, Candy Dog, David M. Berger, Izzy Chait, Stephen J. Kalinich, S. Ti Muntarbhorn for her photo, Elliot Kendall, Bill Bentley, Richard Derrick, Denny Bruce, Peter Piper, Bob Kushner, Ryan Jansen, Nancy Rose Retchin, Graham Nash, Jeff Gold, Rob Bowman, Rodney Bingenheimer, and Andrew Loog Oldham.

This book might not have happened without Wallichs Music City, The Frigate, DisCount Record Center, The Groove Company, Bob and Tom at FreakBeat Records, Tower Records, and Los Angeles AM radio stations KHJ, KRLA, KFWB, KBLA, along with FM channels KPPC, KMET, and KLOS, who introduced me to the sounds of Buffalo Springfield and Neil Young.

Overleaf: Sportpaleis Ahoy, Rotterdam, May 27, 1987.

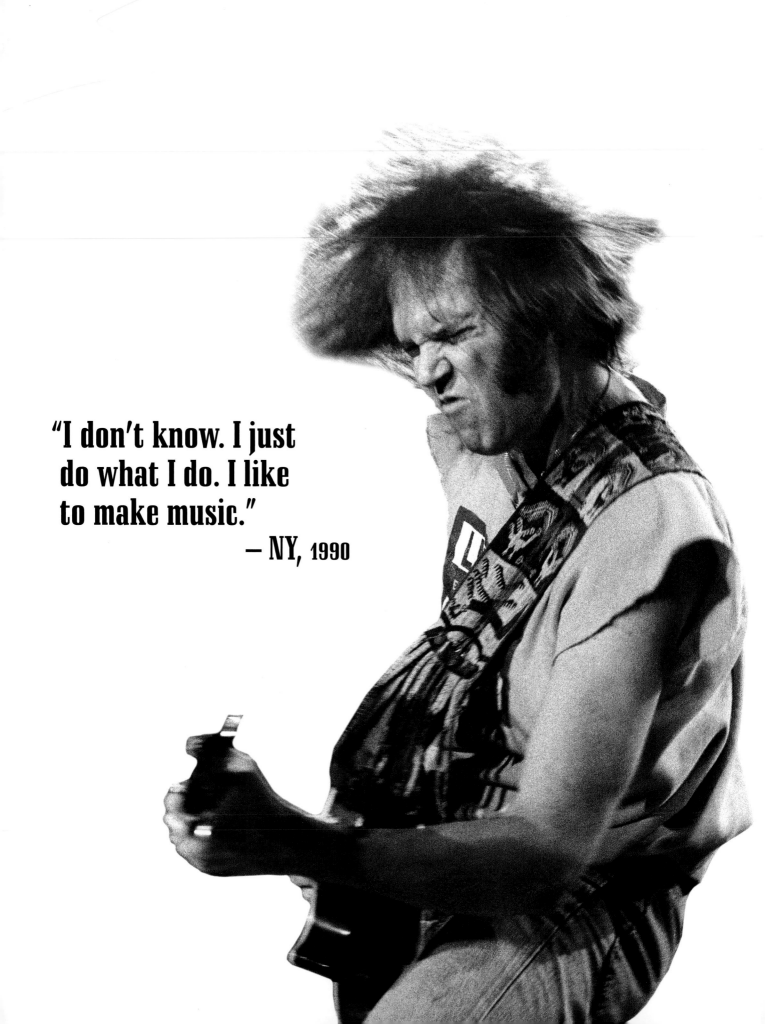

"I don't know. I just do what I do. I like to make music."

— NY, 1990